# The Fighting Pioneers

## Dedication

This book is dedicated to all men, of whatever rank, who served with the battalion during the Great War, and especially to my grandfather, Private Stanley Douglass, who ignited my interest, at a very early age, in the war with tales of his experiences.

# The Fighting Pioneers

## THE STORY OF THE
## 7TH DURHAM LIGHT INFANTRY

## Clive Dunn

Pen & Sword
**MILITARY**

First published in Great Britain in 2015 by
PEN & SWORD MILITARY
*an imprint of*
Pen and Sword Books Ltd
47 Church Street
Barnsley
South Yorkshire S70 2AS

ISBN 978 1 47382 348 8

Printed and bound in England by
CPI Group (UK) Ltd, Croydon, CR0 4YY

Typeset in Times New Roman
by CHIC GRAPHICS

*Pen & Sword Books Ltd incorporates the imprints of*
Pen & Sword Archaeology, Atlas, Aviation, Battleground, Discovery, Family
History, History, Maritime, Military, Naval, Politics, Railways, Select, Social History,
Transport, True Crime, Claymore Press, Frontline Books, Leo Cooper, Praetorian Press,
Remember When, Seaforth Publishing and Wharncliffe.

*For a complete list of Pen and Sword titles please contact*
Pen and Sword Books Limited
47 Church Street, Barnsley, South Yorkshire, S70 2AS, England
E-mail: enquiries@pen-and-sword.co.uk
Website: www.pen-and-sword.co.uk

# Contents

# Preface

This is the story of the 7th Durham Light Infantry (DLI) from the beginning of the volunteer movement and formations raised in Sunderland to its first association with the Durham Light Infantry, when it became the 3rd Volunteer Battalion. With the creation of the Territorial Force in 1908 the battalion was redesignated as the 7th Battalion. It went to France in April 1915 with the rest of the Northumbrian Division (which later became the 50th Division), seeing action almost immediately at the Second Battle of Ypres. In November 1915 the battalion was chosen to become the divisional Pioneers – not always the safe job as some thought – and was sent back to the front line to reinforce the infantry brigades for the German offensives in 1918. During the war the 1/7th Battalion suffered 600 fatalities and the 2/7th Battalion suffered twenty-six. In 1920, when the Territorial Army was reformed after the war, it was re-raised in its original role as infantry. The story concludes on 10 December 1936, when the 7th Durham Light Infantry became the 47th (Durham Light Infantry) AA Battalion RE (TA), whose personnel went on to serve in the Second World War.

My interest in the 7th Durham Light Infantry started at an early age when I used to listen to the tales told to me by my grandfather, Stanley Douglass, who was a pre-war Territorial with the battalion. From there my interest in the First World War steadily grew, and in the Durham Light Infantry in particular. During the 1980s I interviewed a number of survivors from the battalion; sections from these interviews form part of the narrative.

It is now time to write the history of the Sunderland and South Shields Territorial battalion of the Durham Light Infantry.

# Acknowledgements

My thanks go to the Trustees of the Regiment for the use of photographs and extracts of diaries and letters of soldiers of the battalion, which are held by the Durham County Archives.

I am very much indebted to a pamphlet and a series of articles, prepared by Major Mark Storey for the *Sunderland Echo*, which cover the early years of the volunteer movement in Sunderland.

My thanks go to the staff at the Special Collections Department of Leeds University for helping me with the Liddle Collection and their efforts to locate the copyright holders of the papers of Private Wrigglesworth.

I would like also to extend my thanks to the Imperial War Museum for making every effort to contact the copyright holders for permission to use extracts from the papers of Sergeant A. Speight and Private W.G. Miller and for permission to use the photograph of the battalion at Reninghelst, near Ypres, in 1916.

I was able to take the photographs of the Boer War Memorial, which hangs at the Civic Centre, Sunderland, with the help of Trevor Stevens of the City Council, who graciously took time out from his work to arrange for the display cabinet to be opened.

I would especially like to thank the staff of the Durham County Archives, in particular Gill Parkes for her help and patience and the late Mr Malcolm McGregor for his assistance with the honours and awards to the battalion, taken from his book *Honours and Awards to the Durham Light Infantry*, which was printed for private circulation, and his records on the officers of the regiment, held at the Durham County Records Office.

My warm thanks go to Mr Peter Vaux – the grandson of the late Colonel Ernest Vaux, who commanded the battalion for most of the war – for his help with obtaining material and photographs.

My especial thanks go to John Sheen for the prompt to write this book and for his encouragement and support during the writing thereof.

Lastly, and most importantly, to my wife, Gillian, for her patience and support, for her willingness to accompany me across the region to visit museums and archives and for her help with the proofreading.

# Chapter 1

# The Beginning

*Colours of the Sunderland Rifle Volunteers.*

Sunderland has had a long and proud affiliation with the volunteer movements, whose members gave their services to help defend the country. The history of Sunderland's volunteers can be traced back to 1794, when the Loyal Sunderland Volunteers, or Sunderland Loyal Volunteers, were raised during the Revolutionary Wars, when the threat of invasion by France was real. Robert Hayton, a local wealthy coal fitter, raised the volunteers 'for the purpose of manning and defending the batteries at the entrance of Sunderland harbour'. The unit was not officially recognized by the War Office until 1797. Prior to that date the gentlemen concerned hired the services of a regular sergeant to teach them the use of arms.

The Loyal Sunderland Volunteers consisted of three companies of 100 men each. The commanding officer, known as a major commandant, was Major Robert Hayton. He was assisted by two captains, one by the name of MacIntosh, a coal fitter, and the other called Bailey, a solicitor. In addition there was also Lieutenant Irvine and Lieutenant William Wilson. The headquarters of the Volunteers were at Mr Davison's sail loft in West Wear Street, Sunderland. It is believed that parades took place in Villiers Street and drills on the Town Moor, with ranges at Hendon Beach.

It was also in 1797 that colours were presented to the corps on 5 June by Mrs Russell, the wife of William Russell. These colours were returned to her in 1802, when the corps was disbanded because the Revolutionary Wars had come to an end with the Treaty of Amiens, and were stored in Brancepeth Castle. They were thought to be there in 1912, but it is not known where they are now.

As the corps was a volunteer formation, and was raised by local gentlemen and did not initially have official recognition, it had to raise its own funds for the purchase of gunpowder for musket practice, as well as other necessaries. A subscription list was opened, which had amongst its names some of the most prominent people of the town and county. The list was headed by no less than the Bishop of Durham, the Dean of Durham, the Edens and William Wilson, the wealthy owner of Brancepeth Castle, nephew of William Russell. The corps used to march to the tune of *The swine cam jingling doon Pelton Lonin*, the origins of which are unknown.

The Duke of York inspected the corps in 1795, when on a visit to the region, and expressed his appreciation of their military bearing to the commander of the Northern District.

In 1799, with invasion fever at its height, it was decided to have a grand field day with the corps being divided into two divisions, one landing on the beaches at Hendon, advancing inland, and the other moving to meet the threat and forcing them to retreat to their boats. The Volunteers had a great number of keelmen in the ranks, who wore blue pantaloons as opposed to white, who were usually kept apart from the rest. What happened on the day became known locally as the Battle of Hendon. The keelmen landed as planned and advanced and took up position, again according to plan. However, things started to go wrong when the 'friendly forces' advanced. Instead of falling back, as planned, they refused to budge and fired their muskets at close range at the advancing forces, leaving blue powder marks on their faces for the rest of their lives. Hand-to-hand fighting broke out, friends fighting friends. There were a number of serious casualties in the corps on this day, with Private James Sinclair losing an eye. The exercise, as it would be called today, ended when an armistice was agreed.

With the Treaty of Amiens bringing the Revolutionary Wars with France to a conclusion in 1802, the need for volunteer corps subsided. As a result, the Loyal Sunderland Volunteers were disbanded in July of that year following a parade at the Town Moor, where the commanding officer was presented with a silver cup. At about this time, in 1797, another corps, the Bishop Wearmouth Volunteers, was raised, organized by John Goodchild as captain and Robert Biss as lieutenant. Not much is known about this corps except that it too was disbanded in 1802 when peace was declared. Subsequently, Lieutenant Biss continued to serve with the Sunderland Volunteers in 1805.

Unfortunately the peace did not last long and by 1803 Great Britain and France were once again at war with each other. With the war came the renewed threat of invasion. The government was inundated with offers of volunteer service from all over the country to such an extent that it was hardly able to deal with them. County Durham alone raised seven corps of volunteer cavalry, ten of infantry and three of artillery.

One of these corps was the Sunderland Volunteer Infantry, raised in August 1803 under the lieutenant colonel commandantship of Sir Ralph Milbanke of Seaham Hall. This corps consisted of ten companies of sixty men each. The sum of £1,600 was raised by subscription from August to December 1803 to equip them, which was a huge sum in those days, especially considering the size of Sunderland. On Wednesday, 2 November 1803, Lady Milbanke presented new field colours to the corps. The headquarters were once again in Mr Davison's sail loft in West Wear Street. On 25 August 1805, at a parade on the Town Moor, the commanding officer, Lieutenant Colonel Robinson of Hendon Lodge, read out a letter from Brigadier General Ker stating that they may be called upon to serve in other parts of the country. This also meant that the corps would have to be ready to move within an hour of being ordered to do so. The colonel then asked if any man objected, to which the corps responded with three cheers.

Drills took place at Lieutenant Colonel Robinson's plantation, Hendon Lodge, during the summer months. In the winter, drills were conducted in the Seamen's Hall, Church Street. For each drill attended, a private soldier received one shilling. With the threat of invasion receding, the need for the volunteer corps also diminished. They had been ready to fight; fortunately they had not been called upon to do so and in 1813 the Sunderland Rifle Volunteers were disbanded, many men joining the still extant 2nd Durham Militia, which itself wasn't disbanded until 1818.

The colours that had been presented in 1803 were preserved by Lieutenant Colonel Robinson and remained in his family's possession until his son, Septimus James Robinson, restored them to the corps in 1860. It is thought that they were used as decorations when the Duke of Wellington visited Sunderland in 1829.

In 1805, one curious incident involving the Sunderland Rifle Volunteers occurred when Colonel Milbanke placed sentries along the coast near the town. One of the positions guarded was known as the Paul Jones Battery, situated on a sandbank at the end of the old south pier. One night, Private Joseph Dunn, who was in Captain Bramwell's Company, being by himself on duty at the battery, saw a black cat and mistakenly thought it was the Devil. He threw his musket to the ground and ran back to the town. The battery was known thereafter as the Black Cat Battery.

The Volunteer Force then seems to have been mothballed until it would be required again. The next crisis did not occur until 1859. Once again, people perceived the threat to come from France, which was now ruled by Napoleon III, the nephew of Napoleon Bonaparte. There was an initial rush to join what became the Rifle Volunteers. They saw themselves initially as clubs, and that is how they were regarded by the government at the time. To start with, the government did little more than sanction them and provide a small capitation grant for each man. Members of these clubs were of three types: effectives, who subscribed a sum per year and found their own uniform or were assisted from a general fund; honorary members, who subscribed more than the former and attended drills and parades whenever they could; and non-effectives, who merely subscribed towards the running of the corps.

The year 1860 saw the initiation of the volunteer movement and the formation of the Sunderland Rifle Volunteers, which consisted of 180 men divided into three companies. Like its predecessor corps, it was for home defence only. As in the Revolutionary and Napoleonic wars, a subscription was raised from the people of Sunderland. This time the amount raised was disappointing – £400 from a population of approximately 180,000, compared to £1,600 from 20,000 citizens fifty years previously – and various comments were passed. The corps was officially recognised on 6 March 1860, when it became the 3rd Durham (Sunderland) Rifle Volunteers.

In July 1860, Lord Adolphus Vane Tempest was appointed major commandant and in December 1862 he was promoted to lieutenant colonel, by which time a fourth company had been added to the corps. The headquarters were in a former warehouse near Gill Bridge Avenue. Range practices were again carried out at Hendon Beach and there was also a range at Fulwell Quarries. Initially the corps was issued with the muzzle-loading Enfield, but these were later replaced by the breach-loading Snider and Martini rifles.

The establishment of this corps was subsequently raised to 500 all ranks, comprising five companies, with five captains, five lieutenants and five ensigns, with an adjutant. As mentioned earlier, on 17 August 1860, the old colours of the 1803 Volunteers were returned to the corps by Septimus James Robinson, Esquire; they were presented to the corps by Lady Vane Tempest.

When the volunteer movement recommenced in 1860, commissions were by election within each particular corps. This proved to be a very unsatisfactory system, as it was possible for an officer to revert back to the ranks if not re-elected, which did happen on occasion. Later commissions were granted on the nomination of the Lord Lieutenant of the county. These first commissions in the Durham Rifle Volunteer Corps were published in *The London Gazette* of 1860, under the title 'Commissions signed by the Lord Lieutenant of the County Palatine of Durham'.

A review of the northern volunteers took place in Edinburgh on 7 August 1860, with various corps from Scotland, Northumberland, Durham and Cumberland being represented. It took place on a grey and chilly day but this did not stop the crowds gathering to listen to the bands and watch the spectacle, uniforms being evident everywhere. The men from Sunderland mustered at Monkwearmouth Station at 4.30 am; there were members of the Artillery and 200 Rifles present. The volunteers joined other members of the brigade at Newcastle upon Tyne and proceeded then to Edinburgh, arriving at 2.30 pm, whence they marched to the review ground. Queen Victoria arrived at 4.00 pm and drove past the troops, who stood in silence at the salute. When the Queen reached the central dais the march past began. Leading were the Fife Mounted Volunteers, followed by the Artillery, then the Engineers, and finally the enormous mass of Rifles. The whole march past took an hour and a quarter. The end of the review was signalled by cheers and some of the Riflemen waved their caps on the end of their rifles, and when the royal carriage was leaving some broke ranks and surrounded it, cheering all the time. Queen Victoria expressed her admiration to the officer commanding the review on the steadiness and precision that characterized the large body of volunteers whose movements she had witnessed and that their appearance reflected highest credit both upon their officers and themselves. The men of the Durham Rifle Volunteers marched back to the railway station for their train home, arriving in Sunderland at 4.00 am the next day to be greeted by well-wishers.

The 3rd Durham Rifle Volunteers were represented by Captains T.E. Chapman, 3rd Company, T. Burn, 4th Company, and F.C. Huntley, 2nd Company, with Lieutenants J. Barron, 4th Company, A.W. Dixon, 2nd Company, C.T. Potts, 3rd Company, and T. Reed, 1st Company.

By 1864 the strength had risen to 604. It was also in this year that Lieutenant Colonel Vane Tempest died and Sir E.T. Gourley assumed command, with Henry Roberts, late 98th Regiment (later the North Staffordshire Regiment), as adjutant. A rather unique exchange of command took place over the coming years, for in 1870 Lieutenant Colonel Gourley resigned command of the corps to become the honorary colonel. He was replaced by Lieutenant Colonel W.B. Ferguson, who commanded until 1873, when he too resigned and handed over to Lieutenant Colonel Gourley, who had resigned as honorary colonel, the command of the unit having travelled in a full circle.

The number of troops in the new corps tended to decrease as time went by. At the presentation ceremony in the Victoria Hall on 23 January 1874, for the annual rifle competition, it was pointed out to those assembled that in the Revolutionary Wars the number of volunteers were 1,200, whereas there were only 374 effectives out of a population that was now five times its size.

Work on the new purpose-built drill hall at Livingstone Road had commenced in 1879, the money being raised by public subscription and a bazaar. The foundation stone was laid by Mr (later, Sir) James Laing and the building was completed in 1880. Changes to the Army were once again on the horizon and these took the form of the Cardwell Reforms.

Following the defeat of France during the Franco-Prussian War of 1870-71, people of England and their government set about a scheme for improving the defence of the realm. The task fell to Edward Cardwell, Minister for War. Amongst other things, he introduced the short service system whereby instead of a soldier enlisting for twenty years he would now sign on for seven with the colours and a further five with the Reserve. The Reserve would be called up in times of national emergencies to fill gaps in the Regular Army. The purchase of commissions was abolished under these reforms, a system that had in the past hindered the promotion of talented poorer officers. One of the greatest changes occurred in 1881, when the old numbering system of regiments was replaced by county affiliations. As a result, the 68th Light Infantry and 106th Light Infantry (formerly 2nd Bombay European Light Infantry) changed their names to the 1st and 2nd Durham Light Infantry battalions, respectively. The Volunteer Rifle Corps had over the past couple of years been reorganized into administrative battalions, with the exception of the Sunderland Corps, which remained the 3rd Durham Rifle Volunteer Corps.

However, the reforms gave these administrative battalions a real connection with the Durham Light Infantry: the 3rd Corps now became the 3rd Durham Rifle Volunteers. A further change occurred in 1887, when the 3rd Durham Rifle Volunteers became the 3rd Volunteer Battalion Durham Light Infantry.

The change to the new regimental system saw a move away from the club image to one of a more professional outlook. Annual camps started in the 1880s; it is believed that the first of these was at Morpeth. Other camps followed – at Brackenbury Moor, Appleby, Seaton Carew and Rothbury.

The first great challenge for the volunteers came in 1899, when the Second Boer War broke out in South Africa. The volunteers had originally joined to serve anywhere within the United Kingdom in the event of an invasion; they never thought they would be called upon to serve abroad. In January 1900 an appeal went out to all of the volunteer battalions to provide a company for service in the war. Each of the five Durham battalions supplied men to the four volunteer service companies raised during the war. Amidst crowds of well-wishers and family, the first contingent of twenty-three from the 3rd Volunteer Battalion left for the front at 10.54 am on 29 January 1900 via Newcastle, before proceeding on their journey to South Africa. Colonel Peters, the battalion commanding officer, was there to see them off. Sergeant Hunter and Corporal Metcalfe were each presented with a pair of powerful field glasses by Colonel Peters. As a result of the service of the volunteer corps the battle honour South Africa 1900-1902 was awarded to the five battalions (5th, 6th, 7th, 8th and 9th) of the regiment, which they bore on their colours from 1909. A list of the men who served in the volunteer service companies from the 3rd Volunteer Battalion is given in Appendix One. The First Volunteer Service Company joined 1st Durham Light Infantry in April 1900 and remained with them until 9 October 1900, when it was posted to the Drakensburg Defence Force, leaving Durban for England on 8 May 1901. The Second Volunteer Service Company joined 1st Durham Light Infantry on 23 April 1901 and stayed with them until relieved by the Third Volunteer Service Company in April 1902, leaving Cape Town in May. The Third Volunteer Service Company's stay was short, the war finishing in May 1902; they left South Africa in July 1902. The Fourth Volunteer Service Company left England in May 1901 and was initially attached to the 2nd Buffs, it later being attached to 2nd Northumberland Fusiliers before finally leaving South Africa in May 1902.

While serving in South Africa the volunteer companies were attached to the 1st Durham Light Infantry and helped to protect the lines of communications and garrison blockhouses throughout South Africa. Although the garrisoning of the blockhouses – 'iron mushrooms' to the troops – was a necessary step to limiting the movements of the Boers on commando, it was a tedious job. There was an unofficial competition between the blockhouse garrisons as to who had the neatest, many of them having little gardens. Those along the railway lines were able to receive local and other newspapers from passing trains, but for those on the veldt, time passed more slowly.

Each blockhouse had between ten and twelve loopholes, from 5 feet to 5 feet 4 inches off the ground, and just outside the blockhouse was a trench of between 3 and 4 feet deep and 2 feet broad. Each blockhouse was connected to the next by barbed wire fencing. Each blockhouse was within rifle range of the next and they formed a grid system across the land. By the end of the war there were more than 8,000 of them, at a cost of £16 each. In a letter to the *Sunderland Echo* from J.F.A. Brown, E Company, 1st Durham Light Infantry, he stated the only amusement and exercise they got was when they were digging trenches on each side of the barbed wire that connected the blockhouses. He went on to praise the trenches and wire because they checked the rush of horses and killed the effect of a stampede of cattle, which were used to breach the wire. Fastened to the wire, to give warning of anyone trying to cut or climb it, were jam and milk tins, which would rattle and make a noise if disturbed. Private Brown mentioned a poem the troops had: *Tinkle, tinkle little tin, And stop the Boers from getting in.*

On their return to Sunderland each contingent was greeted by the mayor, Colonel Peters, and crowds of townspeople. The last contingent arrived on 5 June 1902, after landing at Southampton the day before and stopping to have breakfast at the barracks in Newcastle at 6.00 am before proceeding to Sunderland, arriving at 1.30 pm. It was hoped now that the men, lately returned from South Africa, would instruct their comrades in modern warfare.

A special meeting was held on 6 November 1902 at the town hall for members of the volunteer units who had served in the war. In attendance were members of the Imperial Yeomanry, 3rd Volunteer Battalion Durham Light Infantry, Telegraph Contingent and nursing staff. The freedom of the borough was granted to the volunteers in recognition of their services and each received a vellum certificate. This was followed by the unveiling of a commemorative plaque, and a dinner. Gold medals were also to be issued, which were to be paid for by the officers. The commemorative plaque now hangs proudly on the wall in the Sunderland Civic Centre.

The age of the volunteers was now coming to an end. As with the end of any war, an analysis of what went wrong and what steps were needed to put things right for the next war took place. These came about in the Haldane Reforms of the early twentieth century.

One of these reforms had great repercussions within the volunteer movement. From 1 April 1908 the volunteer corps were reorganized to become the Territorial Force, whose organization was in the hands of the county associations that had been formed across the country under the Territorial and Reserve Forces Act 1907. The associations were responsible for the organizing, equipping and maintenance of the battalions and the upkeep of their drill halls. The reforms were designed to give the Territorial Force a definite position among the forces of the Crown. The old volunteer battalions of the Durham Light Infantry were renumbered and became the 5th, 6th, 7th, 8th and 9th Durham Light Infantry. The 6th, 7th, 8th and 9th battalions of the Durham Light Infantry were subsequently brigaded together as the Durham Light Infantry Brigade, part of the Northumbrian Division, later to become the 50th Division (the 5th Durham Light Infantry formed part of the York and Durham Brigade). The Territorial Force became the second line of defence. Service in the Territorial Force was voluntary; soldiers enlisted into the battalion, a procedure similar to regular soldiers. The age

Sunderland Boer War Memorial.

The names of men from Sunderland who volunteered for service in South Africa.

Pictures on the Boer War Memorial.

*Camp at Ripon, 1907.*

for enlistment was between seventeen and thirty-three years of age, for a period of four years, which could be extended upon re-enlistment. None of the existing volunteers were compelled to join the new force. They could opt to transfer if they so desired; they had until 30 June 1908 to make their final decision.

Infantry soldiers had to attend either an eight-day or a fifteen-day annual camp. Mounted troops had longer camps. In addition to this there were also weekly drill nights and other parades and exercises.

To mark the end of the old volunteer corps and the formation of the new battalion, on 31 March 1908 the 3rd Volunteer Battalion Durham Light Infantry held a smoking concert in the sergeants' mess, all officers being invited and many attending. The concert finished at eleven o'clock and the proceedings then moved to the Garrison Field for a service to welcome the Territorials. The officers and rank and file then marched twice around the field. The flag of the 3rd VBDLI

*Postcard from a series of regimental colours.*

was then lowered, while the band played *Auld Lang Syne*, and then three volleys were fired. Following this the Last Post was sounded. A few minutes after midnight, Reveille was sounded to announce the existence of the 7th Durham Light Infantry.

# Chapter 2

# The Early Years and the Outbreak of War

*Postcard of the battalion colours.*

There were twenty-two volunteer officers serving on 31 March 1908, all of whom transferred to the Territorials: Honorary Colonel Thomas Reed; Lieutenant Colonel J. Evans (the headmaster of the boys' High School); Major E.S. Strangeways; Captains Maurice Moore, Joseph Spain, Charles W. Hines, Robert B. Harrison and Frederick Wawn; Lieutenants William Priestly, G.S. Waller, Farrow, Charles E. Thompson, A.H.P. Squance, Robert Dawson, Mark Storey, M.E. Mail and J. Lowes Thompson; Surgeon Major Beveridge and Surgeon Captain Milbanke, Chaplain Reverend T. Randell; Adjutant Captain Oakes and Quartermaster and Honorary Lieutenant John Lyons.

The 3rd Volunteer Battalion DLI had consisted of six rifle companies and a cyclist company, the latter being later absorbed by the Northern Cyclist Battalion. The 7th Battalion Durham Light Infantry now had an establishment of eight companies – six at Sunderland and two at South Shields – with the headquarters remaining at the Livingstone Road drill hall. The two companies at South Shields had at one time formed part of the 5th Volunteer Battalion Durham Light Infantry.

Thus the newly created Territorial Force was different in many ways to the old volunteer movement. The formations were now more closely linked with the Regular Army, becoming part of the regiment. The primary role of the Territorials was still to provide for home defence of the United Kingdom and to release regular soldiers for overseas service. The new terms and conditions of enlistment into the Territorial Force meant that a soldier could not be made to serve overseas.

The new Territorial Force helped to improve the organization of the battalion. Instead of a series of individual units to be mobilized as the need arose, they were formed into brigades and divisions throughout the country. As already mentioned, the 7th Battalion Durham Light Infantry found itself brigaded with the 6th, 8th and 9th battalions of the Durham Light Infantry to form the Durham Light Infantry Brigade, which during the course of the war became the 151st Infantry Brigade. This brigade, along with its two sister brigades, the Northumberland Infantry Brigade (later, 149th Infantry Brigade, comprising four battalions of the Northumberland Fusiliers) and the York and Durham Light Infantry brigades (later, 150th Infantry Brigade, comprising 4th East Yorkshires, 4th and 5th Yorkshire Regiment and 5th DLI) formed the Northumbrian Division, which later became the 50th Division.

Annual camps became a permanent feature of life with the Territorials, with the 7th Battalion holding camps at Blackhall Rocks in 1909, Rothbury in 1910, Strensall, York in 1911, and Scarborough in 1912 and 1913. Camps were seen as a chance to have a holiday by members of the battalion, who would possibly not have had one otherwise. Local photographers also looked forward to the Territorial camps. Many of them did good business with group photographs or a series of scenes. This was especially so at Scarborough. Recruitment for the battalion was ongoing and often they would have specific recruitment drives to make the battalion up to establishment. Once in the battalion, like in every other formation, training would commence to turn the recruit into a soldier. The training was similar in many respects to that of their regular counterparts with regard to marksmanship, signalling, first aid and all the other duties that go to make an efficient battalion.

*Blackhall Rocks camp.*

*3rd Volunteer Battalion, Rothbury, 1910.*

*Marching to Rothbury, 1910.*

*Church parade, Rothbury, 1910.*

*The band and bugles, Scarborough, 1912.*

*Scarborough, 1912.*

*Durham Light Infantry church parade, Scarborough.*

*A Company, Scarborough.*

*Marching through Scarborough.*

Private Joe Robson, 2210, a signaller with C Company, remembered:

I joined the 7th Durham Light Infantry in November 1913, I don't know the exact date. I was working at Osborne & Graham Shipbuilders, I was serving my time. At that time I was seventeen years old, almost eighteen. You could not join until you were eighteen. At the time it was like a rage to join the Territorials, the lads had nothing to do much and it was an encouragement to go to camp at Conway, North Wales.

When you joined you had to put forty drills in before the camp in July, fire your course on Whitburn range twice, from 100 yards to 600 yards. Then after you did that you had to have what they called the mad minute, rapid fire, the target moving, fifteen rounds. They used to mark it with signals what you were getting, Bulls eye, Maggie, wash out. We used to have a canny time at Whitburn. Nice range. I've been firing there, I've been in the butts marking for them. You used to get your turn. Terrible in the butts, you know! You could hear the bullets hitting the targets, just a crack like a whip.

*Band members, Scarborough. Private Frank Surtees is kneeling, front left.*

*Durham Light Infantry Brigade at Scarborough.*

*Kit inspection, Scarborough.*

*Battalion officers at Scarborough camp.*

Times were hard in the early part of the twentieth century, and there were other reasons why men joined up, as related by 1068 Private Frank Surtees, of No. 2 Platoon, A Company (initially E Company before the reorganization into a four-company battalion), who served as a bandsman before and during the war:

> I was born on 12 September 1895, at Low Pallion, Sunderland. My father was a shipyard worker. There were six of us in the family. The living conditions were bad, the six of us in one house, built before Napoleon's time, I think. We were crowded, then we had typhoid. How that came on, was one or two ships came home, troop carriers from the Boer War, and my father working in the shipyard in Sunderland, and they just sold the blankets off the ship. My father got a couple. They were thrown in the washing outside and we were playing on them. Typhoid fever. One boy he died, he never got over the fever and my eldest sister had it very, very bad, she pulled around.

While at work my father knew one of the foremen, he happened to mention to him about us taking music lessons. He said, 'Why not let the lads join the Territorials in the band?' He was a sergeant, this feller. So Thomas, my elder brother, joined as a boy. [He was later killed in action with the 9th Durhams on 2 June 1918.] I joined when I was old enough, mostly for the music. I joined in July 1909, the 7th Durhams.

Band practice was our Drill night, on the same night as the others. Band practice was on Garrison Field, in the centre of Sunderland. It was a proper big square for training. People went out to the Crimea from there. I played the cornet and violin. The band sergeant trained us. He was a pretty good trainer for the ordinary person. But we had a regular soldier for a camp conductor, he came from the Gordons. Band practice was once a week. The only training I got was the cornet, no drill, but soon as you become sixteen you go onto the range.

Our bandmaster was a regular soldier, one of the smartest men I have seen. He had been stationed in Ireland and then he came out on retirement and he come to our battalion. He was Mr Morrell, he was good to us, the boys. We always had two boys at least under sixteen, that was myself and another one. Camp was practically a holiday. The band went out to meet the troops when they were on manoeuvres and bring them in. You used to go to the officers' mess, in your best uniform. The officers had a marquee; it was small but well done. We used to play waltz's [sic] or whatever they wanted. A great life! We never got any tips, not that I know of anyway. We got extra band pay. At Blackhall Rocks, we went out, down to the seaside, come back and then lie about in the sun. You could see everyone lying outside their tents in the sun. It was the best holiday they ever had. We went out white and came back bronzed. I enjoyed the whole thing. You went and drew your rifle on the Friday night, went home with it and then went over to Whitburn. It had just opened then. We did our shoot there. I wasn't much good at shooting. I didn't understand.

*Members of A Company, Scarborough.*

*The battalion band, Scarborough.*

When Edwin Patterson joined the battalion he was asked which company he would like to join. When he replied 'A Company', he was told he could not join them, and was placed in B Company. According to Private Patterson, there was class distinction in the battalion because A Company 'were all the posh boys of the town, businessmen's sons, etc.' Private Patterson joined the battalion in 1912 at the age of seventeen and, being a tuba player, became a member of the band. He eventually became Frank Surtees' brother-in-law.

Annual camp 1914 would prove to be different from any other that the men of the battalion had attended and in some respects one of the longest. Once again, the camp would be a brigade camp, i.e. the rest of the brigade held their camp at the same time and at the same place, commencing on 25 July for two weeks. This time the location was at Conway in North Wales.

The companies paraded as normal at the Garrison Field, Livingstone Road drill hall, prior to entraining for camp. The train to Conway stopped at different places to change

*Horseplay by A Company, Scarborough.*

engines, but the troops were not allowed out of the train. The camp has been described as 'just a field with tents pitched up'.

Arrival at Conway and the first week are well remembered by Private Joe Robson of C Company:

> The train branched off the main line and into a field which was the camp, there were no platforms you just had to jump down off the train. The camp was full of tents. We settled down as best we could, it was late at night by that time.
>
> The next morning we were called up early, about six o'clock, to do physical jerks, etc. We had to march up Mount Snowdon, which was not far away. There is a main

*7th Durham Light Infantry camp, Conway, 1914.*

*A Company at Conway camp.*

*Group photograph taken at Conway.*

*The officers at Conway.*

*General view of Conway camp.*

road which goes right round Mount Snowdon and right to the top. Halfway up there is a general dealer's shop. When we got there we used to fall out for ten minutes and we used to go into the shop to get a bottle of pop or a bar of chocolate, whatever we wanted. We used to march up Mount Snowdon and go to other places.

You could see right across to Llandudno from Conway and when it was low tide you could walk across to it, it was only about 2 miles away. Conway Bridge was a marvellous bridge, it was a chain bridge. If one person was walking over it you could feel the vibration.

Training and camp life, with officers' mess dinners accompanied by the battalion band, went on as normal until early August.

The situation in Europe had been deteriorating since 28 June, when Archduke Franz Ferdinand, heir to the Austro-Hungarian throne, and his wife, the Duchess of Hohenberg, while on a state visit to Sarajevo were assassinated by Gavrilo Princip, a member of the Serbian terrorist organization the Black Hand. The Austrians, knowing that they could rely on Germany's support, sent a tough ultimatum to Serbia. The Serbians replied to the ultimatum after they ordered mobilization. The reply did not fully satisfy the Austrians, who declared war on Serbia on 28 July. Russia was pledged to aid Serbia if the Austrians attacked. Consequently, they too mobilized, on 29 July, followed by the Austrians' ally, Germany, on 30 July. Things were moving faster than anyone could have anticipated. On 1 August, France, Russia's ally, mobilized, and this was followed by the Germans declaring war on the Russians the same day. Although there had been border incidents between French and German troops, Germany did not declare war on France until 3 August.

*A pre-war soldier in marching kit.*

The German strategy, known as the Schlieffen Plan, was for a strong right-wing advance through Belgium to attack the left flank of the French Army and seize Paris, and then swing round to take the French Army on the frontier in the rear. The Germans had asked the Belgians to allow their troops through their country, and the request had naturally been refused. The Germans invaded anyway to put their plan into operation and consequently declared war on Belgium on 3 August. The Germans had altered the original plan to avoid invading the Netherlands. Britain, a signatory of the 1839 treaty that guaranteed Belgian neutrality, protested to the Germans and on 4 August gave them an ultimatum to withdraw their troops from the country. The Germans refused and as a result Britain declared war on Germany at 11.00 pm (British time) on 4 August. Anticipating the German response, mobilization orders had been sent out earlier in the day and these reached the battalion while at camp.

The story can be taken up by Private Joe Robson:

*The mobilization telegram sent to the battalion, August 1914.*

> We were all settled down for the camp when at three o'clock in the morning of 4 August the buglers sounded Reveille. War was declared. We were mobilized. Orders were issued to get your gear on, full pack and 250 rounds of ammunition. The cooks had been woken up and they did what they could for us before we left. They were cooking meat and potatoes. They put a potato in one hand a lump of meat in the other and we were then shoved into the train. We came straight back to Sunderland, arriving about six o'clock. We had been on the train from about four o'clock that morning. When we arrived back at Sunderland we were marched back to the Garrison Field at Livingston Road.

Frank Surtees remembered: 'On the Sunday night the colonel got the battalion together and told them we were going home tonight, you'll get your call-up papers in a couple of days. We got them on Tuesday.'

1310 Sergeant G. Thompson, who was in the transport section, in a record of his experiences written for his family in the 1920s and deposited with the Durham County Archives, wrote: 'We got

*Joe Robson, C Company.*

packed up and started off for Sunderland again. It was a long ride; about twelve hours it took us to come back. We marched up to the drill hall, crowds of people were waiting for us.'

Once back at the drill hall there was a lot that needed to be sorted out in accordance with the mobilization instructions. No one was sure what was going to happen; were they to go off to war straightaway or was something else planned? Private Robson continues his story:

*Lance Corporal Frank Surtees.*

We stood around for about two hours, they did not know what to do with us. We were just young lads wondering what we were going to do, we thought we were going straight to war. The CO [commanding officer] sent out some men to get bottles of beer, bottles of pop or sandwiches or a pie. When they came back I had a pie and a bottle of pop. This was about nine o'clock, we were absolutely worn out with our packs on, we grounded our rifles until we had eaten our food. We had just finished when it must have been about ten o'clock, the commander got in front of us on his horse and said, 'You can all go home but don't take your clothes off, you can be called up any minute.'

We were glad to get home, 'course it was all trams then. I lived in St Luke's Terrace at this time, my mother was a widow. I had lost my father when I was two years old, she used to look after me. When I got home I told my mother we've got to keep our clothes on, we might be called up at any minute.

'Oh my God. You're not going straight away?' she said.

'I don't know!'

*Battalion stretcher bearers.*

So I took my pack off my back, my pouches with the 250 rounds of ammunition and water bottle and laid them on the floor. I did not take my tunic or trousers off. I took my boots off and put my slippers on. I lay on the settee all night and nobody came. Nobody came the next day. I thought I would be at home for a while so I decided I'll go to bed that night. I was just going to get ready, I was worn out, it was about nine o'clock and they came round and said we had to report to the Garrison Field.

At this time Private Patterson was still a member of the band but on returning to the drill hall he was posted back to B Company as a stretcher bearer. When they returned to Sunderland things were a bit chaotic, as he remembered, but the situation could work to one's advantage: 'We had a red dress uniform, it was badly organized with the QM, he had that much on, he said, "Just throw them in the band's room, throw them in there." I never threw mine in, I kept my red coat and boots and everything.'

Others, like 1957 Private Stanley Douglass, of B Company, remembered that he was sent on guard duty to Hendon Banks before being allowed home. When the battalion reassembled at the Garrison Field and the companies were sorted out into order, they were marched off to various places around Sunderland to fulfil their role, which for the division as a whole was to guard the north-east coast and various other vital installations, such as the shipyards and collieries, against saboteurs.

*Private Stan Douglass, B Company.*

For the next three weeks the companies were distributed around the town. One went to the roller-skating rink, in Park Lane, another to Hudson Road School, a third to Hendon Valley Road School and the last to the Granary, at the docks.

Sleeping bags were not part of the kit issued in those days and the men had to make do as best they could, many just sleeping on the floor of the schools etc. in blankets. The quartermaster went round the town commandeering blankets – colour did not matter in the emergency – to be issued to the troops.

As part of the training route marches now took place around the countryside and through towns and villages to get the men fit and as an encouragement for other men to join the colours. Another activity that the battalion undertook was trench-digging practice, which would set them in good stead when they went to France, although they did not know it at the time.

Private Joe Robson, C Company, well remembered these route marches, and how the men tried to make them more bearable:

We used to form up and march through Sunderland, bayonets fixed and band playing. We marched around the town a few times and we had a favourite tune, it was the Durham Light Infantry marching tune. We used to sing our own words to it when we were marching:

*Oh look at the soldiers,*
*Oh look at their feet,*
*Oh look at the soldiers,*
*They can't get now't to eat.*

Other aspects of the men's health were considered, as Private Robson remembered:

We were going to march to Ravensworth Castle [Gateshead] to be inoculated and vaccinated. So we marched there and a lot of soldiers' relatives walked with us. I had already been vaccinated so I was just inoculated. Well by the time we got back we were aching. They gave us twenty-four hours off duty.

With the move now to their war establishment and subsequent increase in equipment scales, the quartermaster's department and transport section took charge of a number of additional horses and wagons that had been requisitioned by the War Office. The horses had to be given a health check and the wagons inspected to ensure they were in good working order. Any repairs would need to be done before the battalion deployed overseas.

After a couple of weeks on guard duty in Sunderland and the surrounding area the battalion was concentrated at Scots House, on Newcastle Road. It was here that an important incident took place, as recounted by Private Robson:

The battalion marched to Scots House on the Newcastle Road. We were billeted in there. We were there for two or three days when Colonel Vaux, the commanding officer, came in on his horse, we were all lined up in the grounds. He asked for drafts to go to France, all the boys were quaking. Volunteers had to take three paces forward. I was one of them and they took our names.

It should be remembered that as Territorial soldiers they were under no obligation, at this stage, to serve outside the country. The need of reinforcements in France was becoming apparent; most of the Regular Army were involved in the war and the number of trained soldiers remaining was sparse. All the Territorial formations had been directed to ask their troops if they would volunteer to serve overseas in their own units. Those members of the Territorial Force who did volunteer for overseas service were issued with a badge, which was inscribed 'Imperial Service' and it was worn on the right breast.

According to Sergeant Thompson, who had now been drafted into the transport section: 'At Scots House they called a parade of every man belonging to our battalion. It was for volunteers for France. I think there was 600 put up their hands … I was one of the 600.'

The precise number of those who volunteered varies; suffice to say a good number did, but not everyone volunteered for service in France. Not everyone could. Some members of the battalion were in final years of university and others had other obligations they had to fulfil. Private Douglass remembered that those who did not volunteer were made to march at the rear of the battalion when they went to Sunderland and they were booed by the crowd.

The Durham Light Infantry Brigade now concentrated at Ravensworth Castle, Gateshead. The training here became more serious, with company and battalion manoeuvres, which now included night exercises.

Private Patterson related: 'We used to go out on the morning in the fields on manoeuvres and say we were going to capture that farm over there. The whole division might be in it. We used to use blank cartridges.'

*Non-commissioned officers at Ravensworth Castle, 1915.*

*Officers at Gateshead.*

As well as practice attacks, the ordinary skills that every infantryman had to have were not neglected, as Private Douglass remembered:

We did our training at Windy Nook, which was bayonet fighting. Bayonet fighting is all dummies on a line all strung out like goal posts and you had to charge at them and hit them in certain places, chest and that, and dash into them and all that. From there we were at Ponteland, where we did more training, rifle shooting.

When war was declared Private Surtees, like Private Patterson, was sent back from the band to his company, where he became a rifleman once again. He not only remembered the training but, typical for a soldier, also the food:

I was in 2 Platoon A Company. I was just an ordinary rifleman then. We would go out on long marches and training on the 'battle area'. We would go out to the range at Waterhouse. We were in tents at Ravensworth Castle. The food wasn't too good. Dinner used to be in dixies; 'skilly', we called it [thin stew usually prepared in workhouses], cut-up meat all put into the pot together. You took your own plates, knives and forks. You got used to it.

The training was worked out by the colonel or the brigadier, whoever was running the manoeuvres. You would go out about 9 miles, that's where you would meet your opponent. When you got to the start of it you got so far, to where the real battle was supposed to be, some blanks fired. Then everybody went to his own company, and then away back home again.

The battalion, along with the rest of the brigade, remained at Ravensworth Castle for about a month until the weather worsened as winter approached. As they were under canvas at Ravensworth Castle, which would not do during winter, the battalion was once again billeted

*Route march through Gateshead.*

*Pistol practice, 1915.*

*The battalion band, 1915.*

*Group photograph of Room 4, Gateshead, 1915.*

*Group taken at a school in Gateshead, 1915.*

in various schools, this time in the Gateshead area. Training and guard duties were carried on as best as they could until orders were received in April for the division to move to France. Those who were not going overseas went to form the second-line battalion. All Territorial battalions were ordered to form second lines, as a training formation and as a reinforcement battalion.

The orders to move to France were supposed to be confined to the officers of the battalion, but word did get out, as Private Surtees recalled:

*R.T. Brotherston, killed in action 6 May 1915.*

> When we were ready the captain came round the schools in Gateshead when we were doing bayonet fighting. I don't think he was supposed to tell people and said, 'We are going to Flanders.'
> Before we went to France we got leave, in batches, it might have been a fortnight or a week. I never said anything to my mother or brother.

*Chapter 3*

# The Second Battle of Ypres

O nce orders had been received things started to step up apace and new kit was issued, ready for the front. As Sergeant Thompson wrote:

> The local transport which we had was taken from us and sent to our second line. We were fitted out with real service gear. Each man had to have two horses in this case.
> We went over to Newcastle and got a pair of horses and a limber wagon for each man. I was No. 1 Driver. There were about sixty horses and mules on our strength and about fifty men. All drivers were taken to the 50th Division Royal Field Artillery and went through a hard week's training to learn to ride and drive. They gave us some stick I can tell you. First riding bareback and then with saddles on. We were sore for days.

The advance party of the battalion, which comprised the transport and machine-gun sections, left Gateshead for Boulogne on 17 April 1915. It consisted of three officers and eighty-six other ranks. The train travelled to Southampton, where the advance party embarked for the Continent. Sergeant Thompson takes up the story:

> I remember well that night we sailed from Southampton. It was a grand night, full moon before we left. That night I was detailed for picket duties, and my orders was to see that nobody came up on deck and that no smoking went on. The Germans had been reported in the Channel with their submarines, so we were nervous about it.
> However, we sailed out of Southampton. We were not long at sea when we joined the convoy of other ships that was waiting for us. We had escorts of four destroyers, they were looking out for our safety. See them sweeping around us, it was a grand sight. My duties on deck allowed me to see everything that was going on, there was no lights to be seen anywhere. Sea was rough a bit. So I finished my four-hour watch and I was relieved and I went and tried to have a sleep but nobody sleeped [*sic*] that night, excitement was to [*sic*] great.

Meanwhile, the main party left Gateshead and entrained at Newcastle Central Station, between 9.20 and 9.50 am on 19 April for the same destination as the advance party. Private Surtees remembered the padre coming round giving words of encouragement to the men and the train pulling out of the station before he had finished. Private Tindle occupied his time on the journey by writing the following verse:

*As the train left Newcastle Station*
*With Col. Vaux, Officers and men of the 7th DLI*
*We knew our leader and destination*
*And our hearts were filled with pride.*

The train went off to King's Cross, then Victoria, and they waited there a good while before finally setting off for Folkestone. Their journey took them along the pier straight to a waiting ship for passage to France. On embarkation each soldier was issued with a message from Field Marshal Kitchener, extolling them to uphold the honour of the British Army and to treat their allies with the utmost respect by maintaining their discipline. Kitchener went on to say: 'In this new experience you may find temptations both in wine and women. You must entirely resist both temptations, and, while treating all women with perfect courtesy, you should avoid any intimacy.' This may well have fallen on deaf ears!

Private Douglass recalled:

We embarked for France on 19 April 1915; they didn't tell you that, not in our language. We were only soldiers; we were all shoved onto a big troopship. There were a couple of destroyers that we could see. We were all in the hold. The whole battalion was on one troopship. It was one of the liners that they used for holidays because all the fancy work was boarded off with wood so that we could not damage it with our rifles and things. We got over to Boulogne, we went up to a place called St Michael's Mont and we slept there overnight.

Escorted by two destroyers, the journey was swift and the battalion arrived at Boulogne that night. After disembarkation they stayed in a rest camp just outside the town. As can be imagined, some of the troops had suffered from the effects of seasickness during the crossing and it took a while to get their land legs back. The facilities at the rest camp were basic, the troops being allocated to tents and issued with a blanket. The next day they marched to Pon-de-Briques, which was not a proper station, to meet up with the train carrying the advance party, which had preceded them by two days. The battalion entrained (settling into the usual horseboxes, which were common for British soldiers travelling in France) at 5.10 pm on the 20th for Bavinchove, near Cassel, where they stayed the night. Throughout the night the men could see the front line around the Ypres Salient, which was outlined by the Very lights sent up by both sides. Very lights were rockets that were used by sentries to illuminate no-man's-land at night to check for any attack or to see if one side or the other had working parties or patrols out. They were also used for signalling to the artillery if the front line needed help.

The battalion began to settle into the routine of army life in Belgium, taking time to sort themselves out after the journey from England. One of the first things they discovered was that water was scarce in the area; as a result the water carts were deployed to collect safe, clean drinking water. The opportunity was also taken by the commanders to read out army orders to their companies with regard to discipline. As the battalion was now on active service instructions were given about the special care the troops had to take with their weapons, ammunition, equipment and iron rations.

When the division landed in France it should have been allowed to concentrate behind the lines for a further period of training. After this they should have been introduced to trench warfare by taking over a quiet part of the line after being attached to another division for instruction into trench life and routine. Unfortunately, this was not to be the case, as the Germans were planning an attack at Ypres.

During the period when the battalion had landed in France and moved up to Cassel, everything at the front was quiet, but it was not to remain so for long. It was on 22 April at 5.00 pm that the Germans launched their chlorine gas attack against the Canadians and the French 45th Algerian and 87th Territorial divisions. The gas came as a surprise to the troops manning the front line and unfortunately the French gave way, creating a gap of 5 miles in the line. The Canadians on the other hand formed a defensive flank and continued to resist and man their trenches, although their left flank was in the air. Luckily, the Germans did not press their advantage, as the way to Ypres was clear. During the night the Germans consolidated their position on the ground vacated by the French. The next day they advanced cautiously into the gap, while at the same time pushing the Canadians back towards St Julien.

On 22 April, for the battalion there was a medical inspection of the troops and their health was rated as good. It was with visions of a catastrophe that the Allied leaders started to look around for whatever available troops there were to plug the gap left by the French. Enter the Northumbrian Division. Later that day the divisional commander received orders for all units to be ready to move immediately to the front.

On 23 April the battalion suddenly received orders to move to Steenvoorde, where the 6th, 8th and 9th battalions of the Durham Light Infantry were also concentrating. When they arrived the battalion was ordered to dump their packs in a field, which were to be collected by the transport section later, and to march up to Vlamertinghe. They set off at 4.30 pm.

Private Douglass remembered the approach to the front:

> There were the four battalions in the brigade; we lost the toss, the other three [in fact it was only the 6th and 8th] battalions went up in London omnibus's [*sic*] and we had to march in full pack with ammunition. We had our blankets carried. I believe it was 36 miles we marched with all that clobber on. We ended up in a place called the Granary, up by Poperinghe. We were told to bed down, no equipment to be taken off, except your packs, you had to keep in battledress. 'Loosen your boots but don't take them off.'

*Portrait photograph of Private Stan Douglass.*

This was also confirmed by Private Patterson:

We marched so far and then we met the 6th Durhams, they were in this village and they had been waiting for us coming for the colonels to throw up [to see] who went up in buses. We lost the toss, which we were lucky and they went up. When we got up we were meeting them coming back wounded. We were halfway there and we were standing ready with our tins to get our dinners. 'Pack up!'

If they had given us ten minutes we would have had our dinners. Pack up, off to the front. We marched from dinner time until one o'clock the next morning. You couldn't expect us to fight after that time. Next day we got a slice of bread and bully beef. That was to last us for five days.

In a letter home, Private Corder stated:

We had a very stiff march last night from five to 10.30 (Friday 23rd) and for about three hours we had not a halt. We were billeted for the fight in a huge four-storied hop warehouse, and as our blankets were on the transport we had to get along without as best we could. Personally I had plenty of very dirty sacking and kept fairly warm. It would be about twelve o'clock before we finally turned in, and we were up at six.

The division was not going into the front line as a complete formation; instead it was being used to plug the gaps. The battalion belonged to the 151st Brigade, along with the 6th, 8th and 9th battalions of the Durham Light Infantry. Each battalion was ordered to a different part of the salient to help other formations and they did not come back together as a brigade for some time.

According to Private Surtees, before the battalion moved off,

the colonel called us all around and he said we were going up to the line. And he said 'Some of you won't come back.' My brother-in-law [Private Patterson] told me that. He was in the front. Instead of pulling you right in beside him, they always had to have a big square, that's no good you can never hear anything there. ...About eleven o'clock, 'Fall in'. We fell in, in our order, full pack and everything again. We marched up the main road, up to Ypres. Before we come to Ypres we went into a field and took our packs off. Everybody's pack was put in the field in order, put in proper A Company, B Company and that. We got into fighting order, then we started the march up, it was a long way.

The 7th Battalion, along with the 9th, were ordered to march to the front, which in the event proved lucky for them both. While on the march up to Ypres they received a cheer from the other two battalions in the buses as they passed by. On the 25th, the battalion bivouacked for the night at the White Chateau at Potijze, just outside Ypres.

On the way up the troops had to pass through Ypres, which by this time was on fire from the constant bombardment by the Germans, who were aiming to make the movement of troops to the front difficult, if not impossible, especially in daylight. The vast majority of supplies and reinforcements for the salient had to pass through Ypres. It was the first time the battalion had come under shellfire.

Private Douglass remembered: 'We get to the White Chateau and told to dig in there, which I think was a mistake. It teemed with rain all night and we found ourselves lying in holes full of water.'

Others were slightly luckier, as Private A. Green remarked in a letter to a friend:

We billeted, or should I say slept, in a wood and the five of us were fortunate in finding a dugout all ready for occupation, and though there was a fearful squash we were as cosy as could be and escaped the rain which soaked through everyone who had to sleep out altogether.

The next day at 2.00 pm the battalion came under the orders of Lieutenant Colonel Bridgford, King's Own Shropshire Light Infantry. At dusk, the battalion was ordered to advance to Verlorenhoek, which they did, moving out onto the Menin Road in extended order and, moving via Frezenberg, bivouacked in a field on the south side of the road. On the way up the line they passed the wounded coming back down. Some of them were from the two Durham battalions that had been bussed up. This first sight of battle came as a shock to some.

While the Durhams were at the White Chateau, the Germans had been applying steady pressure on the Canadians, to the effect that they were driven from the Gravenstafel Ridge. At about noon a staff officer, Captain Carpenter, galloped up to Colonel Vaux and handed him some orders and then left. In order to stabilize the situation, a series of counter-attacks were to be made, and to support one of these the battalion was ordered to advance at 2.00 pm on the

*A.J. Green, killed in action 26 May 1915.*

26th towards Gravenstafel and Zevenkote. Colonel Vaux then called the other officers together and gave his orders for the advance. This was to take place over open fields, in full view of the Germans. The battalion marched off in artillery formation in three lines and gallantly pushed on and came to the place ordered, where they commenced to dig in. After the rain of the past few days the sun now began to shine. This was the battalion's first attack and Private Surtees remembered it as follows:

I always remember it was cold with white frost on my shoes. We were going in now and the wounded were coming down, I think they were from the 8th Durhams. I always remember Second Lieutenant Bell turning around to us; we were in the first line of our platoon, saying, 'Well boys, I hope we do better than that.'

Next afternoon, they don't tell you what you are going to do, the officer said, 'Fall in'. We didn't know we were going into action. Somebody said keep together Frank. That was Jimmy Wilson. He said, 'I'll look after you.'

As we got up a little incline it was level, you could see right the way up to the ridge and so we were in proper military order, open order. Then we got ordered to lie down and fix bayonets, I don't know what for, but we fixed bayonets and at that range I thought we would never get through there. The gas, when He [the Germans] gassed the Canadians was lying heavy on the ground, you got a mouthful of that and you got the smell off the shells, you got all that into your lungs. We got settled down and we hadn't been there ten minutes when a German aeroplane came. He went right along and left a smoke line for his artillery to get the range. As soon as he flipped off, then he started. Then we went on. I was glad when we had to go as the lad next to me got hit, I went to him and opened his jacket to see the blood coming out, pumping. I thought it was his heart but it was a bit further down but they sent for the doctor, he was at the back. He came up with a face like a turkey cock. He said, 'You'll have to do the best you can I have all the wounded at the back to attend to.' I don't know what happened to him after that, the stretcher bearers will have taken him away. Another lad on the other side, I don't know what happened to him. A lot got hit at the same time; He was dropping His stuff on us. We were in open order, three steps between each one, it was perfect order, I can say that these casualties were being caused by shrapnel. We tried to dig in, just about 6 inches or so, if something came across it would go over your pack or into it. We must have lain there about an hour or probably more and then we got the order to go. There was a few got killed, just in the line in front.

You're frightened until you get used to it, you can get used to it. We got ordered to move forward, I've never seen so many shell holes and we were jumping from one shell hole to another. We went through Zonnebeke and parallel with the line and we got a good way. We got off the road and had to face the enemy, He wasn't far away. He must have wasted some stuff, light stuff, rifle fire. He was dropping the shells all over, the sods were coming down on you and there was the colonel [Vaux] right at the head. He was standing with his shepherd's crook. There he was standing. I thought, 'Look at that, there he is and they are pelting shells all over the show.' But he came out alright. He never budged, I looked out again as soon as one had gone off, I had a quick look up again, he's still there, he never got wounded.

The Germans were firing all night, it was buzzing over your head and you just lay on your pack waiting for the daylight. It must have been about two o'clock in the morning, maybe later, all of a sudden, when it was dead quiet, the colonel came past, he knew where we were lying. 'Come on lads you've got to get the Hell out of this as quick as possible or you'll be blown to bits in the morning. Hurry up and fall in on the road, not in fours or twos but single file. Get away back where you come from.' It was quite true because we had no trenches, we were on the top just behind the support. We went back to where we came from, we didn't get in the front line.

In the afternoon He started shelling us in these slit trenches. So some of the lads, as soon as there was a break dashed back to where we were in the morning, about 200 yards back. So I thought to myself, I'm not going to keep rushing about I'm going to stop in this little billet until He stops. I put my rifle down and my kit was about a yard away, then all of a sudden, I was just going to get up and make a dash across to where we were before. All of a sudden BANG. I got up and had a quick look. My water bottle was slit right through the centre and He blew my spare shirt out my pack. We had the long Enfield rifles then, the rifle was smashed. I got another one, there were plenty to get. I was lucky.

Lack of communication or knowledge of what you were going to do was a common theme amongst the men, as recorded by Private Douglass:

> We advanced, lay down, advanced again, fall down. Nobody knew what we were doing mind, it had not been explained. The third time we lay down the order came along, 'Fix bayonets'. Nothing happened before that but as soon as them bayonets went on all Hell broke out. He tossed everything at us. No rifle fire mind, just shellfire. The first experience I saw of it I took to be rags flying through the air, they were men really.

Reports were made by a number of officers and men that during the advance a German aeroplane was circling overhead and sending information back to their artillery as to the British position, including that of the battalion.

Lieutenant Philip Austin Kirkup, who would be killed in action in 1917, wrote to his parents in Cleadon:

> You will be interested to hear that we have had our first share of the fighting in this terrible war, and I am proud to say that the good old 7th Durhams behaved like veterans. We made an advance towards the firing line, and came under very heavy artillery fire, but we had a few casualties. My own men behaved magnificently. I lost my poor lance corporal. I came through scatheless myself, except for a rare old smack with a shrapnel bullet.
>
> I will say that they get the range very quickly. Generally an aeroplane comes over us, and a few minutes after we have to look out for squalls.

The only lance corporal killed on this day was 2446 Ogilvie Thomas Nairn, of Sunderland. Another officer of the battalion, from Shields, wrote to his parents:

> Since Sunday I have had the time of my life. We slept in a field on Sunday night after attempting to attack, and yesterday morning we had a nice dose of shrapnel. Then we were all in little holes, and fortunately only had two men injured – not seriously. About 2.00 pm we were ordered to advance. I was detailed with the first line. Everything went well for almost a quarter of a mile, when we halted. An aeroplane spotted us, and within ten minutes it was all Hell. We rushed to a trench and lay like rats. This lasted about half an hour. Then we were ordered to close up on the right and change direction. We started again over open country. Of course, no Germans were seen. Have not seen one yet, except prisoners. It is the artillery. We hadn't been going many minutes when aeroplanes gave us away, and they started again. They used the poisoned shells, and they are awful. The fumes make you blind and daze you. I got the men to wet their handkerchiefs and this helped matters. We reached a village that had been wrecked by our shells and halted to find our bearings. We had just started advancing

when the shells again tickled us. I lay flat, and you could hear the whistle of the shrapnel flying over the trench. They burst just on the front of the trench and covered me with earth, and the fumes fairly choked me. When I had recovered the first line had advanced 500 yards – so I had to follow on my own, and it was rotten, I can tell you. It isn't so bad when a few of you go, but alone it is different. It is surprising how you get used to shells. If you hear them burst you are all right.

Well I found the company all right. Errington's company had joined us. We were all mixed up. In the end we reached our ridge we had to hold. That was after eight. How we came through it with so few casualties I don't know. When we rallied Wawn and Errington and I were the only officers up. We dug ourselves in, and during the talk, rifle fire was opened, and the bullets didn't half fly. We fixed bayonets and replied. I honestly thought we had been surrounded and were done for. We had our revolvers, and intended to have a real cut-in, but it was not to be. We saw nobody. It was dark and fire ceased. Our reserves didn't turn up, but two more of our company's officers and more men turned up. They had got lost.

Then after all our trouble we were ordered to retreat to trenches over a mile behind. We had worked for this position and would have had a real cut-in today. The rest of the battalion turned up. This was 3.00 am and in the end we reached our original starting point at seven this morning. We had a good many casualties but not many killed, mostly wounds in hands and legs. Four officers slightly wounded.

In a letter published in the *Sunderland Echo* dated 24 April 1928, the author describing himself as T7 told of his experiences and what he had witnessed that day. He said that his position during the action was on the extreme left of the third line:

One shell fell right between the feet of an elderly man just 10 yards in front of my brother and I, and when the shower of clods had ceased falling on our heads and the smoke had cleared away the poor fellow was lying dead – disembowelled, the stretcher bearers told me afterwards.

Near us was a windmill, at the foot of which lay a dead man, whom I recognized as one of our buglers [Bugler Emms].

The 'decoy' attack now seemed to be over, and the shell slackened with the coming of darkness, although rifle bullets constantly whistled across the road. Not far away along the road I saw Lieut Hickey lying on a stretcher with his head wrapped in bandages and Lieut Jacks sitting in the ditch smoking a cigarette with his foot bandaged up and from him I learned that the adjutant had been hit by shrapnel; my own platoon had been lucky in losing only three men wounded.

The battalion remained here along the hedgerow until it was ordered by Colonel Bridgeford to retire, which it did, and returned to Verlorenhoek after dark.

The gas that a lot of the officers and men complained of was not caused by gas shells but was the fumes from the explosives. The attack was the first blooding for the battalion and luckily the casualties were light, with only four officers wounded – (Captain and Adjutant R.B. Bergne, Captain H. Jacks, and Second Lieutenants Hickey and Hopper) – and seven

*Corporal Graham (marked with a cross), wounded April 1915.*

other ranks killed (2446 Lance Corporal O.T. Nairn (36), Privates 2648 Thomas Telford Edmundson (20), 2124 Victor Rodley (20), 2376 Percy William Sollas (26), 334 Frederick Thompson (46), 2078 William Thornton (age unknown) and 2094 Bugler George Emms (18). There were also fourteen missing. Frederick Thompson was originally buried near Zonnebeke, but his grave was lost in later fighting and he is now commemorated on the Menin Gate Memorial.

Private James Donaldson Gray died on 27 April from wounds received the previous day. He was a painter by trade; he and his wife lived in Canterbury Street, South Shields. He had served in the Boer War and had been awarded the Territorial Force Efficiency Medal while serving with the old 5th Volunteer Battalion Durham Light Infantry. In addition to this he was also an honorary freeman of South Shields.

In a letter Captain W. Carswell-Hunt stated that Captain H. Jacks had been hit in the foot. The exploits of Captain Jacks in the action stand out in the memory of many soldiers who wrote letters home shortly afterwards. A lance corporal made a remark to an officer from the Northumbrian Division, which was reported in a local paper:

Captain Jacks was wonderful; a shell landed close to him and blew off his cap and broke his glasses, he went on, and next a shrapnel bullet struck him in the leg: still he went on with the first line, until at last he had to give up exhausted.

The same officer talked to other men of the battalion and reported back to those at home in a letter that said:

When Capt Jacks had to give in he called out, 'Go on boys! Keep going on. Don't mind me.' Capt Mail, whom I met later, said that he saw Capt Jacks when the shell burst beside him. His cap flew one way, his glasses another, and he was simply smothered from head to foot with earth. His eyes, nose, mouth, eyebrows and hair were full of it, and he came tumbling into a 'Jack Johnson' hole, where the others were lying, complaining that he couldn't find his specs. Capt Mail saw him later passing by with the stretcher bearers, as cheerful as you like, his chief anxiety being how to get his valise home.

Captain Harold Jacks, a solicitor from South Shields who had left England on 10 April in advance of the battalion and subsequently joined it when it arrived on the 19th, wrote to his mother shortly after the action. In his letter he told her that he was wounded by shrapnel in the left leg, just two hours after the advance began. Prior to being hit he had had a lucky escape as a 'Jack Johnson' nearly claimed his life. A 'Jack Johnson' was a German 5.9 artillery shell that, bursting with a cloud of black smoke, was named after the Negro boxer Jack Johnson.

Unfortunately, Captain Jacks was not to survive the war. After being wounded he became the adjutant of the 3/7th Battalion Durham Light Infantry, moving onto staff appointments later. In 1916 he was placed back on the active list and appointed to the 4th Nigerian Regiment. He died of septicaemia in Lagos, Nigeria, on 27 January 1919. He is the only officer of the regiment to be awarded the African General Service Medal 1902 with the clasp Nigeria 1918.

Private A. Raumph was one of the men wounded on this day and he described his experiences in a letter to his mother:

After getting into open order to skirmish up to our trench, a German aeroplane sighted us and at once the German big guns were pouring shells of every description among us, the shrapnel being the most prominent.

I was lying flat on my stomach when a 'Jack Johnson' dropped a little distance away and just about smothered me, but this I would not have minded if just as I had got my breath a shrapnel burst overhead and sent one scrap just about into my head. Here I lay a while, stunned but as soon as I came round I off with my equipment [*sic*] and crept into a gut [ditch], wending my way along on my stomach until I came to a dressing station, where I got my wound dressed.

I then walked back through the cursed Ypres, where the shells were dropping most furiously and it was only by Divine help that I got through without being hit. Then I managed to catch a motor ambulance and after five hours' swift riding I was brought to a French hospital.

Lance Corporal Burns, who was a private soldier then, receiving his promotion shortly after this engagement, also had a narrow escape, as did those who were near to him:

That morning we advanced in companies, then in platoons and after in open order. The enemy's bullets and shrapnel flying all about us, but still we pushed on through all this though. I saw two or three fall in this scrimmage. After we had advanced so long a time, a rider comes that we had to dig ourselves in as the enemy was in front dressed in khaki. I was digging myself in for all I was worth when I heard a buzzing noise and felt the wind. It was a shrapnel shell which just missed my neck. It stuck in Laverick's pack. He might have told you about that, this is where I got my first wound. A piece of shrapnel about an inch long entering my sole of the right boot, luckily it did not break the skin but caused a painful bruise. One of the chaps was wounded just after I got mine. He laid just at the other side of a shell hole where I was lying. I got to the dressing station where Captain Wawn took my boot off. I then saw our A [who A was is not known] getting his wounds dressed.

Private Hunter Laverick of B Company, who went on to become a company sergeant major, was wounded during this action and was unfortunately wounded again on 24 May. There was one other casualty that day, which was often remembered in letters home, and this was Colonel Vaux's horse. In a letter from Colonel Vaux he related that his hunter had been killed and that fortunately he was not on him at the time, saying that the front was no place for horses.

*Colonel Vaux.*

44

The battalion transport was also having a hectic time of it. For some reason they had been positioned between Potijze and Velorenhoek and just to their rear was a battery of Canadian artillery. This resulted in the transport receiving a few shells due to the Germans trying to find this battery, and so the transport was ordered to withdraw. The advance and retirement of the battalion was made in good order and, in the words of the war diary, 'all ranks behaved splendidly.'

The day after the attack was spent quietly, but things changed that evening, as Private Douglass recalled:

> The next night after that, after we'd been pulled out, we were mustered up together. We were going up in the darkness on a burial parade. And that unnerved us all because we saw there fellas blown to bits. There were scores of bodies; we were really just covering them. I don't know how far we were off the line; we just saw the Very lights. We were working there at nights burying the dead, what dead they were we could not tell you, we were too scared.

Co-operation between neighbouring units took place, each helping the other where it could, together with compassion shown by the Germans, as described by Private Patterson:

> When we advanced up there was an officer of the Princess Pats [Princess Patricia's Canadian Light Infantry], he came along and said, 'Would you mind coming along, I've got some wounded men.'
> 'I can't leave without permission, I must find my officer.'
> I found him, he was at the bottom of the trench.
> 'Have I permission to go to the Canadians to tend to their wounded?'
> 'Yes.'
> Off we went.
> When we got on the top to advance the Canadians were dug in. When we stopped walking we had got into the middle of no-man's-land; in the finish I found them. The sergeant, Sergeant Fletcher, 'Well I'm sorry boys but I'll have to leave you.'
> I said, 'You can't do anything else here, leave it to us, we'll get him back, if we can.'
> You could hear the guns were firing right over our fellas; if he'd shortened his range he'd have caused some bother. Anyhow, when the party came into view he stopped firing. I thought it was a good thing of the observer. He must have seen it was a stretcher party. But that was different to the Menin Road. We got him back and sent away.

However, at another time and on another part of the front, the Germans were not as merciful as those mentioned above. Fate could intervene. Private Patterson continues:

> About two or three days after, we were sent further up the line. The Menin Road went into Ypres. This chap got hit in the head and I said, 'Can you walk?'
> 'Yes I can walk down.'
> 'I'll come down with you.'

I got him on the road.

'Oh, I'm going to faint.'

Well I went back and got another two men and a stretcher and we started off down that road. Well it was alright until we got into view of the observer; he turned the guns straight at us. Bang!

'Keep moving, don't stop whatever you do.'

But he was spot on; he came onto the stretcher and hit the road. I said, 'We're lucky for a start.' That was the second time, but it just shows the difference between the two observers.

Casualties were unfortunately not only confined to the 1st Battalion, they were also occurring with the 2/7th Battalion, which was still in England. Private Frederick George Matthews died in barracks at Hendon, Sunderland, from an accidental gunshot wound on 22 April. His body was taken to Harton Cemetery, South Shields, on Sunday 25th, carried on a gun carriage and covered by a Union flag, upon which were his cap and bayonet. The coffin was accompanied by men of the battalion.

Back at the front, for the next couple of days the companies were engaged in digging near the front line and performing fatigue work for the troops in the trenches north-east of Frezenberg. Private Green wrote home to inform his reader of some excitement that occurred on 29 April:

Thursday 29 April – We did nothing very much during the day yesterday, except in a negative kind of way. Aeroplanes (German) have been hovering about more or less all the morning and their artillery got the range of our position to a nicety. In the afternoon we were shelled with shrapnel and one or two houses nearby set on fire. Two casualties occurred in the hedge side where we had dug ourselves in, but not at all near our party. The over-daring, however, of one of the enemy machines proved its own undoing and flying too low it came within range of our maxim guns. They made no mistake and it was with indescribable relief that we saw the Taube come slanting slowly but helplessly to earth. The two occupants were at once relieved of their responsibilities by the kindly British who, always eager to help, saw to it that they did not do themselves (or incidentally, anyone else) any further injury.

There were three men killed on this day, namely 1516 Private William Hamilton, 2870 Private John Storey Pescodd, of Hendon, Sunderland, and 2386 Private Richard Henderson Vipond, who was a painter in civilian life. It would seem that Private Pescodd was not one of the two deaths mentioned by Private Green, as the following letter to Mrs Pescodd from his Captain makes clear:

I am sorry to have to inform you that your husband John, was wounded in the head by a rifle shot last Thursday, April 29 and is now in hospital. John was busy digging a new trench quite close to the German trenches – about 75 yards when a bullet hit him in the back of the head. This occurred in the dark and John received immediate attention from the ambulance men and was taken away at once to the doctor.

Although mention is made of his going to hospital, Private Pescodd has no known grave and is commemorated on the Menin Gate, Ypres. Lieutenant H. Stewart was wounded, on the first of three occasions, on 30 April, at Zillebeke, by a bullet in the left shoulder, while laying sandbags in a trench. It was also on this day that 1346 Private J.D. Craig of the transport section, who was from Taylor Street, South Shields, was also wounded. All that he could remember was his horse being shot from under him and then nothing until waking up in hospital.

Private John M. Blanchflower described in a letter to a friend in South Shields what it was like to go up to the front to dig trenches and the tension it created:

> We left our dugouts about midnight, to go and dig a trench right in our first line of trenches. Every movement had to be done with the least possible noise. We set off across country in single file, with full equipment and spades, and crept along deserted railway tracks and through ruined villages, taking cover every time the Germans sent up one of their powerful star shells, which light up the place for miles around. Arriving at our destination we set to work, some to dig the trench, others to fill sandbags and pile them up in front. One slip and we would in all probability have been wiped out.

Private Blanchflower, who was a teacher at Dean Road School, South Shields, and was also the secretary of the Laygate Primitive Methodist Bible Class, went on to say that when the work was finished they retired to some dugouts belonging to regular soldiers and they were amazed by their comfort. They were stocked with chairs, tables and stoves, liberated from nearby ruined houses. He also went on to say that he had not had a hot meal since coming to the front, nearly three weeks previously, as fires were banned in the open.

The men of the battalion were learning quickly and adapting to conditions at the front. Private J. Robson, who was a signaller in C Company, told of the motto that was instilled into them:

> You had the one motto when you were in France, they used to tell you, 'You're over here now, kill or be killed.' I only happened to bayonet one chap or else he would have bayoneted me. We were both signallers; we must have been because I was circling over, it was a moonlit night. I was crawling along on my stomach when I saw this German coming towards me with his bayonet levelled. He made a lunge at me and I parried it with my rifle. His rifle went on the ground and I just took a chance and bayoneted him, in fact, it was that far in, the rifle must have been against his stomach. He pulled me over as he fell; I had to put my foot on him to pull the bayonet out. He pulled me over with him there was that much suction, but I never let go of my rifle. He was only a young lad like me. He would be about eighteen years old.
>
> We did not know much about fighting; you just had to fight the best way you could. When you were hand-to-hand fighting you were just fighting with anything, feet or fists or anything, use the butt of your rifle to the jaw or anything like that. Terrible hand-to-hand fighting. You were all mixed up; you did not know if you were fighting Germans or your own men.

Private Robson also related an episode that amused both him and his colleagues, which showed the tenacity of the Belgian farmer:

> We were at one farm, at one time, we were stationed there about a day, about two dozen of us there and we used to laugh at the farmer. The Germans were always shelling; every now and again they would put two or three shells over putting holes in his field. The shelling had just stopped and out went the farmer ploughing his field, hardly had he got in again when they started shelling again.

Private Robson was gassed on 26 May and invalided to England, where he remained on various light duties until 1918, when he was posted back to France, rejoining the battalion.

Digging new trenches, which were often quite close to the front line, had its surprises at times, as Private T. Stafford found out and mentioned in a letter to his wife at 14 D'Arcy Terrace, Sunderland:

> I had the experience of my life on Monday at midnight. We were under very heavy fire when we found one of our officers lying in a trench by himself badly wounded, and my officer asked me to stay behind and dress his wounds, which I did. After that this officer and I made up our minds to try and find the dressing station. We had not got very far away when we thought we heard someone behind us and to our horror there were five German snipers almost on top of us. They started firing at us as fast as they could, but after a while we made our escape. I was carrying my own pack on my back and the officer's as well, but when I saw what was going to happen I threw both packs away. We got through the fields firing all the time.

On 3 May the battalion left Ypres to move into billets at Watou for a well-earned rest, arriving there at 1.30 am after a 12-mile march. There were a number of foot problems after the march but the troops' spirits were excellent. Before the battalion left the trenches on the 3rd, Private Robert W. Smith was wounded in the foot. After his wound had healed sufficiently he was sent home to work for the engineering firms of Armstrong Whitworth Company and Messrs Wm Beardmore & Co, joining them in July 1916. He had served just fifteen days at the front with the battalion. However, in July 1918 he returned to France, serving this time with the Royal Engineers.

Before the battalion left the trenches for its well-earned rest tragedy occurred, followed by a most poignant scene. Private J.G. Southern of the machine-gun section, who was himself to be killed before the end of July, described it in a letter as follows:

> Last Sunday night (2 May) when the people at home would be in the churches and chapels we were in the trenches under shellfire. Shortly after we received orders to shift our position. During this operation two of our lads were killed. Our colonel asked us to sing a hymn or two while those two brave lads were buried in a rude but Britisher grave. They died honourably.

Private Southern's story is corroborated by Signaller C. Potts, who stated:

They bombarded our positions and two of our chaps were killed. Well, we buried them at dark and I was one of the party, and a touching scene it was. We put them down, took off our hats and said the Lord's Prayer. Then our colonel said a short prayer and we filled up the grave. Every now and then a star shell would go up and light the place up and made it look ghostly. I shall never forget that service. The wonderful part of it was that not one shell came over the whole time, yet after we had finished they fell again like hailstones.

The two men referred to were 1759 Private Thomas Hardy Bond and 2687 Private Joseph Robinson. The burial of the dead meant a lot to the men, who were now becoming used to seeing other dead men left lying unburied and seemingly uncared for.

One complaint that comes through from letters and discussions with members of the battalion was that they had little opportunity for bathing due to the circumstances existing at that time. Consequently the men took what chances they could get to freshen up, as related by Private Douglass:

When we were at Watou it was very hot, we were billeted on a farm down there. That was the first time we had been pulled out of the line, the first rest we had after landing in France. It was a big farm and we were all billeted sleeping in straw. Anyway it was that hot this day, I was coming down the road with Billy Brodie.

I said, 'There's a great big pond and I'm going in there Billy.'

There was a little slime. I just chucked my tunic off.

He said, 'Look at the dirt man.'

'I don't care.'

I jumped in and all of a sudden, the noise. Hundreds of frogs came up, great big frogs. I'd jumped into a frog farm. They all came to the surface, great big ones. The slime was hanging on me like a hat and all over the rest of me. Mind I did get cooled off, but the noise. They bark like dogs you know. I had to clean myself the best way I could. We went into the farm yard and used the pump and he wiped all the slime off me. When I got to the billet they didn't half laugh at me. I had to dry in the sun, there was nowt else for it. I said that if I'd done that in England I'd of died with fever or something. I'll never forget that frog farm.

Private Brodie returned to England later in the war. Before the war he had been a fitter at Clarks.

The battalion was in for a pleasant surprise on 5 May when they were ordered to form three sides of a square, to be addressed by Sir John French, who complimented them on the work they had done. His address was reported in the *Shields Daily Gazette and Shipping Telegraph*, by a Tyne Dock soldier who was present, as follows:

Officers, Non-Commissioned Officers and Men of the Durham Light Infantry, I wish to state briefly my appreciation and admiration of your splendid work during the last week. Drawn straight from home, you were placed in the most difficult position in the whole line, and the most highly trained of regular troops could not have displayed greater bravery and cheerfulness. This was the first occasion on which the Germans used poison bombs against the English, but we have fought savages before and we can fight them again. As Territorials you could have remained in England, but you chose to leave home, wives, families and friends, to come to the battlefield of Europe. We men of the Regular Army will never forget the splendid work done by the Territorial forces during this campaign. I am proud of you.

This visit by the commander-in-chief was much appreciated by all ranks of the battalion and the scene was described by Signaller C. Potts:

What a fine-looking chap he is. He looks absolutely in the pink, and his left breast looks like a ribbon counter on a bargain day. As he came into the field we all presented arms and he came to the salute and kept his hand there till he had looked at all those in the front and on both sides of him. Then he motioned for our rifles to go down and us to stand at ease.

The rest of the time was spent in short route marches around the countryside to toughen the troops.

A move to woods at Brandhoek followed, where they camped for a few days. It was noted during this time that enemy aircraft were active and strict precautions were taken to keep the men under cover during the day and thus avoid detection. On 8 May Private Mathew Smith Mallam, who was a collier and worked at the St Hilda Pit, South Shields, died of his wounds in a hospital in France.

During this period the Second Battle of Ypres continued and the need for new trenches and defences was constant. As a result the 7th Durham Light Infantry were called upon to do their bit. On 9 May the division was warned to be ready to move at short notice, while the Durham Light Infantry Brigade was put on one hour's notice to move. The next day the brigade set off for the woods north of Brandhoek, where all units were to bivouac. At 7.30 pm on 11 May they left Brandhoek for Zillebeke, where they met an officer of the Royal Engineers who indicated a line of trench they had to dig. Tools for the job had been issued previously. The battalion was distributed along the indicated line and worked until 2.30 am, working for five and a half hours. After this the battalion went to the GHQ [general headquarters] line, which at this time had become the second line.

This line was described in the *History of the Great War* (usually referred to as the *British Official History*) as follows:

It ran from Zillebeke Lake, where it was 1½ miles behind the front, northwards to a point half a mile east of Wieltje, where it was 3 miles behind the front, thence it gradually turned north-westwards to join a line covering Boesinghe village and railway bridge. It consisted of well-constructed text-book redoubts, of some 30 yards face, with their flanks turned back, each for a garrison of about fifty men. These redoubts were from 400 to 500 yards apart and were eventually joined up by fire trenches. The line was exceedingly well sighted from the point of view of a good field of fire, sometimes on a reverse, sometimes on a forward slope, but not overlooked owing to the general flatness of the ground. The real strength of the line lay in its wire – a continuous belt some 6 yards wide with openings only at the transverse roads and tracks.

The battalion remained in the GHQ line during the 12th, being heavily shelled all day, losing an officer killed (Lieutenant Cree, who was a barrister in the North East circuit and Chancery Bar) and twelve men wounded. It was also on 12 May that the brigade and division changed its designations. The Durham Light Infantry Brigade became the 151st Brigade and the Northumbrian Division became the 50th Division. Another working party of 500 men was sent to the 3rd Field Company Royal Engineers to work on a new line of trenches 50 yards east of the GHQ line, returning back to that line during the day. The battalion left the GHQ line on 14 May, becoming the reserve to General Kavanagh's Cavalry Division, the company commanders going forward to look at the ground they would have to move over in the event of the battalion being called upon to make a counter-attack.

Private Frank Surtees remembered an incident that occurred doing one of these trench-digging operations:

We went up to Zillebeke; that was when we started digging the trenches for the new battle line. He shelled us very heavy. Coming into the main trench I thought I'm going to go into the slit trench, but I changed my mind and thought I'll go and sit on the fire step and there was Freddie Bell, Peter Dowd and somebody else standing near. As soon as I got up out of this place somebody took my place. He [the Germans] put a terrific one over, heavy shell, what we call 5.9s. I saw it burst about 50 feet away, terrible noise. A lad called Peter Dowd, standing opposite, said, 'Ah! I'm finished.' I don't know what happened really, he might of got a splinter in the brain. He was buried about half past six behind the trench because then they used to bury them where they fell. After that we used to go down the main road to a big cemetery. Where I was when I got up the fella got hit. It was remarkable. I think he got hit in the feet. I never saw him again.

A follow-on to this story occurred in the 1920s, when Private Surtees was contacted by the War Office:

About five years after the war a buff-coloured letter arrived; it said, 'Could you please help, we've found a groundsheet here at Zillebeke behind the trenches and a body is wrapped in it. Could you tell us who it would be? It said it was marked in indelible pencil Frank Surtees 7DLI.' I said it could be Peter Dowd, who was in our section; it could be him because we just buried him behind the trenches. The stretcher bearers took them down to headquarters and buried them there.

As the body could not be formally identified as Private Peter Dowd, he was listed killed in action on 15 May and, as he has no known grave, he is commemorated on the Menin Gate. The other two men killed on that day were Private William Plews and Private John James Bailey. The latter had been employed at Forster's Forge, Sunderland, and left behind a 2-year-old daughter. The next day Private John H. White was wounded, which resulted in him losing an eye.

The battalion remained in reserve until the 17th, but they still had to provide working parties of up to 450 men nightly, to extend and deepen trenches. This did not change when they moved to huts at Brielen, arriving in the early hours of the morning of the 18th. If they thought they would be marked down for having a rest, then the thought was short-lived because every evening they still had to provide working parties for the 3rd Field Company Royal Engineers. This work was not without its hazards; men were still being killed and wounded. It was a steady trickle, which took its toll on the battalion.

During this tour of duty – digging trenches and suchlike – in the period from 11 to 17 May the battalion had eight killed and forty-five wounded; ten or so of these subsequently died of their wounds. It was now time for the battalion to learn the routine of the front line. This took place on 21 May. A and B companies were attached to the 3rd

*J.J. Bailey, killed in action 15 May 1915.*

Royal Fusiliers (85th Brigade), being split up among the Fusiliers by platoons between Bellewaarde and the Ypres to Roulers railway. The rest of the battalion, comprising HQ and C and D companies, was attached to the 3rd Middlesex Regiment (85th Brigade), taking over a section of the line, relieving the 20th Hussars, this being the first time these companies had been in the front line. The battalion adapted themselves to the new circumstances splendidly. That part of the battalion attached to the Middlesex Regiment was withdrawn on 23 May to the huts at Brielen. A and B companies remained in the line with the Fusiliers. In a letter home to South Shields, a private of the battalion wrote that the trenches contained a lot of water and the parapet offered only scarce protection. He said that on the Whit Sunday he had occasion to stand up and stretch his legs when he was hit by a bullet from a sniper, although he remained unseen, or so he thought, the bullet apparently passing through a sandbag. He was hit at seven o'clock in the morning, but was not removed from the trenches until ten o'clock at night because of the danger.

The day of 24 May 1915 began as fine and hot. Nothing especially interesting had been noticed during the night by the sentries on duty in the front line. However, to be on the safe side, stand-to was ordered for 2.15 am. Thirty minutes later, the troops in the front line saw four red lights, followed a little later by two others fired from the German trenches. It was then that the German artillery opened up, together with machine-gun and rifle fire, along the whole length of the V Corps' front. In conjunction with the bombardment the Germans released chlorine gas from their trenches. In some parts of the V Corps' area the trenches were so close together that the British could hear the hiss of the gas. The front held by the 3rd Royal Fusiliers, which still included A and B companies of the battalion, was further away from the Germans. The wind was light, which fortunately resulted in the gas moving slowly. The gas came as no surprise due to the alertness of the troops who had been standing-to for a while.

The trenches of the 85th Brigade had suffered somewhat from the weather as they were knee-deep in mud, which made movement difficult and life unpleasant. The initial attack by the Germans was repulsed on most parts of the front; the only success they achieved was the capture of Mouse Trap Farm, which was held by two platoons of the Royal Dublin Fusiliers.

This meant that the left flank of the Royal Fusiliers and 7th Durhams was open, and the enemy pressed their advantage. Telephone communication with brigade headquarters had been all but severed; runners continued to operate to maintain contact.

The *British Official History* said this of the start of the attack:

> All telephonic communication was now cut, observation was nearly out of the question, as the enemy had the advantage of the higher ground and the front line was shrouded in a black pall of smoke and dust formed by the continuous shelling with heavy howitzers.

The continual pressure exerted by the Germans on the Royal Fusiliers and Durhams forced the British from their trenches, back to the third line, just in behind Railway Wood. Counter-attacks were not successful in retaking the lost ground and the first batch of reinforcements from the 2nd Buffs, which had lost heavily on the way up due to the artillery barrage, helped to stabilize the front. Later in the day the remaining two companies of the 7th Durham Light Infantry arrived to help their comrades and halt the Germans.

Private Douglass remembered the attack:

> On the Whit Monday of 1915 the gas attack started. We didn't know what it was. All we knew that morning was that it was a nice calm day with a breeze. We saw this smoky stuff coming over. Just before that Lieutenant Stockdale on my left, Brodie, my mate, was on the left of him. Stockdale dropped in the trench with a bullet right through his head. Rifle fire started to break out all over and still we didn't know it was gas. Then everybody started to cough and retch and retch and that's what happened to me. I got a sniff of it and I was retching and retching. All that I can remember is I saw the Germans coming. We had no gas masks. They were just like monsters to us because they had big snouts. It was a gas mask, just like a pig's snout. And all I remember is one of them bending over me, in fact he pulled me up and dropped me down again. And I was still retching and retching and groaning and I must have passed out. I don't know how I got out of the trench, but when I came to I was lying in Wipers Square, waiting for an ambulance to take me down to the Canadian Hospital. The next thing that I remember I was in the Canadian Hospital. I don't know how I got there. How long I'd been there I couldn't tell you. But there was one morning the nurse came round, I was just beginning to get conscious and I heard her say, 'Doctor, here's one recovering, here's one making a movement.'
>
> There were two chaps beside her and she told me later they were specialists.
>
> He says, 'You're a very lucky chap.'
>
> I remember the song that was playing on a record somewhere; it was the *Eton Boating Song*, 'Rowing down the river'.
>
> One of them says, 'Have you ever been a smoker?'
>
> 'No I've never smoked.'
>
> 'Well you can put that down; it's probably saved your life because nearly everyone we got down here died.'
>
> It was useless really taking them down. They moved me from that hospital to a

big marquee for gas patients. We just had the marquee roof up, no walls around, for fresh air. They used to take us out in coaches for fresh air. 'All gas patients fall in.' It was about six weeks I was down there.

In a letter to his parents Private Douglass wrote:

I am now in hospital, gassed. We were attacked on Monday morning by the Germans. They put poisonous gases into our trenches and we were forced to retire, leaving our men poisoned. I got into the dressing station and we were shelled out. And I don't know how I got away, but I managed somehow and got into a train. I shall never forget Whit Monday. We lost everything we had.

The experience of Private Douglass, B Company, following his gassing was not unique, as related by Private Edwin Patterson, also of B Company:

Whit Monday I got gassed. We couldn't do nothing about it, we just had to hold on. He got in the front-line trench, I believe. A Company was about wiped out, but we gave as good as we got. I had to go into hospital. It was like having a red hot flame run down onto your lungs. I was in hospital for six weeks. I found out there what good nurses are and what bad nurses are. We had an ambulance from the trenches, they took them down to the train and the ambulance trains took them down to the Base. I was there six weeks. The doctor said, 'We don't know the effect this gas will have on you when you get old.'

'Get old! You're lucky if you live a fortnight up there.' He started to laugh.

They (nurses) used to put you down as a man, you're too lazy to work and all that. This woman came along and she had a Canadian. I was sitting in a deckchair and she says, 'Get up!' I got up and she put this Canadian down, puts his pillow round. She went and he looked at me, enough to say, 'Not my fault!' That was that, I had to lie down on the grass.

This was when I was gassed. VADs, they were alright, you could tell the difference.

The men's appreciation of the Germans' marksmanship with the rifle changed with this attack. Private R. Lovell, writing to a friend from a Woolwich hospital, after having been wounded in the head, expressed his admiration for their ability. Quartermaster Sergeant Grayston was wounded by two bullets; one caused a flesh wound on his left hand, the other grazed his right leg. To top this he was also shot through his hat, the bullet luckily missing his head. Other bullets were found to have hit other pieces of his equipment.

Part of A and B companies had been held back in reserve, just behind the front line. Private E. McIntosh was one such soldier, as he put in a letter home:

You will gather from the address that I have been put out of action at last. I got it all right early on Monday morning. The Germans attacked our front line under cover of the heaviest dose of gas that has been experienced here, and our men were compelled, after a stubborn resistance, to retire. Our platoon was lying in reserve and we were rushed up. Shortly afterwards we were cut off and hemmed in on three sides. It was slaughter then. Our fellows stuck it against terrible odds. There seemed to be thousands of Maxims and thousands of guns. I got through it somehow with a nasty smack on the nose, which is not worrying me at all. It might spoil my manly beauty, that is all. I don't know how my chums got on. I was lucky to get away as I did with Maxim and shellfire all the way down to the dressing station.

2613 Private Wilfred Raine, the youngest son of the late Reverend Foster Raine of the United Methodist Church, Thornhill Circuit, writing to his mother, who lived at Oaklands Terrace, Sunderland, from the Royal Herbert Hospital, Woolwich, told her what had happened to him:

On Whit Monday morning we had at 1.00 am finished a trench, 50 yards behind the first line, 3 miles through Ypres and near Hill 60, for our men to retire to, when a terrific shelling, rifle firing, and gassing commenced at 2.45. We were supports, (50 Durhams and some 3rd Royal Fusiliers) and about 3.30 am were supporting in the first line trenches. The Royal Fusiliers should have been there on a stretch of 100 yards, but had been gassed out. After wading through a communication trench with 30 inches of sloppy mud in it we got to the deserted trench, rather nonplussed.

About forty of our platoon got in and the rest were cut off. We settled down to wait for what happened with fixed bayonets. Sergt Collingwood looked over the parapet (the trench was 7ft deep, with a ledge to stand on 2 feet higher) and saw about sixty Germans coming; so we all got on the ledge and let them have it. In a mob they advanced, although we thinned them out by rifle fire, and receiving reinforcements they got in the trench when there was no one defending – on top and at the back of us.

Soon our men were lying thickly. I fired fifteen rounds and saw four Germans drop as the result, and then I was hit.

Private Raine had been hit in the left shoulder by shrapnel. Fortunately he survived the war.

Another Private Raine, 2163 Wilfred Arthur, of 3 St Albans Street, Sunderland, who had enlisted in May 1914, was initially reported as missing on Whit Monday. He turned up on 26 May 1915 at No. 12 Stationary Hospital suffering from gas poisoning. Later in the year he was transferred to the 23rd Provisional Battalion Durham Light Infantry and in 1916 returned to work as an engineer at John Dickenson & Sons Limited, Palmer's Engine Works, Sunderland.

The Germans did not have everything their own way. Although the men were suffering from the gas and the bombardment, they managed to put up a stout resistance. Sergeant Norman Saxon, B Company, described his experience to an acquaintance back in Sunderland:

I will describe what happened on Whit Monday.

Tom and I were separated from the other two so we stuck together. At last we reached the first trench, and I may say the worst end, as we had to fire front and side. We were soon busy, for the Germans were upon us. It was when the fight was at its height that Tom said to me, 'Well Norman, we have stuck together so far, let's fight together.' And we did, shoulder to shoulder. At one time four of us fired together for about eight rounds and checked an advance on the left. After that Tom and a chap called Middleton and myself were the only ones who could fire on the left and we let them have it hot. Then we moved our positions and did a bit more damage.

It was at this point that I lost my partner. I spotted a Hun who seemed to be their crack shot. We could only see his helmet and I instantly told Tom I was on him and fired. I missed him and got a bullet through my hat from him in exchange. Again I fired at him, and he hit me through the hat, nearly knocking me off. Then Tom said, 'I'll have a shot at the beggar,' but the brute was ready. In the meantime I had to reload and did so quickly and up again at him. I must have downed him with the first two shots, for he disappeared. I then turned to look at Tom and found him lying on his back with a bad wound through his head. He must have passed away instantly.

*Group taken at Gateshead, 1915, including Sergeant Norman Saxon. Some of the men are wearing the Imperial Service badge, denoting they have volunteered to serve abroad.*

There is no indication who Tom was from the letter. However, on this day two men called Thomas were killed. They were 2911 Private Thomas Goodfellow and 2449 Private Thomas Straker.

Although a lot of soldiers were wounded, in many cases their story did not stop there, and neither did it end when they reached the regimental aid post, as described by Sergeant Herbert Walton, of A Company, who was later commissioned. In his memoir he wrote:

Whit Monday 24 May. I was slightly wounded when the Germans made an onslaught in front of Ypres when, for the second time, they used poison gas, for which we had no protection except a small pad to place over our mouth and nose.

Shortly after I had left the trench to go to the first aid post and after being patched up, the first aid post was forced to evacuate because the Germans had overrun the front line. It was a case of those who were able to walk having to look after themselves and with others I set off to walk to Ypres, which was about 3 miles distant. After walking nearly 2 miles I was picked up by an ambulance and taken to the casualty clearing station at Watou, not far from Ypres.

After recovering, Sergeant Walton rejoined the reserve battalion. On 15 September 1916 he was gazetted second lieutenant and did not rejoin the battalion in France until November 1916.

During the retirement from the front line it was inevitable that some men would become separated from the main body. One such soldier was Private Frank Grey, who somehow attached himself to the Dragoon Guards and ended up making a counter-attack with them before rejoining the battalion. There were reports of narrow escapes from being captured, as Private Nicol reported on his experiences:

I had sent the wounded back helping each other. I had only one wounded left, an officer, very bad, when the Germans rushed past shouting as hard as they could. They were too busy rushing our boys to notice me behind a house, bandaging the officer, so I was able to get away down a ditch and through some young corn.

The way the Germans treated the wounded and prisoners varied. There were some who treated their prisoners humanely and there were some who committed what would be today called war crimes. The following are instances of both kinds that happened on that Whit Monday.

Lance Corporal G.H. Cogden, managing to keep his sense of humour, was one of the lucky ones because not only did he face danger from the Germans but he also faced danger from his own side, as he said when he wrote home:

I have been wounded in a fight here, which was not a private affair, so we could all join in. I don't remember much about it, only feeling a smack in the jaw as if a train had run into it. However, I rose to time, and wakened up with my face in a pool of blood, a few teeth in my mouth, a small hole in each cheek, and a black eye. You bet I was fortunate. The rifle bullet had gone in one cheek, lifted the ivories, and gone out at the other, quite a pretty movement.

I was going to get up and run back, after I went down for the count, to our lines, when I saw a Bavarian shooting the next wounded man to me, so you can imagine what I felt, as I was not 20 yards away. I promptly wriggled into a hole, where I was later captured by three Germans, who treated me awfully decently. They gave me water and coffee and also tried to bandage my wound, but at the same time I was their prisoner, and it took me a good hour to slip them.

I afterwards crept along the ground for half an hour, and finished up about 30 yards in front of one of our trenches and yelled for help, and stood up, and was mighty near being shot again, this time by our own men.

Reports of atrocities began to circulate. Private G. Atkinson, of B Company, told his parents in a letter:

> We were in action again on Whit Monday, and had a bad time of it but I might tell you the Germans got it very hot. When our Jasper [a brother who was also in the 7th DLI] comes home he will have a nice tale to tell you. I was looking for him for two days before I could hear of him, but, I saw him well again. Well so far as I can tell you about it, there were about six of them trapped by Germans and they made them throw their arms away and their kits. When they got about 20 yards away they began to shoot at them, hitting two, but the others got away safe and sound. I hope it will be a long time before we have such a time of it again. The boys will not forget Whit Monday for a long time. I can tell you it was like being in Hell for a few hours.

Private H. Horn, in a letter to his brother, also reported seeing 'one Prussian giant, about 6ft 8ins, tell one of our men to put up his hands. The man did so, and then the Prussian seized the prisoner's rifle and blew his brains out. I may say the German lived only about three seconds after, for one of our fellows who saw it at once stopped retiring and shot the man dead on the spot.'

While the Whit Monday attack was taking place Private Frank Surtees had been in hospital suffering from the effects of gas received in April. When he returned to the battalion he was told the following tale by those who were there and had survived:

> This is a good one. Freddie Bell and Jack Reay [*sic*], two big lands, both 6-footers. He caught them in the May when He was attacking and our battalion was in the front line. I wasn't there; I was down at Rouen at the time. Well He caught them; He must have come down the trench, broken the flank. What He did, and this is true from the ones which were there. Jack Reay and Bell and some more, the Germans made them take off their equipment and told them to run for it across to our lines and when they ran for it they shot them down just like pigeons. It's true that. Tommy Wilson I think got away, he got wounded in the legs I think, but he got away.

The two companies in reserve, C and D, together with battalion HQ, were ordered forward to the support trenches. As the wind was light the gas lingered longer and moved slowly. This meant that although the reserves were a couple of miles behind the front line, they too suffered from the effects of the gas.

Private Roger Wilson described his experiences:

> We lay down in our trenches to sleep at 2.00 am but as it was beginning to get light it was time to get the letters. I volunteered with two others to get the mail and parcels. We returned to our trenches heavily laden with the parcels and our pockets full of letters. It was now 2.30 am. I had to give out all the parcels and letters and being out of bed myself commenced to open my parcel from Aunt Emily. During this process I looked over the parapet of the trench and to my astonishment I saw perhaps a mile in front of me, stretched from left to right as far as the eye could see, a thick cloud of

yellow gas. I gave the warning to half our platoon and shouted to get on the respirators – no time was lost in doing this either.

We were now standing to arms and all at once there started from the German lines a perfect hail of bullets and shells. We had to keep well down in our trenches; shells were coming thick and fast and bursting all round us. It was terrific. On looking through a peephole in the parapet a most terrible scene was portrayed. The gas, although gradually dispersing, was coming slowly towards us. The sky seemed clouded by the smoke and fumes from the bursting shells, and as it was not yet light one could see the red flash the shells made on bursting. We could not see the firing line in front of us, but on looking hard I could see men staggering back over the fields. These were the poor English soldiers who had been gassed. But our artillery was soon at work, and although I did not see its effect it did excellently. On our right the firing line was only about 200 yards away and it was here that we had to keep on the *qui vive* more particularly. Soon from these trenches wounded and gassed men came crawling. They had to pass the back of our trench to get onto the road, so we saw the poor chaps – some all cut with shrapnel, some wounded by bullets, and others gasping like madmen for breath. These latter were the gassed, and they were in a pitiful condition.

We remained in this trench for some hours before we got the order to move, when it was known to us that we had to reinforce the firing line. Then in single file we passed up the trench to a communicating trench leading up to the firing line. How slowly we moved! We could not do otherwise, as the trenches were 2 feet deep in water and mud and at every step we took our feet and legs were submerged to above the knees, so you will see how patient we had to be. It was a trying job, too. It required all our energy to withdraw our legs and it got worse as we went along, for the liquid was gradually being worked to a thick, deep dough. The captain led the way.

We were now in the firing line and we saw the Germans not more than 200 yards in front of us. We immediately opened fire on them, but there were hundreds of them and they kept advancing all the time. They came nearer and nearer and were being shot down all the time by our chaps, who were firing away magnificently, although, unfortunately, not without loss. Soon the Germans, big fat men with their helmets and huge packs and fixed bayonets, came within 10 yards in front of us. Fortunately for us there was barbed wire between the enemy and our trench. This was a great advantage for we kept up such a rapid fire that they did not attempt to cut it. As a matter of fact our fire was so hot that they had to retire on our front for 100 yards or so. But the worst was yet to come. The enemy tried to surround us and cut off our retreat. They extended on their right, came round on our left, and many of them got to the rear of us. So that left us with only one way of escape from them and that was the trench on our right.

However, we dealt with the enemy on our side and rear and it was here that I realized what I came out to do. Taking a careful, steady aim each time, I could see the man I aimed for fall over at every shot. I accounted for many a Hun during the time we were in the trench. I can't say that I was glad, but I will say that I was satisfied.

It would be seven or eight o'clock now and we were still here fighting away with all our might. Bullets seemed to come from all directions and the shelling had not ceased at all. We were truly in a hot place. I dare hardly bring the scenes to memory again even now. It wrung my very heart strings to see my comrades fall, but, alas, it could not be helped. Well, we had lost all thought of time. The only thing that made us believe it was near twelve was hunger. I myself had had nothing since about four on the previous day. I could feel the gas on my stomach and it made me nearly double up. So when we retired, the one or two who were left, I got on the road in some miraculous way, for the very air seemed nothing but obnoxious gasses, shells and bullets. I went trudging along feeling as weak as a babe and as sick as a dog. What horrible sights beset me as I made for the hospital. Men were lying about the road dead and wounded in pitiful condition.

On Whit Monday evening I had to go to a dressing station to get put right. They put me in a motor car and took me to hospital, out of which I came on Thursday evening, feeling a lot better.

The transport section also had an interesting time during the battle. Sergeant Thompson wrote the following account of that day:

It was on Whit Monday 1915 when our battalion were in the thick of it. The Germans sent over some gas, of a yellowish colour, and we had to put on our respirators to save ourselves from being gassed. We went through something at this place, the shellfire was awful. Our transport got orders to move out of the White Chateau. Shellfire was bad. Just before we left we saw a batch of German prisoners, Prussian Guards they were.

We moved to a place called St Jean and the Germans shelled us all the time. Here was to be our transport lines for a while.

The treatment of the wounded and prisoners could vary from unit to unit and individual to individual, some good, some bad. Lance Corporal Alf Burns, writing to his wife from his hospital bed in Switzerland in August 1916, recounted his time during this battle from the moment they entered the trenches until he was evacuated to Roulers awaiting transport to Germany:

We received sharp orders to proceed to the first line of trenches, which we got there at night, after a long march. When we were going into them we were pestered by snipers but I don't think that they hit anybody. We were very glad to get into the trenches as we had had no sleep for a long time. I was feeling very much done up myself by now; things seemed to go on alright here. We past [sic] our time in filling sandbags to strengthen the trenches which was blown in bits in some places and in taking pot shots at the enemy in front. In the enemy's trench they were walking about with a dummy in the air; of course, we had to have a shot at it. But what we did not like was the water in the trench. One night it was thundering and lightning and raining very heavy. When in these trenches (which was my last as you will see later on) we could not get any water, so we just had to dig a big hole in the trench and drink the dirty water which came into the holes, putting a cloth over our mess tin to stop the dirty water going down our throats and we were very hungry.

The rations and fresh water had just came up when the attack started. I happened to be on look-out in our trench when I saw a red light go up in the air followed by another one. Well the rations had to be left as we had to fight for our lives. This was the 24th of May, Whit Monday morning. This red light was a German signal to attack, their artillery began sending shells over into the trenches and behind, doing a lot of damage to our reserves. After their artillery quietened down, then they began to send the gas over to our trenches. We suffered very much with this stuff; it was just like a lot of dirty greenish white smoke rolling towards us. After they gave us a good lot of this, they started to come over for us, for all they were worth, time and time again, until they broke through our trenches in two places. That morning we could hardly get up the reserves on account of the heavy shelling from the enemy. Two men on my left, who was in my trench, got it very bad with the gas, one of which I saw wounded after. We got the order to retire and the men were coming past me with Germans at their rear. This is the time I saw Wallace and he stopped to speak to me. I saw him later on in the morning. [The Wallace, Lance Corporal Burns mentions is 3151 Private Wallace Eggleston, of B Company, who was killed in action on 25 May 1915.] Things was beginning to look terrible and very black for us. So in my trench we thought it about time we got out of it as the Germans was quite on top of us. Well we started but it was very slow work, as there were dead bodies lying about in the trench and the trenches was knocked about very much. I got to the communication trench, which was half filled with mud and water. I came to the end of this trench, which was very deep; it reached up to my waist. After two or three tries to get out on the top onto the roadway at the end of this trench, I was feeling very much done up for want of sleep, also with the gas.

When I got onto the road I saw lots of men take cover, but I went on and on seeing me making down the road the men started to follow. We got a bit down this road when the Germans saw us and they let drive with their machine guns. I saw the men dropping on the road and just then I got one across the head, which began to bleed freely. By this time I was left by myself. I then began to look round to see where I was when I got another one through the left arm and when I came to look at myself I was nothing but a mass of mud and blood. The skin was off my right thumb, with using my rifle so much that morning. I was beginning to lose a lot of blood and I was feeling weak, going further down the road I came to a ditch, which I fell into, on my face. I got out the best way I could, but found after I had got up at the wrong side of this ditch, I was going back into the trenches I had just left. Finding my mistake out, I tried to get back but it was too late. I saw the Germans coming for me shouting at the top of their voices. I just had time to toss my rifle and pack into a small dugout just behind me when they came up to me, some going on and a few stopping to take charge of me. I was then told to take off my jacket and undo my shirt. I was wondering what was coming off. I thought they were going to do me in, but I don't think I cared, for I cannot tell you how I felt about this time. Well it seems they only wanted to see my disc, what regiment I belonged to. Then they went through my pockets, but only took from me my knife. They then took me over and stood me against the wall of a large house. I thought they were going to shoot me but they only came round to see a [*sic*] Englander and to get cover from our shells which was being put into them to keep them for advancing any further. They got hold of me and took me inside of this house where I saw about ten men and an officer lying wounded. I looked after them and dressed their wounds as much as I could as I was in a very bad way myself. After I had finished with them I went over to a wall against which a German was standing. I was just beginning to slip down on the floor, through weakness, when one of our shells burst inside of the house. There was two of us hit with this shell. I got a bullet right through the knee, smashing the bone, and the German was killed.

Well when I got hit with this bullet I did drop flat on the floor but jumped up and ran outside. I don't know how I did it but I got outside and dropped. One of our men, who had just been brought in, came and dressed me and propped me against the wall. The shells were coming over now thick and fast. I was getting hit every time with bricks, bits of trees, etc. I will never forget these two days and two nights. I stayed in this house lying wounded with nothing to eat and nothing to drink but dirty water. I laid outside all that Monday watching our artillery blowing up everything around us. Sometimes a shell would come right through the walls, making big holes and sometimes burst inside and cover us all with bricks.

The German in charge of us was very kind, going out time and time again with a water bottle for water for us. He told me that their Red Cross would come for us when our artillery gave over. Well our artillery stopped sending shells over on Tuesday night but it was very late at night when the Red Cross men came for us. They took me on a stretcher and put me down just behind their first line trench. They were just beginning to relieve each other and they were coming and going out of these trenches just where I was lying. Some of them were very kind to me, giving me cigarettes, sweets and coffee. Our shells was beginning to burst just a bit from where I was lying. I would be an hour at this place when they picked me up and went on but we had not gone far when we heard the sound of machine guns and rifle fire. Then the bullets came dropping around us. They dropped me and ran for some trenches which was at the side of us. They went on a little further when the same thing happened. I believe it was our company making an attack. By now I found there was one of our officers walking beside us. He had his left arm in a sling. I don't know who he was as it was too dark to see. Well they got me to a broken-down house, there a German doctor had a look at me but he did not touch me at all. They then carry me up some stairs and put me down beside a window, all the panes being out. It was very cold. I asked one of the Germans for something to cover me as one of my trouser legs was gone. I got covered over with some nice remarks but I did not care as I did not understand what he said. They put another wounded Englishman beside but you could see he was not for this world long, he was asking for water, water all the time and every time the Germans gave it him he would kiss their hands, poor fellow. You could see he was properly gone. They shifted me early in the morning and took me to a small wooden house on the road. They then put me into a horse ambulance and took me to a town called Roulers.

Lance Corporal Burns went on in his letter to describe his further treatment in the German hospitals. Unfortunately, his leg became worse and needed operations, although the bullet had been removed earlier. The leg still did not heal and this resulted in him being repatriated to England via Switzerland.

Sergeant J.W. Campbell, in a letter to the *Sunderland Echo* published on 26 May 1928, related that when they took over the trenches the regulars said that it had been quiet, and nothing seemed to contradict this. However, it was a false security. He and his party had been digging a communication trench and just returned to their own dugouts when an alarm was raised and they stood-to, only to find out it was a false alarm. Shortly afterwards another alarm was raised; this time it proved real, the Germans having broken through the flanks. Sergeant Campbell's party were ordered to man a deep communication trench that was knee-deep in water. He takes up the story:

> Owing to the depth it was difficult to see over the top, much less get a rifle over to fire. Shells were now bursting on our trench with deadly effect, and to our horror we saw a great cloud of greenish-yellow gas drifting over the trenches to our left. We were firing with great difficulty owing to there being no fire step, and lack of orders only added to the confusion of the moment caused by the sudden and heavy attack.
>
> The spare bandoliers which we had carried with us since landing in France now became of real use, and were passed over to the men who occupied a small advance trench and also a ruined farmhouse, from which they were able to do some sniping with much success.
>
> A few of our chaps were now *hors de combat*, having been shot through the head, and wounded by shellfire, while other poor fellows were slowly choking through the dreadful effects of the chlorine gas, as the respirators in use then were of a most primitive order. Eventually we got the order to retire from this position and work back a bit. We were now being pounded from all sides, and momentarily everything became confusion. The enemy began to pour upon us from both flanks and we were in great danger of being surrounded. Gradually, and with difficulty, we managed to get out of this communication trench and work down towards a support line. Our people got scattered and mixed up with other units who had come up in support.

Captain Bradford, the new adjutant who had joined the battalion at Watou in May, placed himself at the crossroads near Potijze Chateau and by his coolness was an inspiration to those troops coming up to the front. It was as if he were a policeman on point duty, even though bullets were flying past him and shells landing close by.

Sergeant Thompson goes on to recount an incident a little later:

> One day they (the Canadians) saw someone in a church and some of their men went over and brought this man over to the Canadian CO. When they searched him they found out he was a spy. They soon put him out of the road. A few of our drivers went over to have a look at him. He was a very tall chap with French clothes on top of his German uniform.
>
> Next day an order came for a limber wagon to proceed for rations. The driver

was off for duty, poor fellow, he had not long started on his journey when a shell burst right on top of him and blew him and his horses to pieces. This happened near Hell's Corner; we buried him in St Jean.

When the officers reported back to the battalion during the evening, they said that the companies had behaved in a valiant manner. Back at Brielen, the remainder of the battalion were roused by the guard when they noticed the first traces of the gas used by the Germans. Respirators were donned and luckily no casualties were suffered. The battalion stood-to all day, leaving Brielen at 9.00 pm and moving through Ypres – which was being heavily shelled – to the GHQ line at Potijze. The battalion was still under the orders of the 85th Brigade.

All through the 25th, the battalion remained in the GHQ line. What remained of A and B companies rejoined the rest of the battalion during the night. During the fighting some men had attached themselves to other units and rejoined when things quietened down. It was after this that the battalion was withdrawn to Brielen, first to a field and then to the huts for a well-deserved rest. It was while they were here that Brigadier General Martin inspected them and expressed himself thoroughly satisfied with the state of the men and their equipment. Bugler Thomas Sanderson, who had attended the Rectory Park Boys' School, died of wounds on 25 May. His mother received a letter to say that he was buried at the farm of Monsieur Henri Tallyn Vantares, which was situated on the western side of the Poperinghe-Westoutre road, 3,000 yards south of Poperinghe. After the war his grave was moved and he is now buried at Klein Vierstraat British Cemetery.

This effectively was the end of the Second Battle of Ypres. Both the British and German troops were exhausted and each side was concerned about the amount of artillery ammunition used as their reserves were getting low. The British only had a little shrapnel left; Sir John French had confirmed to the War Office that he would have to cease offensive operations until the situation was resolved.

The battalion lost Major C.W. Hines, Captain F.M. Wawn, Lieutenant J. Meek and Second Lieutenant A.W.S. Stockdale killed, Lieutenants A. Rhodes and R.W. Adamson missing and Second Lieutenant C. Pickersgill wounded,

*Bugler Thomas Sanderson, died of wounds 25 May 1915.*

along with 25 other ranks killed, 75 wounded and 181 missing on 24 to 25 May.

Captain Wawn had been an accountant with Bolton, Wawn & Co, Sunderland. After finishing school he had been to France and Germany to study their languages. He had originally been commissioned into the 3rd Volunteer Battalion DLI and had served during the Boer War. Second Lieutenant Pickersgill had enlisted as a private in the 6th Durham Light Infantry. For a few months in 1916 he was attached to the Inland Water Transport, Royal

Engineers. He was also a cricketer for Durham County. Lieutenant Arthur Rhodes was a solicitor with his father's firm, F.S. Rhodes of Manchester. In December word was received that Lieutenant Rhodes was a prisoner, held in the camp at Wahn, near Cologne. Unfortunately this was not the case and it was presumed that he had been killed on 24 May. He is buried in Bedford House Cemetery, Ypres.

*Second Lieutenant R.W. Adamson, killed in action 24 May 1915.*

Private Surtees was informed by survivors of his company that Lieutenant Adamson had ordered his men to retire during the attack while he remained where he was, giving them covering fire until he was killed. Lieutenant Adamson had been educated at Durham School and had volunteered for service with the North Staffordshire Regiment during the Boer War, later being employed by the National Provincial Bank at Sunderland. His brother, Captain C.Y. Adamson, was killed in 1918 on the Salonika Front while serving with the 8th Royal Scots Fusiliers. Lieutenant Adamson has no known grave and is commemorated on the Menin Gate, Ypres.

It was also reported in the *South Shields Daily Gazette* that Major Hines, of Boldon (a solicitor with Hines & Son in Sunderland who had been commissioned into the 3rd Volunteer Battalion Durham Light Infantry on 24 March 1897), when last seen was the only living man in one of the trenches, firing steadily away at the advancing Germans until he was killed in the final rush near Wittbroke Farm. Lieutenant Colonel Vaux explained how Major Hines died in a letter to Canon Smith, the Rector of St Mary's Roman Catholic Church, Sunderland: 'He [Major Hines] always loved soldiering, and died one of the bravest men who have lost their lives out here. He would not retire; he could have left his post, but his duty was to stay, and the last anyone saw of him he was firing away at the enemy.' Private Tindle, who was severely wounded during the battle, was orderly to Major Hines. He was near him when he received his fatal wound. Private Tindle was rescued by a comrade, Private Black, who, noticing his helpless condition, grabbed him by the collar and dragged him over wire entanglements to safety, amidst a hail of shrapnel. Private Black was recommended for the DCM but unfortunately did not receive it.

Lieutenant Meek was a bank clerk, working in Newcastle upon Tyne, and a keen member of the Sunderland Operatic Society. Lieutenant Arthur W.S. Stockdale was a solicitor, in business with his father. He played cricket for the Sunderland Ashbrooke Club. Lieutenant C.O. Sayer, of Kirkby Stephens, Cumberland, was last seen with a broken left leg lying in a trench just before it was rushed by the Germans. Lieutenant Sayer died of his wounds on 7 June 1915 in the German military hospital at Courtnai, while a prisoner of war. Prior to the war he was mathematics lecturer at the Sunderland Day Training College. He left a widow and an infant daughter. He was the eldest of five brothers on active service.

Lieutenant W.S. Sanderson, the battalion transport officer, also ended up in hospital by the end of the month. He was a former mayor of Morpeth. He had been taking up some wagons in the dark, loaded with food for the battalion. They met other wagons coming back down from the front and, out of a side road, a motor convoy of ammunition wagons. Lieutenant

Sanderson's horse was between them and became excited and slipped, jamming Lieutenant Sanderson's legs against the wagons and throwing him off. Luckily he was only shaken up and bruised, but still needed to be referred to hospital.

The casualties for the division for the period 22 April to 31 May were, according to the *British Official History*:

> Military Operations: officers, 40 killed, 121 wounded and 25 missing. Casualties for other ranks were 596 killed, 2,963 wounded and 1,459 missing.

E. Cook, killed in action 26 May 1915.

The following are some of the fifty-nine men of the battalion who were either killed or died of wounds from 24 to 26 May:

2254 Corporal William Mustard Charlton. He was educated at the National School and found employment at Priestman's Yard, Sunderland, joining the battalion on 5 May 1913. He left behind a wife and two sons, the youngest being born on 28 February 1915.

2642 Private James Edward Cook, who was an assistant schoolmaster at Thornley Council School at the outbreak of the war. Although his body was found six weeks later and buried by a comrade, his grave was later lost and he is commemorated on the Menin Gate Memorial to the missing.

Private Wilfred Morton was wounded and taken prisoner during this period; he subsequently succumbed to his wounds on 30 May 1915. Before the war he had worked for his father, who was a quantity surveyor.

2066 Private Thomas William Fox, who was educated at St Mary's RC School and employed in the Engineering Department of Lynn's Forge, Pallion, in Sunderland. He had joined the battalion on 12 May 1914.

2416 Private Robert Usher, who was wounded in the right knee, as well as being gassed, was captured on Whit Monday. In his report to the authorities on his release in 1918 he mentions five other men of the battalion (including R. Dixon, W.H. Bowman, W. Leavesley and J. Stephenson) who were with him at Friedrichsfeld. The other mentioned was Alfred Burns, who is quoted earlier.

W.M. Charleton, killed in action 24 May 1915.

Some of those who were wounded during this battle were: 2233 Private Joseph Liddle Fairley, who was wounded in the head; 2230 Private Robert Duncan Jameson, who was wounded in both hands; and 2593 Private John Marshall, who was hit in the chest; 1993 Private Charles

Christian, who was gassed and suffered a gunshot wound to his left arm/wrist. Private Christian, who had enlisted in February 1914, spent the next nine weeks in hospital before finally being discharged in 1917 as permanently unfit. Unfortunately, he died on 17 August 1918, possibly as a result of his disabilities.

By the end of May 1915, the battalion mustered only 16 officers and 538 other ranks, after having landed in France on 19 April at full strength. The full strength of an infantry battalion at the start of the war was 30 officers and 992 other ranks.

After the war, at the unveiling of a war memorial in Sunderland, Colonel Vaux described an incident that took place during the gas attack. He said that the men of the battalion were standing in the trenches when they saw a gas cloud approaching and other men retiring from the front line. Colonel Vaux gathered these men together telling them, 'It's no use running. Come up here and sing a hymn.' They stood on top of the trench and sang *Abide with Me*. Colonel Vaux related that the cloud passed over them and not a man was gassed. This incident inspired Captain Wade, who had served as a private in the battalion, to paint a picture of the scene. The painting became known as *The Miracle of Ypres* and is still in the possession of Colonel Vaux's family.

Private H.H. Tindle, who was wounded in the right thigh during the action on Whit Monday, penned the following lines about the battle:

*2438 Private William Allan, killed in action 24 May 1915.*

*The Miracle of Ypres*, 1915.

It happened on Whit Monday
We knew what was in store
And our chaps God bless them
Knew twas to be bore.

Why the battle came off on Whit Monday
And all men to their posts
We poured lead into the Germans
And they poured it into us.

But when they saw they were beaten
Their gas shells they did try
And for four and a half solid hours
We had the orders 'Stand By'.

They had me in a sniping post
I stuck there 'til at last
While the Germans sent their gasses
As if they were from a blast

I was just about suffocating
When the order came to 'Charge',
I stood up with fixed bayonets
And over parapet sprang.

While only a few yards off them
I heard the hideous yells
Of the dying and the wounded
A bullet hit me and I fell.

As the orders rang out 'Retire'
We were outnumbered six to one
The boys gave them a D**ned good hiding
That's all we could have done.

As they had gassed our men that morning
Quite half of them had died
The rest of them had done their best
Or poor fellow they had tried.

*Chapter 4*

# Summer 1915

After the fighting of May had died down and what became known as the 'Second Battle' had come to an end, the battalion found itself in reserve to three divisions, namely the 28th, 6th and 3rd.

Experience was now beginning to tell in the battalion and lessons had been learnt from the recent battle. On 30 May orders were received – issued by headquarters as a result of the recent battle – to take readings of wind direction in the mornings and evenings. If the wind came from the German trenches, gas helmets had to be worn in the 'alert position' in case of a potential gas attack.

Since April, when the division had landed in France, it had been split up to assist other units, especially during the fighting. Orders arrived on 1 June that the division was to reassemble and take over a sector of the line, after relieving the 3rd Division. This was something new for the various battalions; they would now have to learn about trench warfare. Consequently, orders were issued for the concentration of the division: the 150th and 151st brigades came under the orders of 50th Division at 6.00 am on 2 June; the 149th Brigade joined it on 5 June.

There now followed a quiet period when the battalion was withdrawn to Poperinghe, where training in the form of short route marches and the like took place. The battalion bombers – thirty-six in number – were also given some practice with live bombs. The time to return to the salient duly arrived and on 6 June the battalion found themselves in the support trenches, west-south-west of Ypres, with the 150th Brigade holding the front. The work of strengthening the defences went on. The work comprised improving the wire, digging communication trenches and constructing strong points, all with the help of the brigade in the front line. On 6 June a company of the battalion was sent to Maple Copse to put it in a state of defence. Three days later, the 9th Durham Light Infantry relieved the battalion, which then proceeded to Ouderdom. Even when relief had taken place, the journey back to billets was at times far from safe. Private Long remembered that during one such relief, as a platoon was marching back a shell landed amongst them. Luckily it did not explode and no one was injured. He also remembered a rather ironic incident that had taken place during the recent fighting when one of the men had half his head blown off by a shell, and a few minutes later a parcel from his wife arrived. Private A. Bell wrote in a letter home that when the battalion was passing through the ruins of Ypres, a shell came through a house and wounded nearly all of one section.

The men at the front had not been forgotten by those at home in Sunderland. Not long after their arrival at the front collections were started for comforts for the men. Lance Corporal T. Lawson received such a parcel on 10 June, sent by a schoolgirl from Hendon. She had worked hard and saved her money to buy razors, shaving straps, foot powder and other useful

*In the trenches.*

things. Lance Corporal Lawson was so touched by this gift that he named his benefactor, in a letter to the *Sunderland Echo*, as Miss P. Hood of 33 Hendon Road.

The men of the battalion were being introduced to new sights and sounds. Private Bert Oliphant, in a letter to his mother in Sunderland, mentioned that there were a lot of Indian troops billeted close to them. The Sunderland men were fascinated by their customs and rituals: 'Sometimes they are on their knees praying and uttering the most blood-curdling cries.' However, friendly relations were maintained through the international medium of football, with inter-unit matches being held.

Although the battalion was out of the line on rest, accidents did happen, as related by Private J. Potts in a letter to his brother: 'We had got orders on Monday morning for rifle inspection when a poor fellow got a stray shot right through his thigh. I was not a foot off him. If he had not just stood up the bullet might have gone right through his heart. What a lucky man.'

On 12 June 1915, the battalion took over its own section of the front line, 2 miles south-east of Ypres, relieving the 4th Yorkshire Regiment. Life continued quietly in the front line, the men being employed in improving the parapets and dugouts. Things livened up on the 16th, when the 3rd Division made an attack at 4.15 am on the German trenches on Bellewarde Ridge, about a mile to the battalion's left. The battalion was ordered to co-operate by bursts of rapid fire at the German trenches to their front. It was not known what the results of the 3rd Division's attack were but the battalion did not escape without loss. The casualties that day amounted to one killed (2127 Private Ernest Stuart Livingstone Fenton, of D Company), fifteen wounded and one missing, those wounded apparently being the victims of a trench mortar bomb. The next day, the 5th Yorkshire Regiment relieved the 7th Durham Light Infantry, who moved back into dugouts at Sanctuary Wood, remaining in support of the 5th Yorks. For the next few days digging parties were supplied to construct a new communication trench in the rear of the fire trench. The battalion was relieved by the 4th Yorks in the support dugouts and moved back, with 149th Brigade, to Dranoutre. It is here that the battalion began to be split up again, for two companies were sent to support points behind the trenches occupied by the 8th Durham Light Infantry. The rest of the battalion left Dranoutre to go to billets near Kemmel. The machine-gun section was sent up to the front line with the 9th Durham Light Infantry.

It was at this time that news of the death of Captain C.B. Woodham DSO of the Duke of Cornwall's Light Infantry reached the battalion. Captain Woodham had been the adjutant for the 7th Durham Light Infantry for seven years and was very popular with both the officers and men. He had left the battalion a few years earlier to rejoin his regiment at the end of his appointment. His death was a sad one for the battalion.

Because of the losses sustained during the fighting of April and May, and due to the fact that no reinforcement had as yet been received from England, the 6th and 8th battalions Durham Light Infantry were amalgamated and became the 6/8th Composite Battalion. This meant that the brigade was now a battalion short. Consequently, the 5th Loyal North Lancs arrived to bring the formation up to strength. This battalion stayed with 151st Brigade until the end of November. Another unit became part of the brigade group on 20 June, which would work closely with the 7th Battalion in the future, and this was the 7th Field Company, Royal Engineers.

The second of the Nairn brothers to be killed with the battalion died on 22 June. He was 1366 Private Walter Nairn. Private Frank Surtees remembered that he had been on the fire step when he was shot through the head by a sniper. He died almost immediately of his wounds. Private W. Nairn had joined the 7th Durham Light Infantry on 26 March 1911 as a boy soldier; he had previously been employed at Priestman's Yard, Sunderland, as a blacksmith. He was one of four brothers to see active service. One of his brothers, Lance Corporal Ogilvie Thomas Nairn, had been killed on 26 April 1915.

Kemmel Hill, where the division was located, seemed like a health resort compared to the Ypres Salient. The front-line trenches were good and the communication trenches deep and dry. Behind the lines some farms still stood; they were yet to be the target of the German artillery. As a result those still standing had been converted into strongpoints. Even more unusual to the men of the division was the fact that some of the cottages at the foot of Kemmel

*The Nairn brothers. Ogilvie Thomas Nairn was killed in action 26 April 1915, and Walter Nairn (far left) died of wounds on 22 June 1915. Two other brothers served as regulars in the Army.*

Hill were still occupied by their owners. The day of 27 June saw the battalion relieve the 6/8th Durham Light Infantry in the front line. The relief began at dusk and took two hours to complete. This was their first tour in the front line at Kemmel. A quiet time was had by the battalion, the enemy causing no trouble, the artillery fire being mainly the morning and evening hates (a hate was a bombardment). As there was very little wire in front of the trenches, it was decided to rectify this and to generally strengthen the defences; the Germans were doing similar work on theirs. Private William Edward Dunn, 2730, died on 29 June from wounds received while on listening post duty. He had joined the battalion on 5 September 1914.

The first reinforcements from England arrived on 30 June, comprising 160 officers and men who were immediately allocated to companies. On this day, 2337 Private John William Reid, from Sunderland, was killed. He left behind a wife and four children. He had worked as a miner at Wearmouth Colliery, Sunderland. It was also about this time that rumours of leave started to circulate throughout the battalion.

One evening, 3123 Private J. Tasker was detailed to form part of a working party to erect barbed wire in front of the trenches. The job, he remembered, was considered a particularly hazardous one, to the extent that all his friends shook his hand before he climbed over the parapet. Fortunately he survived to tell the tale. Various stories and myths circulated around the trenches and some eventually found their way into print in local newspapers. One such was related by Corporal W. Trenholm, who mentioned that the battalion had been bothered by snipers, particularly at night, some of which used explosive bullets. He related what happened to a particular sniper caught by the Canadians:

At one place they [the Canadians] had to fetch water from a pump after dark, but the men one after the other were mysteriously killed near the pump handle. After twelve men had been killed an investigation party was formed, and they captured a German sniper. He told them he had got his rifle correctly trained on the pump handle and then fixed it in a vice. During the night when he heard the handle moved he simply fired and killed the men seeking water. This sniper was not made a prisoner but shot with his own rifle and one of his explosive bullets. He deserved it.

The reinforcements were sent to the front line with their companies, the men who had landed with the battalion were considered old hands by now. Private S. Douglass remembered the arrival of the reinforcements and their sensitivities to their new environment:

When we first got our reinforcements there was a young lad, we were all only boys really, he came in the trench. I had been out three or four weeks, I was seasoned. They put him in the bay beside me. There was a dead man lying in the trench, we hadn't time to get them all out and there were men lying on top of the trenches.
He says, 'Can you not do something for that feller, he's lying there staring?'
This is his first time in the trenches. I said, 'Chuck some muck in his eyes.'
'He's moving.'
'Chuck some muck in his eyes man!'
It was rats moving him really. The captain came along, Captain Forster.

He says, 'Captain, I've got a complaint about this man.'

'What is it sonny?'

'He's making game of the dead, he's telling me to toss muck in that man's eyes.'

He was quite serious. Captain Forster says, 'Sonny, before this day's out I hope that there's somebody left that can joke.'

The day of 3 July saw the battalion relieved by the 6/8th Durham Light Infantry. The battalion then marched back to a bivouac area at Kemmel. The trenches at Kemmel, although much more comfortable than those in the salient, were described as a bad place for sniping, which resulted in a number of head wounds. The trenches themselves were in part situated down the hill. Private T. Keelin told of some risky work carried out on the evening of 5 July. The battalion had had to dig a communication trench in a particularly dangerous location. The men had to crawl on their hands and knees to the area they had to dig. When the order was given, he remembered, they dug as they had never dug before; it was completed in record time. During this operation the Germans were continually dropping flares amongst them, but they did not notice them. In Private Keelin's words, 'Only one chap stopped a bullet and I am sorry to say that he has since died.' This was Private Robert Welsh, of Ryhope Colliery.

A few days later, on 10 July, Lieutenant Walter Leslie Campbell was wounded. He had been the secretary of the Sunderland Working Men's Building Society at South Hylton. The next day, 11 July, 3514 Private Douglas Robson was wounded for the first time, receiving a gunshot wound in the thigh. After recovering from this wound Private Robson went on to be wounded in the shoulder, back and head on the Somme and again in April 1918, receiving another gunshot wound to the thigh. Surprisingly, after all this, Private Robson survived the war.

Private Surtees remembered an event that took place while he was in the trenches at Kemmel:

We were going to have a shoot one night. We were getting the big guns up then from England; there was one about 3 miles behind. It was a thing we used to hate. The captain of the artillery battery come up with his soldier carrying the box and what have you. He was looking quietly, they had a look over and he says we are going to have a fire. So he got the range for the shell and he said it's fired. You could not hear it. A great shell came over, dead in the German trench. Just what our fellas wanted.

The Germans would have to come out at night to repair their trench, we knew that. At night we thought we were going to have a shoot on that place, from left and right, because it's got to be filled up. A sergeant come along, Sergeant King I think it was, he might have been in No. 1 Platoon. He put a match right in line with it on the top of the trench, he put out three and you put your rifle on a line with that. At night, nice and dark, 'Right Oh lads go on. We'll have the shoot.' We started, about fifteen each, right along. The listening party on the flank said that there were some Germans out.

Mind he was smart. The bay in which we were standing, machine guns started, nearly cutting your hair, by goodness gracious that was near. We fired our fifteen off and got down again.

It was here at Kemmel that one of those curious incidents that can only happen in the Army took place. It involved the battalion transport, as Sergeant Thompson related:

There was a shortage of horses for the artillery and they took from us twenty of our horses and gave us twenty mules in their place. They gave us some beauties, we had some game on to get them broke in. We got rid of them after a while and we got back horses again.

One of the officers of the battalion wrote home and gave an account of a typical relief and of the daily routine in the trenches:

Orders arrive that the 7th DLI will take over certain trenches, all numbered from another regiment. The CO and captains go out, see the officers of the other regiment, examine the trenches and the ground, arrange for guides, get all information about the enemy, find out where bombs and ammunition are kept, where telephone dugouts are, and with which big gun batteries the telephones are in touch, also what saps are being dug, what patrols go out at night, which part of the trench is enfiladed, which part of the trench wants making up, and other things to do too numerous to mention.

The CO arranges to arrive with his battalion at dark. The outgoing battalion is very anxious that we won't be late. In many cases there is difficult ground to go over to the trenches, and always under rifle fire, as the enemy knows all the roads. In some parts the regiment has to march in single file, tumbling over obstacles, getting tied up in telephone wires, or caught by the hair like Absalom. You can quite understand the language is not the best.

On arrival at the trenches the company officer takes over a list of stores, log book, tools, etc., and his men file in at one end, while the outgoing company files out at the other, down communicating trenches. This takes everything up to three to four hours, and one is lucky if one gets away from the trenches before one am. Then the men go on duty. One in every three is a sentry, the rest keep on all equipment, ready to turn out at a moment's notice.

Patrols are sent out and working parties start to prepare the parapet where it has been knocked about during the day. Then at the break of day all stand by for an hour. After this men not wanted for sentry duty are allowed to lie down and sleep until morning, when the first duty is to clean all rifles, then breakfast. Work on the trenches (too many things to mention) until noon, then dinner, and more work if necessary.

Front-line men are never taken out of trenches for any other work. The reserve companies do all the carrying of rations and water and very hard work they have every night. Rations are brought up by transport ponies or in carts, just as the ground suits, from the transport line some miles away. The reserve company also digs trenches during the day – one may say that work on trenches never ceases – they have always to be improved.

Captain N.R. Shepherd also described a relief, in a letter to his parents. During the takeover the officers checked over the inventory for the 'Trench Dump', which included items such as maps, shovels, sandbags and so on. Copies of the inventory would be made and the stores signed for. Before leaving their billet, on the afternoon the relief was to take place the area would be cleaned, and the same applied to the trenches. An outgoing battalion would try to ensure that the trenches were left as clean as possible. Failure to do so would be reported up the chain of command. The platoons of the departing battalion would leave by the lateral communication trench, then move into the main communication trench to their rendezvous point. Here they would form up for the march back to their billet.

Changes to the command structure took place about this time, with Brigadier J.S.M. Shea succeeding Brigadier Martin in command of 151st Brigade, and at divisional level Major General Lord Cavan replaced Major General Lindsay.

It was while at rest that the battalion furnished further parties of one officer and fifty men for working parties to dig other trenches and work on supporting positions. The circle was complete again on 9 July, when the battalion relieved the 6/8th DLI in the front line. The first few days were quiet. On the 12th, Lord Cavan, General Officer Commanding the 50th Division, made a visit to the line. Things started to heat up on the 13th, when the enemy showed great activity by heavily bombarding the trenches of A and D companies. The battalion retaliated with rifle grenades, but unfortunately they did not have enough of them to seriously inconvenience the Germans. Even more happened the next day, when the enemy exploded a mine about 100 yards to the left of the battalion. At the same time, in order to keep the heads of the battalion down, they opened rapid fire on the trenches for about ten minutes. One of the rumours going through the battalion at the time was that the Germans were looking for one of our tunnels known as the Berlin Sap. Private Patterson, who had been sitting on the floor of the trench, was lifted 2 feet into the air when the mine exploded.

While the battalion had been holding the front line, patrols had been sent out for the purposes of gathering information, cutting wire and ensuring the German patrols did not get too close. As with any activity of this sort, it was highly dangerous work and the battalion did not always have it all their own way, as Private Douglass described:

> We had men out just the same as them, in case there was an attack, what you would call recce patrols, listening and observing. I was out on recce patrol; I had to creep out at night, no rifle or anything, just wire cutters and your bayonet. I was out one night; about five of us went over, listening patrol and all that sort of thing. We didn't really know what we were there for.
>
> The Germans had theirs out as well and that was a chance you had to take, running into each other. It was silent fighting then. If you made a noise both sides would open up, they don't care who's there.
>
> Anyway, the Germans started to shell. 'Course that scattered us. I was on my own.
>
> That's all I was doing when I jumped into the shell hole, that's the duty I was on, just between the lines. The Germans kept men between the lines in listening posts, listening, just creeping about. Generally cutting wire really if we could get up that far to their lines without being seen we used to cut wire. Of course when the shelling started naturally we dived into the nearest cover we could find. No-man's-land was full of shell holes; you could hardly walk around them. I jumped into the first shell

hole, it was full of water and this Jerry jumped in beside me, he was on the same game as me. He thought he would get out of the way of the shellfire. So we both started to fight when we saw who was who. I thought it might have been one of our fellers at first, he would think the same probably 'til we started to fight and try and drown each other. There was a struggle. I was trying to shout between gasps. Then I had to fight for my life so I twisted his neck and kept him under water and I don't know whether I broke his neck or not. He nearly had me, I tell you I got out alive; he didn't. I was just about exhausted myself. In fact I don't know how I got out of that shell hole yet. I was soaking; you would think I had been overboard. I was soaking when I got back into the front-line trench again and I had to explain what was the matter.

Private Surtees was also involved in observation and patrol work on the Armentières front, as he recalled:

In the trenches at Armentières, I was sitting there, when the sergeant came along the trench and said that he had to put seven men out tonight, outside on the front, in front of the wire. We went out on listening post. There was a big house just in front of the trench, amongst the wire. This night my pal and I were in this outhouse, it was quiet. In the wall facing the Germans there was a small aperture and some sort of fire step. When he put Very lights up you could see that alright, see through it nearly. I was standing there on look-out; he was dropping Very lights about. When all of a sudden BANG. It hit the bottom of the brick, just above my head. There was a flash in my face and a sprinkling of the stuff went in my face. My mate got a bit of a fright, he was there waiting for me to drop, he thought I'd gone. When we come in at daybreak, one of the sergeants says, 'I'm sorry boys, I've spilt the rum.' His nose was red raw, he'd drank it.

I had been out all night and was tired. If you had been out all night you could stop in your dugout and get a rest, that's if there is nothing doing. How he started, trench mortars, you could see them come up from his trench and when it hits the bottom it shakes the trench. Very strong shelling. This is because we fired our trench mortars. He dropped a very big one just behind the trench and he knocked a lieutenant out and one or two more. You shook in the trench and Lieutenant Hardy said he was bouncing like a pepper pot. [Lieutenant Richard Thompson Hardy had been commissioned into the battalion from the 6th Durham Light Infantry, where he had been a sergeant.]

I was sitting in a little dugout, and heard a whizz and there's the back of the trench, as if someone had cut it with a knife. As soon as he stopped I was out of that dugout and onto the platform and looked to see if anyone was coming over.

Relief came on the 15th in the form of a battalion of the Welch Regiment, the Durhams being moved back to Locre. The stay here lasted for only one day; the battalion proceeded to Pont de Nieppe, thence to Armentières, where they went into billets.

During the second week of July leave commenced and two officers and three other ranks left the battalion for a well-earned rest at home. Leave in the early days started from the time

*C Company, Armentières.*

a soldier left the battalion, so you would in effect lose precious time from your leave if you missed your train connections or the cross-Channel ferry, and a soldier's leave ended when he arrived back in France. This was shortly changed and leave started when a soldier had their pass stamped by the embarkation officer on the quay at Boulogne. An extra day was added if the soldier had to travel to Ireland or Scotland.

The battalion reached Armentières on 17 July. The town was only partially damaged by enemy shellfire at this time; factories were still working, as well as a brewery. The billets, as a consequence, were excellent. A visit was paid to the swimming baths but the water was found to be dirty, and consequently the battalion did not pay a return visit.

The trenches here ran east and north-east of the town. They were approached through wide communication trenches that were entered in the suburbs of Chapelle d'Armentières and Houplines. It was a peaceful sector. The trenches ran through farms that had been hastily abandoned by their owners, and it was still possible to obtain vegetables from their fields. The troops could also buy bread, butter and eggs at the entrance of the communication trenches.

It was also at this time that a divisional concert party was formed. They were called the Jesmond Jesters. The battalion also reformed its band. Private Surtees remembered how it came about:

> I was brought out of the trenches, at Armentières; there were two or three of us. We had lost that many bandsmen that were killed. A ship owner at Sunderland presented the battalion with a set of instruments. This day, I think I had been out all night, there was a lance corporal, but I think he played the trombone before the war and I had to come out. I was a cornet player. 'You've got to get down to headquarters and Bradford's going to see the two of you.' So we got down, full kit and everything. He [Captain Bradford] said, 'Take your caps off, get your hair cut.' We'd just had it cut off!
>
> He said, 'I'll tell you what is happening; you don't go on the fire step anymore. We are going to have a band, we are having instruments sent and I've brought out this other two. You go with the stretcher bearers when they come out. You can put your rifle in the quarter's stores and ammunition.

The instruments for the battalion's band were donated by Mr James Westoll, late High Sheriff of County Durham, at his own expense. Entertainment in the trenches at Armentières was provided by a piano, as described by Private Surtees:

> At Armentières some unit had got a piano and dragged it up and got it in the trench. I don't know how they did it. This day, the sergeant started playing this piano. We were shouting and we had only been doing it for two or three minutes when He [the Germans] turned a battery on us. I've never seen the sergeant shift so much.

The noise created by the piano and chorus had been heard in the German trenches, which resulted in the information being quickly passed backwards up through the lines. It seemed that the Germans thought that the battalion was forming up for an attack or a raid.

The battalion's next turn in the front line came on 24 July, when they relieved the 9th Durham Light Infantry, the relief being completed by about midnight. All was quiet. It was during this period that it was decided that each battalion would have its own intelligence officer. In the 7th Battalion Captain Hunt was appointed to the position. His duties comprised observation and the collection of all information regarding the enemy that might prove to be of interest and send it to brigade HQ by 12 noon daily. Innovations were constantly being tried and the commanding officer, Colonel Vaux, tried an experiment. He had some of the rifles bound with cord below the band near the backsight and some done with canvas. This was done to enable the men to catch hold of their rifles, after firing, if required for a charge.

While on the Armentières front a curious incident happened in the transport lines, situated in a large racing stable. This was related by Sergeant Thompson:

> I remember one of our best horses killed at this place. The driver had been out late one night with rations and in the grounds there was some very large and high railings, to keep people out of the grounds. He had fed his horse and fastened the head rope high up on the railings. He had forgotten to tell the picket that was on duty to halter the rope so when the picket went round to see all was well, here was the horse lying dead. He had hung himself. We had a parade for this and every man was warned for the future.

Life in the transport lines was also full of dangers. Sergeant Thompson mentioned that known dumps were shelled at times during the night by the Germans and wrote of the following experience:

> I remember one night going up with rations to the trenches. One whole street of houses was on fire. What an awful sight it was, we had to go at full stretch and gallop. The horses were very frightened. We got through it and to where the battalion was. That night we had some of our drivers wounded with shellfire.

It has often been said that the senior officers never visited the trenches to see the conditions the men were working and living in. Reading the war diary of the battalion it would seem the opposite was true. There are frequent references to Sir Charles Fergusson, the brigadier, and Lord Cavan, the divisional commander, coming round the front. On 31 July, while the battalion was in the front line, they both made an appearance, and Lord Cavan expressed his appreciation of the work done by all ranks.

3097 Private John George Southern was killed in action on 30 July. He had enlisted into the battalion on 9 November 1914 and landed in France with them on 19 April 1915. He had previously been employed at the Hylton Colliery. Private Southern had been a regular Sunday school teacher at a Primitive Methodist church and it had been his ambition to become a foreign missionary after the war. His mother received the following message in a letter from one of the battalion's officers: 'In the past his presence among us inspired all that was good. In the future, if God spares us, we will retain a lasting memory of his goodness.'

This tour in the front line came to an end on 1 August, when the 4th Northumberland Fusiliers and 5th Border Regiment relieved the 7th Durham Light Infantry. The relief was completed by 11.00 pm and the battalion then marched back to billets at Pont de Nieppe. On 4 August, one officer and twenty men from each company were selected as Grenadiers, and these men had to parade daily under the Grenadier officer.

Another change of command came on 5 August, when Major General Sir P.S. Wilkinson took over command of the 50th Division from Lord Cavan, who had been appointed to the command of the Guards Division.

In August, Sergeant H. Langford came to the attention of J.W. Jackson of the 1st KOSB when he wrote home, praising the sergeant's bravery:

*Private J.G. Southern, killed in action 30 July 1915.*

> I may mention in all due respect and praise Sergt H. Langford going out at night alone, scouting, and with listening patrols, etc. There is absolutely no fear in the man. Only the other day one of his superiors was telling me of a very daring manoeuvre on his part. As soon as it was dark enough he vaulted the parapet of his trench and crawled almost within an ace of the enemy's lines. On returning he destroyed the German wire entanglements. When asked where he had been and what he had been doing these last three hours, he coolly remarked, 'I have been looking for the Kaiser.'
>
> I trust he will pull through to the end, and if so I feel sure that it will be with honour.

Sergeant Henry Langford, who had previously been wounded on 30 April 1915, and was to be awarded the Military Medal later in the war, eventually became temporary regimental sergeant major of the battalion.

On 30 August, the day before the battalion was relieved in the front line, Captain J. Errington was killed. Private Surtees recalled the event:

> This captain, he was in the South African War [he had served in the ranks of the Imperial Yeomanry], one of the lads that was looking out of a periscope or something. He said there is somebody working over there. Errington I think, come and said, 'Where?' and he goes to the corner where the fella had been standing, straight there and had a good look over and he came down. Simple as that. You'd think they would use more Common [sense]. Move, keep moving never go to the same place twice.

Captain Errington had previously served in the 5th Volunteer Battalion Durham Light Infantry, then joining the 7th Durham Light Infantry at South Shields when the battalion was formed in 1908. It transpired that he had looked over the parapet to confirm the sentry's statement and was consequently shot through the head. He had been employed as a bank clerk with Lloyds Bank, Grey Street, Newcastle upon Tyne, before the war and had resided with his sister at Beverley Terrace, Cullercoats.

The latter half of 1915 saw great changes in the Army in France and Flanders. Not only were battalions of Kitchener's Army arriving in great numbers that needed training, but scientific advances were being made. This period saw the introduction of hand and rifle grenades in large quantities, as well as rifles with telescopic sights, trench mortars and Lewis guns being issued to front-line troops. During September the division received a number of steel helmets for experimental purposes.

The rest of the month followed the usual pattern of front-line duty followed by periods in billets. In fact, the battalion remained in billets until 12 September, when it relieved the 5th Yorkshire Regiment in the trenches, the relief being completed by 9.00 am. The time in the trenches was different from other times. On the 13th, the Germans poured some liquid over their parapet and ignited it. The fire started to move towards the British front line, but luckily the wind veered and the fire correspondingly changed direction, away from the battalion lines. The next day, the Germans followed this up with a barrage of whizz bangs. The 7th Durham Light Infantry were now seen as old hands; consequently they now started to give instructions on trench life and this peculiar style of warfare to the troops of the new battalions arriving in France and Belgium. A party of four New Army officers were attached for duty during this tour. Things remained quiet until 19 September, when the battalion was relieved by the 5th Loyal North Lancs. The battalion moved back to billets in Armentières. Life was not all that restful. Working parties of up to 450 men were supplied nightly to the Royal Engineers for work on the Subsidiary Line. However, on 24 September the brigade became the Army Corps Reserve, which meant that the battalion had to remain in billets and be ready to move at short notice.

Major events were happening further south. The Battle of Loos began on 25 September. This saw the piercing of the German line on the first day but because the follow-up divisions had been kept back some distance from the front and remained under the command of Sir John French, not Sir Douglas Haig, commander of the First Army, they could not be used until the next day. By this time the opportunity had been lost and the divisions suffered many casualties when their assault went in. The 50th Division did not take part in this battle, which lasted until mid-October. It was, though, called upon to play a part in the deception plan for the first day of the offensive. Orders had been received to place specially prepared bundles of straw in front of the division's trenches and set them alight. It was hoped by doing this that the Germans would think the division was about to launch an attack. It is doubtful that the Germans were taken in by this.

In September the following poignant letter, written by Private Delaney of the 9th Durham Light Infantry, appeared in a local paper:

I was wounded at Ypres on 30 April and was lying helpless, when I heard the shout of a child and footsteps approaching. The sounds came nearer, and presently I saw a soldier carrying a child in his arms. Blood was streaming down his face and he walked lame. He stopped, and asked me if I was much hurt and I said yes. Carefully putting the child down by my side, he immediately went back and returned with two Canadians. I was carried into safety. He and I were with the Canadians five days. I got to know that he belonged to the 7th DLI, and that his name was Private J. Scanlon. The man was always with the child, and then the child died, and the soldier wept bitterly. He cried over it as if it were his own. I found out that the child's father and mother had been killed, and that the mother had left the child with him and given him a French medal. The medal he clung to. He would not part with it. One Canadian offered him twenty francs for it, but he would not sell. I hope he is alive and well.

On the 27th, the battalion relieved the 7th Royal Sussex Regiment in the trenches north-east of Houplines, the relief being completed by 9.00 pm. Work was undertaken straight away on the improvement of the defences. Patrolling was the main feature of the battalion's activity during this tour. Patrols went out up to the German wire, obtaining useful information, thoroughly reconnoitring the wire and defences without attracting attention. Sergeants Speight and Waiter crept up to the German wire and brought back a sample of it for analysis. It also appeared that the patrolling was one-sided; the Germans evidently did very little of it. The battalion snipers were kept employed, using German periscopes for target practice. On 3 October, Sergeants Birchall and Thompson crept up a ditch and approached to within 10 yards of the enemy's wire. They obtained useful information regarding the Germans' defences. On 8 October the 7th Durham Light Infantry was relieved by the 9th Durham Light Infantry, the relief being completed by 7.30 pm.

Private Douglass tells of an unfortunate incident that happened one day when they were in the front line, which had fatal consequences:

> I remember going into Kemmel. We were manning the front line one day when he brayed it in [smashed up the trench], just on dawn, until the trenches were hardly ditches, a proper bombardment. We had a lot of casualties. Anyway, then I was picked to make my way down to headquarters to get trench boards and revetting frames to build the trenches up again. You could only move at night time, so I had to make my way down to the RE dump. That was about a mile back. I had a note from the officer to say what we wanted in the trenches and I had to get men from their unit to help me. Well I got about ten or twelve Royal Engineers to help me up. We were carrying U frames and trench boards, sandbags etc. and it was night time. We could not go up the communication trench with them, they were too clumsy, and so we had to walk over the top, to get to the front line. I was in the middle of them. Every time a shell went up, a Very light went up; you had to stand still, no movement at all. You were less noticeable if you stood still than moving. We were getting within a short distance of our trenches when one of the Engineers lit a darned cigarette. You can imagine what happened. Very lights went up all round, pandemonium. Shells came over, smashed all to bits. Shells, trench mortars and everything came at us. They blew all the blooming stuff to pieces we had, and I was banged to the ground with half my clothes torn off me with the blast. When I came back to the trenches after they had me down to the casualty clearing station again for that, I was told there wasn't any survivors of them, the whole lot had gone. All through that man lighting a damned cigarette.

Rest in Armentières had its brighter side. The men could relax for a few days. Fortunately there were only a few cases of drunkenness. One memorable incident involved Private Patterson, who was on his way to headquarters. He kept to the side of the road that was covered from the trenches, but as he crossed the road he looked into a school. To his utter bewilderment he found all the children sitting there singing! And all so close to the front, he thought.

In another incident at Armentières he remembered when he was the butt of the joke by one of his friends:

We took a billet one night over the school. I looked out the window next morning. I said, 'Come and have a look at this!' There was a woman below in the garden next door hanging out her washing and a laddie playing in the garden. You could look across and see the German trenches.

Our billet in Armentières was next door to the fire station, there was an estaminet [café] next door. There was me, Ernie Charlton and Frank. Ernie Charlton was a bugler. How much had we got? Well we managed to scrape, amongst the lot of us, about a tanner up [6d]. So we went in. I'm sitting with my feet on the form; Frank sitting on the other side. Ernie went across to where you get your order. I happened to look across. I didn't realize that Grenadine was sweet lemonade. I couldn't drink that beer, it was half water. She came across, you used to have a little basin of beer, put the beer down then she put the lime down and she stood. Then she said, 'Well Tommy, when are you going to kiss me?'

I nearly fell off the form. She was good looking. I said, 'What have you been up too?'

'I told her you were shy.'

I went in one night just to fill the time in, me and another chap. I got a seat, it was full of Canadians. She said, 'Well you haven't kissed me yet!'

'Hop it, hop it!'

This Canadian says to me, 'You haven't any nerve.'

'I get that every time I come!'

'I wish it was me.'

While on rest in Armentières training and route marches took place to improve the efficiency and fitness of the troops. The battalion bombers went to the Bomb School for instruction in the use of live grenades. At this time there were thirty-two bombers per company. The rest period, however, was short-lived, for on 14 October the battalion relieved the 6th Durhams in the trenches north-east of Houplines. For 3009 Private James Gibson, the return was even more short-lived because the next day he was wounded in the left thigh by a gunshot. Also at this time, three platoons of the 13th Northumberland Fusiliers were attached to the battalion for instructional purposes. Once again, patrolling was the order of the day, although the battalion's patrols brought back a lot of useful information regarding the German defences. They were unable to make contact with the enemy, who preferred to concentrate their activities on improving defences.

Sir Charles Fergusson, GOC 151st Brigade, made one of his frequent visits to the front line, this time on 22 October, visiting the battalion and ensuring all was well. The rest of the month was spent in the usual routine of front-line duty and spells of rest in Armentières. On the 27th, Second Lieutenant W.F. Laing and sixty men from the battalion were detailed to form part of a composite battalion, made up from the 50th Division. This battalion was commanded by Lieutenant Colonel Vaux DSO, and was inspected at Bailleul by His Majesty King George V. The end of the month saw a draft of twenty-five men come to the battalion from the 3rd line 7th Durham Light Infantry.

Meanwhile, back at home in Sunderland, steps were being taken to provide Christmas comforts for the men at the front as well as for their families. An appeal appeared in the *Sunderland Echo* for donations of one shilling and upwards. It was proposed to provide each soldier with a 1lb good quality Christmas pudding (made in Sunderland), cigarettes, chocolates, toffee, a booklet (*The Happy Warrior*) and a heartening Christmas message. While for those at home it was hoped they would receive a 2lb Christmas pudding (depending on the size of the family) and a Christmas message.

As reinforcements continued to arrive the old hands in the companies tried to help them the best they could. But they were not always successful, as Private Patterson remembered:

We went to Armentières, which was full of people. If you got into a quiet part of the line we said, 'If you leave us alone we'll leave you alone.' But there were silly blokes. If I told one, I told a dozen, 'Don't poke your head up.' This particular day we were sitting in the dugout and there was somebody firing and I said to my mate, 'He's asking for it.' Then all of a sudden – woof. 'Stretcher bearers.' Right through, dead cert, you cannot miss them. There he was. I said, 'Who is it? It's no use talking to you. I told you to keep your heads down.'

I had to take him down to the burial ground. A fellow called Bill White he used to be the grave digger; he said, 'What, another one!'

'Aye they won't be told Bill,' I said.

Not a pleasant job. The burial parties take all your belongings off you, identifiers; that's why there's so many missing.

['Identifiers' meant identity disc; initially, each soldier had one with name, rank, number and religion. Later in the war each soldier was issued with two; one red and one green. If they died the red one was sent to the base and the green one left on the body for identification when it came to be exhumed for reburial in the new war cemeteries being established.]

The training sometimes had fatal consequences, again as related by Private Patterson:

Kitchener's Army came out. We used to teach them. This particular night, I said to my mate, 'I'm taking my boots off tonight; I'm going to have my boots off and have a sleep.'

'Something will happen.'

'Hadaway man,' I said.

We bedded down and about three o'clock in the morning, it was just getting daylight. 'Stretcher bearers!'

'I told you.'

We went out. I went in the trench and said, 'What's the trouble?'

'Well there's two men went out on patrol and they didn't pass the word round "Men on patrol" and one of these from Kitchener's Army let blaze, killed one and the other was badly wounded.'

So I said to Jacky, 'We've got to get in and out quick, it's pretty light now.'

We went out and got him and brought him in and the officer started to moan because I'd took his electric torch and the battery had started to run out. We brought him in but left the other one out for the next night. Men were killed because they weren't warned. They reckon the other one died in hospital.

Private Patterson remembered another incident when he was coming out of the trenches with a wounded man, when he met Colonel Vaux:

There was one night when I was carrying a bloke down and I saw this chap standing, carrying a big stick. I said, 'Can you tell me where the dressing station is sir?'
'Oh! Is that one of my boys? Keep straight down and you'll come to it.'
He had a cavalry coat and he used to just stand and the way things had gone for him, Sunderland lads being killed, it was hurting him.'

The battalion band was reformed, as previously mentioned, while the battalion was still in the trenches at Armentières when Private Surtees, with two or three others, was ordered to return to headquarters to see Captain Bradford. When they saw him he told them to reform the band. Private Surtees and his colleagues were ordered to hand in their rifles and ammunition to the quartermaster. Their duties were now to help the stretcher bearers, but not always with success, as Private Surtees related:

I saw one or two nasty things. I said to a chap, called Mark Abbott [1976 Corporal Mark Abbott], 'I don't know anything about medical business.' He said, 'It's alright, there's a medical bag.' I hadn't been in a day, it was quiet, all of a sudden CRACK. 'Did you hear that Mark', a man of about 40. I said, 'Somebody's got it and there's somebody shouting for stretcher bearers.' I just run round the bend and there he was, down poor fella, it went in [the bullet] above the left temple and there he was down, frothing at the mouth, dying. They put a shell dressing on the back. It carries the back [of the head] out you know. I forget his name now, he belonged to Sunderland. He died. He would not know anything about it. He went in a few minutes. Two big stretcher bearers would come and take him out.

For the early part of November the normal routine of front-line work and rest went on. While in the front line and reserve, parapets and parados fell in because of the rain and work to repair them was continuous. Added to this, communication trenches had to be maintained and parties of up to 350 men were sent out to see to them. The battalion was once again in the front line on 7 November, in the Houplines trenches, with the 9th Durham Light Infantry on the left and the 13th Northumberland Fusiliers on the right.

Things were quiet again during this tour, although on the 8th the battalion snipers were particularly active, accounting for four of the enemy. A lot of time was spent with instructing New Army battalions in trench routines, and the battalion played host to the 8th Lincolnshire Regiment before handing over the trenches to the 14th Durham Light Infantry, 21st Division. Then the battalion was withdrawn and spent a night in billets before marching off to the Bailleul area the next day. Headquarters were in a village called La Crèche, which was composed of a number of farms and cottages, the principal buildings being the church and the priest's house. Light training took place here, with local leave into Bailleul being granted, with football in the afternoons.

The care and attention that Colonel Vaux gave to the well-being of the men of the battalion was greatly appreciated by all ranks. Private H. Harrison, of B Company, wrote to his father at Horden Colliery, stating that they had been relieved on 4 November after a week in the front-line trenches, during which time it had rained nearly every day. Private Harrison takes up the story:

> Col Vaux got us fettled up all right when we came out to billets. He got all the goatskins and blankets dried ready for us when we came out, he had big coke fires burning in the rooms, a clean pair of socks and pants and shirt each, and we also got hot tea with rum in it with bread, so we did not do so badly.

Private Thomas Place, who had been wounded, wrote to Miss E.M. Donkin of 10 Fawcett Street, Sunderland, saying that he was feeling better, although his leg was still giving him trouble. He also enclosed the following parody on *When Irish Eyes are Smiling*:

> *When German shells are flying*
> *And their shrapnel starts to sing,*
> *Our lads they keep replying*
> *And they make their rifles ring;*
> *Our lads they feel so happy*
> *In the trenches every day,*
> *If you only send them Woodbines*
> *They will pay you back some day.*

# Chapter 5

# Winter 1915 to Summer 1916

A big change in the career of the battalion occurred on 16 November 1915, when it became the Pioneer battalion for the division. Authority for this had been given on 17 August. Although its role would change the battalion would still be liable to be called upon as a fighting unit when necessary. One of the advantages of becoming a Pioneer battalion was that the troops received extra pay. According to Private Patterson, he received an extra 5d (2p) per day and considered himself well off. Due to this he was able to increase the weekly allowance he sent home to his mother.

Because of the change of role, the transport section of the battalion was expanded to include additional horses, wagons and men. Transport was equipped with General Service Wagons and limber wagons, which were loaded with different tools for the varying tasks to be done on the trenches and roads. However, the vultures were also circling. Colonel Vaux received a letter from 50 Divisional HQ requesting the machine-gun section and Captain Williamson, who were to form part of the new divisional machine-gun section. It was emphasized that good machine-gun officers were very hard to find.

Private Surtees was impressed with Colonel Vaux's determination for the battalion to become the divisional Pioneers:

> We were repairing our trench, making fire steps; everyone had to do their own then. When the colonel came along, he took off his coat and said, 'Come along boys, we'll have to work like Hell. I want that job.'
>
> He didn't say what the job was. Now we didn't know what he wanted. He wanted this pioneer job for the battalion. We were just the battalion for it because we had all types of trades, everything, electrical, joiners, etc. from Sunderland shipbuilding. You had everything that you needed. We had a good battalion for that.

It was on 22 November that the 7th Durham Light Infantry left 151st Brigade to start training as the Pioneer battalion to the 50th (Northumbrian) Division. Two other things happened on this day: firstly, the battalion marched past Sir Herbert Plumer, GOC Second Army; and secondly, A Company was sent to Armentières for a seven-day attachment to the 50th Division Royal Engineers. For the rest of the month the battalion carried on with practice attacks on enemy positions, whilst the company attached to the Royal Engineers was rotated when necessary.

On 4 December, Sergeant S. Howey left the battalion upon being appointed 'G Clerk' at 151st Brigade headquarters, joining a number of other men from the battalion there. In 1917 Sergeant Howey was recommended for a commission and proceeded to England for his

*The battalion on the move during a rain storm.*

course. Unfortunately, after passing the course he died suddenly on 22 May 1918. Back in 1916 he had reported to a field ambulance feeling unwell and had been told that his heart was affected. He is buried in Ryhope Road Cemetery, Sunderland.

With the onset of winter came the colder weather. The troops still had their ordinary uniforms, with which they had landed in France back in April, but now they were also issued with additional clothing to help against the cold, as Private Douglass recalled:

In winter we were in the fighting area, we were in dugouts because I remember having to get out and break the ice. We were in the trenches off and on throughout the winter, where they dished us out with sheepskins. They smelt when they got wet. We had about half a dozen sandbags wrapped around our legs, round each leg.

Throughout December the battalion still carried on its usual infantry training, with route marches, practice attacks and the like. It was on the 15th of the month that General Fergusson visited the battalion to say goodbye and to thank them for all the fine work they had done, as the battalion was now leaving the brigade and they were to become divisional troops. On 17 December the battalion moved from Bailleul to Canada Huts, where it started work as the divisional Pioneers. Companies were allocated on a daily basis to the three brigades of the division or to individual tasks. Christmas was celebrated at Canada Huts, where church parades were held. The war diary does not mention any other work being done. Back in Sunderland, the fund that had been set up in October to provide Christmas cheer for men of the 7th Durham Light Infantry and their wives, widows and children was expanded to include other soldiers and sailors of Sunderland. The aim was to provide, by public subscription, a 1lb pudding, sweets, cigarettes and literature to the men, and for the women, widows and families, puddings and a seasonal message. The goods were subsequently despatched to the front for the troops to enjoy during the festive season.

At the end of the year Lieutenant Colonel Vaux sent the following message:

To the good people of Sunderland – the handsome Christmas presents for the men of the 7th DLI arrived just in time, and after church service, were issued to them. If the donors could have heard the cheers, they would have been more than repaid for their kindness. The 7th DLI deeply appreciate the goodness of the people of Sunderland.

On Christmas Day 1915, Private Surtees spent the day with others of the battalion watching cockfighting, the entertainment being provided by two civilians. It was a display he thought cruel. He also called to mind an incident that happened when the band was billeted at Canada Huts:

The huts we went into as a rest place with our headquarters, there was a sergeant in charge, a Scotch chap. He lived in one of the huts and he used to have a raggy, dirty cloth dividing him from the troops. Someone come shouting Fire! We went out and there was fire; the hut next door to us was on fire, but nobody said about the poor sergeant in the corner. He was burnt to death. All you saw in the morning was his innards bubbling up, poor old fella. I think, myself he must have been tight [drunk], he had a lovely nose and a lovely face [as a result of the drink].

New Year's Day 1916 saw all the guns of the division opening fire on the German front for five minutes. The Germans, for their part, did not reply.

The year 1916 arrived to find A and B companies at the Magazine, which had been built within the town walls of Ypres. This had walls 5 feet thick and could withstand all shells but the very biggest. Now A Company was attached to the 151st Brigade, B Company with 150th

Brigade, C Company was working at Bedford House, and D Company with headquarters, remaining at Canada Huts. It was reported that at this time Canada Huts was a sea of mud, nearly a foot deep and everything covered in mud. During January the battalion remained dispersed among the brigades, being mainly engaged on revetting communication trenches and constructing special dugouts for machine guns. General Shea, Office Commanding 151st Brigade, sent a letter to Colonel Vaux stating that he was delighted with the work A Company had done for his brigade. The men at Canada Huts also received a visit from the Duke of Northumberland on 13 and 16 January, and praise was coming from many sources for the work done by the battalion. It was always borne in mind by the men of the battalion that their work was for 'the lads in the trenches'. Two platoons from B Company moved to Sanctuary Wood to construct special dugouts for the front line.

The following is taken from an unpublished history of the battalion:

Various reasons have been suggested from time to time as the origin of the name 'Sanctuary Wood'. The true origin appears to be as is stated in a letter written by Mr H.S. Jackson, of New York, USA, who served during the war with the 2nd Battalion 'The Queen's' Royals (7th Division). He says, 'When we first arrived in that beautiful wood (October 1914) there was a small pond covered with water lilies with a magnificent shrine on the eastern side. Carved in French in large letters on a monolith was the word "*Sanctuaire*" and below, "*Du bon Dieu*" I believe they read. In a few days nothing was left of the shrine and the pond was filled with earth and trees blown into it by "Jack Johnsons". There were several paths of black cinders leading to the shrine. I remember a dead French Zouave and a British artilleryman lay near it for several days.'

The huts had their drawbacks, as Private T. Warren described:

We are billeted in a hut which is wick [thick] with rats. They are great big ones, just like cats. They actually come in bed beside us. Very often during the night somebody jumps up in alarm because there is a rat under his blankets. We all get our bayonets and a search is made, but they generally get away.

The men of the battalion still shared the dangers of their compatriots in the trenches and when they were returning to Canada Huts on the 22nd, B and D companies were shelled while passing through Ypres. Luckily there were no casualties. As well as the work on dugouts and communication trenches, there were other more specialist and varied tasks to be done. On the 18th, work started on a vehicle repair workshop at Canada Huts under the supervision of Captain G. MacIntyre. Similarly, on the 28th, a cycle repair depot was started under the direction of Acting/Regimental Quartermaster Sergeant Pryce, to repair bicycles for units of the division. Normal daily hours of work for the companies and headquarters were from 9.00 am to 3.00 pm.

The work changed during February 1916. On the 14th, the Germans heavily shelled Ypres and Sanctuary Wood. The battalion lost one man killed, 3429 Private Frederick Thwaites, and four men wounded. Work also took place at night to reclaim obsolete equipment and clear local communication trenches. A rare treat for the troops arrived on the 19th in the form of Miss Lena Ashwell's concert party, made up of four artists – all males – who entertained the battalion at the YMCA hut.

A party of forty-five men, under Second Lieutenant Forster, were ordered to the Royal Engineer Park, at Reninghelst, to practice making dummy assembly trenches. Also on the 23rd, a party of twenty men from D Company, under Second Lieutenant Dalziel, made a fascine (wooden) road in Dickebusch Camp. At 9.00 pm on the 24th, Lieutenant T.F. Forster took forty-five men from D Company to Transport Farm, where they met Brigadier General J. Shea, who showed them where the dummy assembly trenches were to be dug. The party made them quickly and well and received great praise from the division. The dummy trenches were sited at Verbranden-Molen, with the hope of making the enemy believe that there would be an attack in this area. It is doubtful that the Germans believed this but it did result in the area being shelled. The dummy trenches were made by pegging out strips of canvas, approximately the width of a trench, so that if seen from the air they resembled proper trenches. On the last day of the month, the 29th, Second Lieutenant W.A. Bradley went out at 9.00 pm with a party of fifty men from C Company to work on the wiring of the GHQ second line, returning at 4.00 am. The three forward companies B, C and D were working at very high pressure throughout March. Their work consisted of revetting the front-line trenches, constructing machine-gun emplacements and strong dugouts in or near to the front line. During the month, a number of working parties went out at night, under Second Lieutenant W.A. Bradley, to reclaim the obsolete communication trench named Johnson Street and the wiring of the GHQ second line. An important visitor, Sir Douglas Haig, visited Canada Huts on the 23rd of the month.

Another essential duty carried out at this time was taking rations up to the front line. This was not only dangerous but could also be messy. Private Patterson remembered one particular trip in March:

> At a place called the Bluff, at Ypres, they reckon the trenches were that near you could hear each other talking. We were on working party one time and we had to take all the rations up. Up the railway. This night it poured down in torrents. You know the railway sleepers, I thought I'd step on them; hundreds had done the same and gone in between them, where it was about a foot deep. I was carrying a rifle, half a cheese and a sandbag full of bread. Down went the lot, the cheese went in amongst the mud. When I got up to the front line they played Hell. I said, 'You ought to come and try it and fetch the bags up.'
>
> The next night was nice and fine. We used to meet at a farmhouse and our transport used to get us to the line with the sandbags and your rifle and off you went. Very lights went up and all that. You stood still. When you got back you were allowed to lie in/sleep in. That was the best thing about it, a good sleep.

While at Dickebusch Camp, the battalion was subject to the occasional bombing raid by German aeroplanes. However, the danger did not necessarily come from the Germans' bombs but from the splinters and, at times, fragments of shells that were falling to earth as a result of British anti-aircraft fire.

On 28 March the battalion reverted back to its original function as infantry and relieved the 5th Border Regiment in the front line, remaining there until being itself relieved on the 31st.

April 1916 saw the battalion move from Canada Huts to Scherpenberg. The battalion marched in 'threes', instead of the usual 'fours', and this formation was found to be most suitable for the narrow roads. The work here was the same as at Canada Huts, and building overhead cover for machine-gun emplacements was now included in the daily toil. The work had its dangers; often it was carried out under shell and machine-gun fire. Much of the work consisted of repairing the front line after it had been heavily bombarded. On the 26th, the battalion moved to a tented camp at La Clytte, and on the 30th, an official photographer took several photographs of the men in Battle Order (reduced equipment with the haversack placed on their side and no backpacks), wearing their steel helmets.

Life went on more or less as normal in La Clytte. There was an estaminet and two or three shops, including a pleasant bakery, which did good business. Although this was a quiet area the work was not. Although hindered by water in the trenches, which made it difficult for the placing of U frames, normal work continued until 4 May, when the battalion was relieved. The battalion next moved to the Meteren rest area, about a mile due east of Flêtre. The billets here were very good but the companies were somewhat dispersed. Sport and training were the order of the day for the next fortnight. The officers were beaten at cricket by the NCOs and men. Some men managed to visit Bailleul, where they found plenty of shops and estaminets for their pleasure. It was also possible to use the Field Post Office here, which advertised the promise to have letters in London by the next morning if posted by 1.00 pm and by First Class post. The troops were able to obtain good meals at the local hotels and, more poignantly, the leave train left from here, so it was a case of 'look but do not touch' unless you had a ticket.

*Post.*

On top of Mont des Cats stood a Trappist monastery and a windmill. Here, as at other monts, the country lanes and woods were attractive to walkers among the battalion. Looking to the north the men could see 'clouds' floating. These were not clouds but shrapnel bursts, which marked the position of the front line.

Their training was devoted to Handling of Arms and Squad Drill. Sixteen men under Second Lieutenant H. Thompson started a course for scouts. Any spare men were attached for special instruction to the Lewis Gun Detachment, Signal section and Medical Officer. Few church parades took place during this period due to the wet weather. On 20 April the battalion moved back to La Clytte, relieving the 5th Yorkshire Regiment, and work continued on improving communication trenches. The battalion moved to Scherpenberg on 24 April. The work continued on trench improvements during June, although heavy rain hindered the work.

Brigadier General Shea handed over command to Brigadier General P.F. Westmoreland when he was appointed to the command of 30th Division. He held a parade to say goodbye to his 'Tigers', as he called them. Although no longer part of the 151st Brigade, 7th Durham Light Infantry took part and made their farewells.

Other changes occurred. In particular there was a change in adjutant on 8 May and the battalion said goodbye to Captain R.B. Bradford, who had been with them for almost a year. He left to become second in command of 9th Durham Light Infantry and Captain W.F. Laing was appointed to take his place. Lieutenant Colonel Vaux had nothing but praise for Captain Bradford on his departure to the 9th DLI and was sorry to see him go. He wished him the best of luck in his new appointment.

*Reninghelst, Ypres, 29 April 1916. (IWM Q537)*

*La Clytte, 1916. Far rear: Lieutenant Dalziel. Back row: Forster, Dobson, Polge, Birchall, Kierl, Goodrick, Thompson and Readhead. Seated: Laing, Thompson and Heslop. On the ground: Short, Welsh, Pickersgill, McLeaman, MacIntyre, Walker and Scott.*
*[credit] (DCRO/D/DLI 2/7/18/108)*

Most of May was spent repairing the parapets of the front line, which were constantly being damaged by the German bombardments, with the companies of the battalion being shared out along the whole divisional front.

News was received of the following decorations being awarded to members of the battalion in the Birthday Honours List: Colonel Vaux was appointed a Companion of the Order of St Michael and St George (CMG); 2276 Sergeant D.N. Borthwick received a Distinguished Conduct Medal (DCM); and 1720 Private A. Marsh received a Military Medal (MM).

On a sad note, Lieutenant Colonel Stuart of the divisional staff was killed on the night of 4/5 June. He was buried on the afternoon of the 5th at Westoutre. The battalion provided the carrying party, firing party and bugles.

Colonel Vaux received further recognition for his and the battalion's services by being Mentioned in Despatches, in General Haig's despatch.

The Germans opened a heavy bombardment of the divisional front on 30 June, which meant that the battalion was unable to do much work on that day.

Private Edward Tunstall, of 69 Ewesley Road, Sunderland, who was a signaller in B Company, had his poem *The Company's Signaller* published in the *Sunderland Echo*:

He ain't a blooming officer,
He ain't no NCO;
But the regiment will need him,
No matter where they go,
He gets no mighty chances,
His troubles are his own,
He's the chap that marks
The field service telephone.

He was just a plain 'flag-wagger'
Till the war increased his work,
And though he's doing overtime
He's not the chap to shirk;
With his instruments he's busy,
Whether in the trench or out,
In daytime or in darkness,
When there's not a soul about.

When the bayonet work is over,
When he's layin' out the wire,
Well – he's got to get connected
Under hellish German fire;
At his instruments he's busy,
While his comrades are at rest,
And exactly what his thoughts are,
Good or bad, well, he knows best.

The tales he tells are doubtful,
But they're cheerful, without doubt,
And we're always gay and frisky
When the 'telephone's' about,
With his instruments he's busy
Calling up or tapping through,
You will find his bloomin' value
At the final call – 'Stand-to'.

# Chapter 6

# The Somme

The great battle commenced on 1 July, the main aims being to relieve the pressure on the French front at Verdun, assist other Allies in their theatres by tying down German reserves and to wear down the German strength in front of the British. The opening of the battle was a partial success in the south but a failure in the centre and north, with the British Army suffering 60,000 casualties – the worst day in its history. The 50th Division was not destined to take part in the battle for another two and a half months.

In the meantime, work for the battalion continued as normal throughout July, with no particular occurrences being recorded. Events further south, on the Somme, were watched with interest by members of the division and during the course of August, divisions that had been through the Somme battle started to arrive in the area for a rest and refit. The battalion remained at Scherpenberg until 7 August, when they moved to the reserve area at Flêtre, having been relieved the day before by the 5th South Wales Borderers (Pioneers), not for a rest, as thought, but for kit inspections and route marches.

The 50th Division was now to take its part in the fighting on the Somme. The 7th Durhams entrained at Flêtre on 11 August. The following is a copy of the Operation Orders for the move:

**Operation Orders**

| | | |
|---|---|---|
| BM | = | Bailleul Main |
| G | = | Godewaersyelde |
| DN | = | Doullens North |
| FC | = | Fienvillers Candas |

1. The battalion will entrain on Friday morning 11/8/16.
2. 'A' Company and 4 GS wagons (tools) will leave BM at 8.58 am in No. 13 Train and detraining at DN.
3. The GS wagons will arrive at BM at 6.00 am and 'A' Coy will arrive at 7.30 am. OC 'A' Coy will hand in to RTO (Railway Transport Officer) on arrival a complete marching out state showing numbers of men, horses and 4-wheeled wagons. A duplicate will be handed into the Orderly Room as the Company passes. The Transport Officer will render a parade state to OC 'A' Coy by 9.00 pm on Thursday night showing the number of men, horses and 4-wheeled wagons which will accompany 'A' Coy.
4. An Officer from 'A' Coy will report at BM at 5.50 am to an Officer from divisional headqrs to receive instructions as regards the procedure to be adopted when the wagons and company arrive.

5. <u>The remainder of the battalion</u> will leave G at 10.53 am in train No. 15 and detraining at FC.

6. 'B' Coy and remainder of Transport will arrive at G at 8.00 am and the remainder of the battalion will parade at Battalion Alarm Post at 7.15 am. OC 'B' Coy will hand to RTO on arrival a complete marching out state which will be given him by the adjutant when the company moves off. OC 'B', 'C', 'D' Coys and Details will render to Orderly Room by 6.00 am a marching out state showing number of men, horses, 4-wheeled wagons and 2-wheeled wagons and bicycles.

7. An officer from 'B' Coy will report at G at 7.50 am to an officer from divisional headqrs to receive instructions as regards the procedure to be adopted when the remainder of the battalion arrives.

8. The entrainment must be completed half an hour before the time of departure of train.

9. No troops or transport will enter the station yard until authorized to do so by the RTO.

10. No personnel or stores will be allowed in the brake vans at the end of the trains.

11. Supply and baggage wagons will accompany the transport.

12. <u>RATIONS</u> The Battalion will entrain with the unexpended portion of Friday's rations and the Train Vehicles loaded with rations for consumption on the 12th inst.

13. Water bottles must be carried and water carts entrained full.

14. Breach ropes for horse trucks must be provided by the transport officer. Ropes for lashing vehicles will be provided by the railway.

15. Each Coy will detail three men to ensure that once the entrainment is completed no one leaves the train without permission until ordered to do so at the station of detrainment.

16. The approximate time of journey is six hours.

The battalion duly arrived at Berneuil, where it spent 12 August in billets resting. Over the next couple of days the battalion moved, in stages, to Baizieux, which was in a dirty and dilapidated condition. It was here that divisional headquarters were set up, the troops having to be content with tents or other shelters in the wood. Training commenced on the 19th, particular attention being paid to the fitness of the men and discipline, although the weather was foul and played havoc with the timetable. Also because of the weather the troops were found billets in the village, the wood becoming too bad.

Sergeant Thompson remembered a lighter moment when they arrived on the Somme:

> In Albert we saw a large covered wagon which must have belonged to some show people, that must have went away and left it, our captain said. So one night it was very foggy, we took a few horses down and brought it to our new camp, and about twenty of us slept in it. Nobody seen us take it away so we brought it up to our new camp and that was a place called Fricourt. We covered some trees over it for a while. We always used to think we would have got into trouble about it afterwards, but nobody ever said anything. It made a fine billet for us.

Lessons had been learned from the recent fighting during the battle and a new type of strongpoint, which was cruciform in shape, was practised. This allowed for a much extended field of fire with a minimum garrison, compared with other types of strongpoint employed up until then.

*Captain Broadley, Captain MacIntyre and Captain Heslop RAMC, Mametz Wood, December 1916.*

A and C companies, under Major Hunt, were attached to the 15th (Scottish) Division at Becourt on 26 August. The next day they started work on the repair of the tram line from Bottom Wood to Contalmaison and the roads in the Mametz Wood area. The other two companies, B and D, stayed at Baizieux constructing a new road through Hennencourt Wood. On the 28th of the month Lieutenant General Sir W.P. Pulteney KCB, DSO presented the DCM to 65 Company Sergeant Major J. Stoker.

A and C companies continued their work on the tram line and roads for the remainder of the month and early part of September, when on the 4th they were joined by B and D companies, with headquarters moving to Becourt. It was time now for the battalion to move up nearer to the front line. As a result work began on 6 September with D Company repairing and maintaining Bethel Sap and Argyle and Sutherland Trench, and B Company on Jutland Extension and Kerry Avenue. The Germans held the ridge running from Martinpuich and High Wood, which meant that due to enemy observation posts the work carried out by the two companies was continuously subjected to shellfire. A couple of days later, D Company was withdrawn to work on the Contalmaison-Longueval road, which was constantly being torn and pitted by shellfire. On 8 September, Captain H. Stewart received a wound caused by a shell fragment at High Wood.

The following is from an unpublished history of the battalion:

> There was a story, embellished perhaps in the telling, of how one day while Colonel Vaux was watching the companies at work on a road and pleased with their progress, he called out to them, 'That's the way to make a road, boys.' 'Indeed it is not,' came a voice behind him. Round wheeled the colonel with the question, 'And who may you be?' 'Your Corps Commander,' was the reply. Not in the least perturbed – when was he ever – Colonel Vaux at once held out his hand in greeting with the words, 'I'm proud to see you, Sir.'

Captain N.R. Shepherd wrote about working on the roads on the Somme before the attack in September. The road forward from Bazentin was described as 'an 18-foot space of mud' and it was the battalion's job to try to ensure it was clear, which was a never-ending fight against the elements. The battalion war diary sums up the work carried out during this period as 'on roads' – as ever, an understatement. He tells of a work party he was with, that a third of the men were sent to Bazentin to collect bricks. The village had really become a brick store, where the bricks were loaded onto General Service Wagons and limbers and sent up the road. The rest of the party were employed in scaling the surface of mud, once they had found it, removing the mud and then preparing the shell holes so that they could be filled in. Road metal was only allowed for the main roads, so they had to use the bricks that they had collected from the village. Work at Martinpuich was hot because the Germans were able to observe the movements of the British form Le Sars. Captain Shepherd had a cynical attitude towards the road repairs, writing:

*Captain N.R. Shepherd.*

*Bazentin – the colonel and padre buried seventy Durham Light Infantry dead near this spot. The padre says a prayer while the rifle in the ground marks the grave.*

Of course nobody knows anything about building roads, but that is not necessary. As long as we can scrape mud away into sump pits and dump bricks onto the road regardless of their being converted into mush by the endless transport pounding them to pieces, and generally keep up the impression of working for eight hours, then the upkeep of the road is proceeding satisfactorily in the eyes of the Higher Command, and we are left to rest in peace.

Communication trenches needed to be cleaned and deepened, with trench boards being used. Constant work to repair the roads was needed due to their overall bad state and the amount of traffic and enemy action. Heavy enemy shelling continually hindered the work.

As with all work of this type, accidents happened at times. One accident that occurred on 11 September resulted in an enquiry being undertaken by the commanding officer. Three members of a loading party – 4334 Private W. McGee, 2228 Private H. Cooney and 3576 Private C. Atkinson – were loading metal at Round Wood dump, which was a salvage dump near Contalmaison. During a cessation of work one of these men walked across the road and picked up a sandbag containing, apparently, mills bomb detonators, which he threw clear of the dump. An explosion followed, causing minor injuries and pieces of the detonator boxes were found thrown around. The enquiry found that the incident was accidental and no blame was attributed to any of the men. Such were the dangers of battlefield litter.

The next phase of the Battle of the Somme was about to commence. The British held almost the whole of the forward crest of the main ridge that ran for 9,000 yards from Delville Wood to the road above Mouquet Farm. Unfortunately, at the centre of this line was High Wood, only half of which was in British hands. Behind this and extending along the high ground to the south of Martinpuich was a strong German line known as the Switch Line. On 14 September the battalion, together with the rest of the division, moved forward to Fricourt to take part in the offensive planned for the next day, the various companies being attached to different brigades.

The 50th Division formed the centre of the III Corps Front, with the 47th Division on the right, which was to attack High Wood, and the 15th Division, on the left, was to attack Martinpuich. As the division was attacking on a two-brigade front, D Company was attached to 150th Infantry Brigade and B Company to 149th Infantry Brigade, with its objectives consisting of three lines of trenches, all to the east and south-east of Martinpuich. The job of B and D Companies was to make communication trenches between the newly captured lines and the start line. The normal German tactics when a trench or position was lost was to put down a heavy barrage and spray the area with machine-gun and rifle fire. This prevented reinforcements getting up with much-needed supplies of ammunition and water and it made the work of consolidation, putting the trench in a defensible state ready for the inevitable counter-attack, all the more difficult.

This was the first time that the division had been employed in a big 'set piece' battle and it is also worth noting that the artillery fired its first creeping barrage, instead of lifting to new targets at a given time.

The attack proved to be a success and the gains made had to be consolidated and attached to the existing British line. A significant new offensive weapon was employed in the battles of 15 September, namely the tank, two having been allotted to the division. During trials it had been estimated that a tank would make 15 yards per minute over heavily churned-up ground and 33 yards over good ground, increasing to 50 yards per minute downhill. This would have an effect on the timings of any barrage.

*Bivvies on the Somme.*

*One of the main roads running through to Bazentin-le-Petit. Terrible slaughter of Germans took place here in July 1916.*

Both flanking divisions started their attack a couple of hundred yards behind the 50th Division, which meant that the flanks of the 50th Division would be in the air and subject to fire from three sides. The attack commenced at 6.20 am. The first objective was quickly gained and at 7.20 am in order to aid the 47th and 15th Divisions, the 50th continued its advance to capture the second objective. The division lost heavily but the advance helped to capture both High Wood and Martinpuich.

In the afternoon, D Company dug a communication trench from Pioneer Alley to Tangle Trench under very heavy shellfire. Two platoons of C Company with the 7th Field Company Royal Engineers repaired the road from Bazentin-le-Petit towards High Wood, which had now been captured by the 47th London Division. B Company worked on digging gun emplacements and trenches for a Howitzer battery. The next day the work continued unabated. B Company completed Bethel Sap to the Old German front line and cleared Crescent Alley for a distance of 800 yards. All the companies and working parties worked on 12-hour shifts. This continued during the remaining weeks of September to consolidate the gains and clear and repair the existing trench systems. The work was so extensive and important that infantry were used to help the battalion. It was only possible to have the occasional couple of hours' rest at Fricourt. The front was not quiet; local attacks constantly took place to improve the British position. This involved the battalion continuously working on the front in preparation for the next attack.

Private Edwin Patterson remembered the attack on 15 September:

> We were practising and the doctor came in and said, 'You, you, you and you, we are going up the line tomorrow, attach yourself to so and so a company.' We went over with the lads.
>
> It was a Hell of a place High Wood, what they'd done, when they'd bombarded and blew the trees down, they used to wire to what was [left] standing, criss-cross, criss-cross, with barbed wire. You'd never get through that.
>
> The worst part we ever did was on the Somme, we went over with the tanks, the first time we'd used tanks, the 50th Division. We had our own tanks. We had to take High Wood on the end so that they couldn't fire on the division. We cleared that, but if you'd seen High Wood you couldn't get through. A bloke said, 'Don't go in there.'
>
> I said, 'I'm not going in there for nobody.'
>
> Anyhow the division did well that day.
>
> I went over with the first lot. They [the tanks] had two wheels on the back. I was sitting outside my dugout, the night before and I was dozing away and I happened to look up and here's this great thing coming and I wasn't shifting. If I hadn't shifted he'd of run me over. He had to be up in position for the bombardment the guns going would kill the sound and when he got in his position, he stayed out until the attack came up. When they came up we were well across. Blimey if one of the drivers came out, he had a leather skull cap on and little jacket and a revolver, riding trousers, etc. The tanks when they got going they were alright but they soon broke down.
>
> Oh yes I went over. At a place called Bazentin-le-Petit. That was the village, when the bombardment started we had to allow for the lifting of the barrage. When we got right away, it was like walking on a mat of lead marbles, there was that many of them, thousands and thousands of them, lead marbles [from the shrapnel shells]. The farmers made a fortune after the war.
>
> I asked the doctor about my rifle, he said I'd have to take it with me. I slung it. When I came back I just picked one up.

Private Patterson said that he was not allowed to wear a Red Cross armband, only S-B, for stretcher-bearer, and, as related, on the Somme he was ordered to carry his rifle. Wondering how he was expected to carry stretchers, look after the wounded and carry a rifle, he solved the problem by throwing his away and picking up another when he went back to camp later.

Captain Shepherd, in his last letter to his parents, said that he had received orders on 14 September to take up positions in 70th Avenue, preparatory to the attack:

> At noon Bennett, Walker and I went up to inspect the trench – going via Mametz Wood across to Bazentin-le-Petit – up Scotch Avenue and Pioneer Alley – 70th Avenue lay off to the left and 50 yards behind our front line.
>
> We found the trench very dirty with dead and flies and with no depth or protection, but we decided it was good enough together with L—- trench 50 yards farther back.
>
> At 6.00 pm the company moved up with Reed and self in 70th and McKinnon, Walker and Polge in L——.

*Captain Williamson (left) and Captain Forster capture Captain Bennett.*

Captain Shepherd's letters were privately published after the war by his family.

The men were immediately set to work to clear the trench and prepare fresh holes in its side. No one was able to get any sleep that night. At 6.20 am on 15 September the bombardment commenced and straight away the Germans retaliated with 5.9-inch shells, causing some damage to the division. Some men of Captain Shepherd's company were buried and subsequently dug out. Luckily, no one was killed. At 6.20 am the infantry went over the top and successfully captured their objectives. Captain Shepherd continued:

Word now came down from the brigade for us to proceed with connecting up the Eye Trench with the Hook.

I took twenty men of my platoon down, and after some difficulty found the road alongside which we were to dig and started on it, sending back word for the rest of the company.

McKinnon then came down with Company Sergeant Coxon and we walked over to the Boche line.

5.9-inch were now coming on our job frequently, and one burst near us and killed Coxon. We carried him into Eye Trench but he was nearly dead.

1595 John Coxon is buried in Contalmaison Chateau Cemetery. Enemy shellfire increased and for a time the men had to take cover. Work resumed again about 2.00 pm until 5.00 pm.

*Captain N.R. Shepherd's grave.*

*Captain L.G. Shepherd at his brother's grave.*

The work having been completed, the company was withdrawn to 70th Avenue, under a heavy barrage.

Captain Shepherd finished his letter thus:

The brigade being informed of the completion of the work reluctantly allowed us to withdraw to our Mametz billet at 7.30. Everybody was very exhausted – a drink of tea being the only food (excepting a bacon sandwich in the early hours) we had had all day, some of us who had been without sleep for forty-eight hours being very beat.

At the outset of the attack a cinematograph operator filmed the attack from the front line.

There was an absence of the newspaper rubbish. The Jocks just strolled across under our barrage. The Durhams likewise strolled over to their positions. A 'crump' would seem to fall amongst them but when the smoke lifted they would just pick themselves up and walk on.

It is sad to say that Captain Norman Robinson Shepherd was killed in action on 4 November 1916 at the age of thirty-three during the forming up for the attack. He is buried in Bazentin-le-Petit Military Cemetery. Captain Shepherd had initially enlisted into the battalion as a Private on 6 September 1914 before obtaining a commission and joining the battalion in July 1915. He was a solicitor, having been admitted to the Bar in December 1906 and then a member of Graham, Shepherd & Sons of Sunderland.

Private Frank Surtees and the rest of the band were ordered up during the attack to help with the pioneering work:

We went up to repair the roads, to get the guns up. High Wood was on the top and Trones Wood, you could see them right on a ridge. He had all the view. We went up filling in the roads, with knocked down housing, anything to get the guns up. It was hard work.

I remember that day going up and prisoners coming down, being brought in.

We went off to have a look round, we just slipped off for a few minutes, maybe half an hour, coming across the open was all sodden and clarts [muddy], as we used to say then. Here was little faces, coming out of where they had just been washed over, our boys, Scots, not properly buried. If you see some good equipment, you would give it a pull, but the body was on it, you didn't know that.

Private Surtees had come across hastily buried soldiers and the result of the haste meant that the light covering of earth was easily removed, thus exposing the dead.

Unfortunately, in order to forestall the attacks the Germans brought down heavier barrages than was normal, which meant that repair work on the front line had to be done two or three times over. The battalion received the congratulations of the Commander Royal Engineers (CRE) for their splendid work.

It is difficult to stress the difficulty they faced in digging communication trenches, especially where the ground had been heavily shelled and the craters were interlocking. The sides of the trenches had to be supported to stop them collapsing as the work progressed. The barrages on the Somme resulted in the trenches often becoming mere traces on the ground, not being very deep due to being blown in, and filled with debris and the dead. On 16 September B Company cleared 800 yards of Crescent Alley, in addition to connecting Bethnell Sap with the old German front line. However, following a difficult period in the front line, when the infantry came down after relief tired and dirty, a newly dug communication trench afforded merciful protection on their journey.

The following is part of Operations Order No. 2, which was issued prior to the action on 15 September 1916:

1. (a) The Fourth Army in conjunction with the French and the Reserve Army is going to renew the attack on Friday, 15 September.
2. (b) The 50th Division will attack with the 47th Division on its right and the 15th Division on its left.
3. (c) PIONEERS The Pioneer Battalion (7th DLI) will be disposed as follows:-
One Company ('B' Coy) is allotted to the 149th Infantry Brigade and one company ('D' Coy) is allotted to the 150th Infantry Brigade and will be accommodated by them. They will be employed making communication trenches between the successive lines. Infantry brigadiers will order them forward for this work as soon as they consider the situation sufficiently favourable for the work to be carried out.
Two platoons of 'C' Coy will be employed under the 7th Field Coy RE repairing the road through S.8.d – S.8c – S.8.a – S.8.b. They will be situated about X 23d central at zero hour.
The remaining half of 'C' Coy and the whole of 'A' Coy, the Lewis Gun Detachment, Band and Details will be in reserve about X 28 b 6.9.

At Fricourt Sergeant Thompson recalled:

We used to get bombed pretty often. The first thing I saw when I went up the line was a village full of German dead, there were also British, in fact the whole place was full of dead and this was at Bazentin. A place we had to pass on our way to where our battalion was working. The smell was awful. Horses and wagons lying about all over. It was one day when I was in charge of our convoy, we were on our way to High Wood with trench boards. When in front of us was a battalion of Welsh Borderers going up into the line. It was daylight and the German balloons could be seen plain. When all of a sudden they sent a salvo over of shells and caught this battalion. I gave the order for my drivers to unhook and gallop back to where it was safe. They continued to shell for an hour. I helped to dress the wounded and convey them to safety. There were about fifty killed that day. After we got the wounded all away the battalion proceeded to the line and I got my wagons ready and got to where our companies were working. We got unloaded and started on our return journey when they started to shell again. This time we watched where the shells were bursting and then made a gallop for it. I was 'Mentioned in Despatches' at this part of the line by Field Marshal Sir Douglas Haig.

*Blacksmith's shop, Fricourt.*

Another time, Sergeant Thompson's wagons had to go to an unfamiliar dump:

> One day I was sent down to RE Dump in Albert with a convoy of six wagonloads of trench boards. It was the first time we had been to this dump. It was a huge place and to our surprise when we got inside there were hundreds of German prisoners working here and some of them could speak English.

It was always to the amazement of men of the battalion that the prisoners they encountered had a good command of the English language. The reason for this was that quite a lot of Germans had worked in England before the war in a variety jobs, such as being waiters, so it was easy for them to pick up the language.

Private John Williamson Benison was killed on 21 September by a shell explosion. He had enlisted on 21 October 1914 and prior to that had been employed as a stoneman at Ryhope Colliery. He left two young children.

The last couple of days of September were employed in concentrating on preparations for the new offensive to be launched on 1 October.

The month began with an attack by the 50th Division on the afternoon of 1 October; the division was to advance on a four-battalion front. The task given to the 7th Durham Light Infantry was to dig communication trenches, joining the 'jumping off' trenches with the objective when circumstances permitted. Work commenced on North Durham Trench, South Durham Trench and Blaydon Trench after dark on the night of 30 September/1 October. At the same time dumps of bombs, water and ammunition were formed and dawn found the battalion still at work. The division was in position by 4.00 am, and the barrage of the German lines commenced at 7.00 am. The time prior to the attack was employed in improving the assembly trenches. At 3.10 pm the attacking troops deployed into the open and five minutes later the attack got under way. By 3.30 pm, almost without a casualty, all the objectives were taken. The attack had not been without its difficulties. The wire was indifferently cut, which meant that the troops were funnelled into places where they could get through. Luckily, owing to the smoke put down by our artillery, they were screened from the Germans. On the right the 6th Durham Light Infantry had difficulty and were driven out of their second objective. By 11.00 pm, reinforced by the 9th Durham Light Infantry under Lieutenant Colonel R.B. Bradford, the former adjutant of the battalion, they succeeded in capturing the second objective. It was for this action that Lieutenant Colonel Bradford won the Victoria Cross. The citation for his award reads as follows:

> Lieut (temporary Lieut Col) Roland Boys Bradford, MC, Durham Light Infantry, for most conspicuous bravery and good leadership in attack, whereby he saved the situation on the right flank of his brigade and of the division. Lt Col Bradford's battalion was in support. A leading battalion having suffered very severe casualties, and the commander being wounded, its flank became dangerously exposed at close quarters to the enemy. Raked by machine-gun fire, the situation of the battalion became critical. At the request of the wounded commander Lt Col Bradford asked permission to command the exposed battalion in addition to his own. Permission granted, he at once proceeded to the foremost lines. By his fearless conduct under fire of all description and his skilful leadership of the two battalions, regardless of all danger, he succeeded in rallying the attack, captured and defended the objective and so secured the flank.

During the night, under very difficult conditions, A and D companies succeeded in connecting up Rutherford Alley with the final objective. However, due to the barrage and congested state of the trench C Company was unable to establish communication on the left of the divisional front, but this was rectified on 3 October. In order to improve matters A and D companies attempted to complete Durham Trench but were unable to do so on account of the very heavy shelling. B Company continued to work on the roads.

Although the division was relieved on the night of 3/4 October the battalion and Royal Engineer field companies remained in the forward area attached to the 23rd Division in the line working on roads and tramways. In *The History of the 50th Division,* Everard Wyrall has this to say about the field companies, Division Artillery (who also remained at the front) and the 7th Durham Light Infantry: 'Their services were so valuable that they could not be given a rest. It seemed hard to penalise efficiency!'

A Special Order of the Day was issued on 3 October by Major General Sir P.S. Wilkinson, CB, CMG Commanding 50th Division:

> Nobody could be prouder than I am at commanding such troops as you of the 50th Division.
>
> Within a few days of landing in this country you made a name for yourselves at the Second Battle of Ypres. Since that battle you have gained a great reputation on

account of your magnificent defence of a portion of the Ypres Salient during the worst months of the year.

From 15 September to 3 October you have had another chance of shewing your qualities in attack and it is not too much to say that no division in the British Army has, or could have, done better.

You have advanced nearly 2 miles and taken seven lines of German trenches.

Your gallantry and determination on every occasion since you joined in the Battle of the Somme have been worthy of the highest traditions of the British Army.

I deplore with you the loss of many of our intimate friends and comrades.

I thank you all for the excellent and cheerful way in which you have undertaken every task put to you.

Pleasing news arrived on the 7th that 2416 Sergeant T. Coleman and 2566 Sergeant A. Davey had both been awarded the Military Medal. Further news arrived later in the week that Captain M.A. Mackinnon had been awarded the Military Cross and 1702 Private J.A. Grant the Military Medal.

Private Patterson recalled another incident that occurred during his time on the Somme:

One night I was out on a working party, I was attached to this section and they were getting knocked about, past High Wood. One of the officers said, 'I've got a nice dugout for you.' There were four of us. I said to my mate, 'You know what he got us a dugout for?'

'What?'

'Well if he gets hit we're here to pick him up.'

It was about two o'clock in the morning and I was standing talking to my mate and I said to him, 'Can you hear somebody crying?' The guns were quiet.

'No!'

'Listen!' I could hear a faint cry. 'You stay here because I don't want to get lost.' I went among the ruins, I was standing and there was a hole in the side of the trench and there was a chap in there and I heard him cry. I was nearly standing on top of him.

'How long have you been here?'

'I've been here for three days; the others passed me and wouldn't do now't. You will come back wont you?'

'I can't take you at present.'

I went up to the officer and said, 'I want six men sir.'

'What for?'

'There's a chap lying here and it'll take that to get him back.'

When we got to the bombardment area it was like a fine powder, when it rained you sank down to your knees. You'd used to pass him on the walk round, until you got past the bad spot. I said to him, 'I'll need at least six men.'

'Alright I'll order them.'

I got six fellas. When we left him he was sitting on the stretcher. He said, 'Tarrah!' [Goodbye] I think he had a stomach wound. I couldn't do anything at all like that. We put him off at a casualty clearing station, they would look after him. Only by luck I heard him crying at two o'clock in the morning.

Private Douglass always remembered a curious incident that seemed to take everyone, even the Germans, by surprise. He continued:

At a place called the Gully that famous newspaper tycoon came up. He came up and went into that Gully where nobody dared show a finger, it was full of dead, you couldn't bury them. The more you went out the more men you lost. The stench was terrible off them. The Germans had one side of it, we had the other. Horatio Bottomley, they called him, he was just in his civilian clothes and steel hat. We expected him to go up a height at anytime. He walked up there and he walked back again, with just a stick under his arm. The Germans knew he wasn't a soldier because of the way he was dressed, he had a raincoat on and that. We were amazed he came out again. Anything that moved in that place was shot. That was broad daylight at that. Whether he was in ignorance of where he was or what I don't know.

In conjunction with III Corps' scheme, work was commenced on the railway from Shelter Wood to Martinpuich. D Company worked on ballasting and laying junctions whilst A Company prepared the ground for the rails. The ground upon which the battalion worked had recently been fought over. As a result the companies never knew what they might unearth – a bomb or a shell that might go off when hit, giving nobody any chance of reaching shelter.

The rest of the month was employed on the railway and road clearing and repairing, but by the end of the month rain had flooded the communication trenches, and this considerably hampered the work.

News also came through that 4225 Private T. French had been awarded the Military Medal. October seems to have been a month for awards as it was announced that Captain W.R. Goodrick had been gazetted a Military Cross and 2543 Lance Sergeant L.A. Bittlestone and 2284 Private R. Maquire also received the Military Medal. On 10 October Lieutenant C.D. Moon-Ord was wounded at Martinpuich. Unfortunately, he died at No. 3 Durham Hospital, Sunderland, on 1 December 1916 of pneumonia, which he contracted while convalescing. He had attended Aysgarth Preparatory School, Harrow. While there he became the Junior Gymnast Champion 1901-02 and senior champion in 1902. Colonel Vaux said that he was 'a most promising young officer, devoted to duty, very popular with his comrades'.

On the 17th, work was commenced on the erection of huts at the eastern end of Mametz Wood. The work progressed so quickly that within five days they were occupied by B Company, followed on

*Lieutenant Moon-Ord, died 2 December 1916.*

the 24th by D Company, and battalion headquarters the next day. It was not long before the camp was complete.

The weather changed during the last few days of the month. All the hard work the battalion had done on the roads around High Wood was cancelled out as the roads became a sea of liquid mud, 2 or 3 feet deep. There was the additional danger of the shell holes being filled with liquid mud; it was possible for anyone who fell into them to drown. Raised duck board tracks had to be built to overcome the problem.

Work continued for the companies on clearing trenches and repairing roads. Trenches and communication trenches were in a shocking state due mainly to the weather and enemy shelling. It was found to be easier to dig new communication trenches rather than try to repair existing ones. All elements of the battalion were engaged in engineering work. The companies have been mentioned already; the Lewis gun detachment and bandsmen were employed on constructing a new divisional headquarters at Sabot Copse. Work continued until 3 November and because of the impending offensive operations, the 4th was declared a rest day.

The division was once again in action on 5 November, Inkermann Day, in an attack on the Butte de Warlencourt. (Inkermann was a battle fought on 5 November 1854, during the Crimean War, which the 68th Light Infantry – which became the Durham Light Infantry in 1881 – celebrated up and until the day they were disbanded.) The Butte was thought to be a Gallic burial mound, built of chalk. During the months before the attack the constant shellfire had removed the vegetation, leaving only the bare white chalk face. The attack of the 50th Division was not the first assault on the Butte. The only tactical advantage the Butte possessed was that it permitted observation of the front back to the ridge from High Wood to Martinpuich.

The attack was carried out by 151st Brigade with two battalions of the 149th Brigade attached. B Company 7th Durhams, under Captain N.R. Shepherd, were attached to the right sector and C Company, plus a platoon of D Company to the left. The task of B Company was to continue Pioneer Alley from Maxwell Trench to Grid Trench, and the work of C Company was to continue Tail Trench and join it with Butte Trench. Both companies were in their position in Hexham Road and Abbaye Trench respectively, suffering heavy casualties before the offensive took place. Captain N.R. Shepherd was killed and Second Lieutenants J. McLeaman and A.H. Polge were wounded. Second Lieutenant McLeaman had enlisted in 1914 as a private in the Scottish Horse Field Brigade Ambulance before being commissioned. In 1917 he left the battalion and returned to his medical studies at Edinburgh University. Second Lieutenant Arthur Herbert Polge originally enlisted in the Inns of Court Officers' Training Corps (OTC) on 3 June 1915; he had worked for the Guardian Assurance Company Limited.

Once again, the weather was bad, for during the night of 3/4 November there was rain and a gale blowing, which made the trenches appalling. It was thought that the attacking troops may not be able to climb out of the trenches, but they managed, those at the front being lifted out by those behind and then in turn lending a hand to their helpers.

C Company proceeded to their position for the attack by way of a communication trench, whilst those of B Company proceeded overland by a track to the Flers Line from High Wood. In addition to their fighting order, the companies also carried the tools of their trade – mainly picks and shovels – so it was not unusual to see overburdened men slipping and falling off the track.

The attack opened with a barrage at 9.10 am on 5 November 1916, followed quickly by the infantry assault. The left flank of the attack occupied the Butte de Warlencourt and passed beyond it. Unfortunately, the right flank of the attack was held up by machine-gun fire and the German counter-barrage. Hand-to-hand fighting followed as the Germans tried to regain the ground they had lost; eventually, by about 11.00 pm, the men of the 151st Brigade had been forced back to their original positions. The attacking force displayed great gallantry and captured the Butte and Quarry, but they were unable to hold on to their gains. Attempts were made to link up with the troops on the Butte before the counter-attack.

B Company could do little on the right flank, where the attack failed. Instead they were employed on clearing Pioneer Alley, which had been badly damaged by the German fire, and then they withdrew to the Flers Line.

C Company and the platoon of D Company tried to link up with their comrades of the brigade holding the Butte but had to give up the attempt after the successful German counter-attack.

Although not as heavily engaged in the fighting as the men of 151st Brigade, from 4 to 5 November the battalion lost two officers (Captain Shepherd and Lieutenant H.J.T Bannehr), seven men killed and twenty-two wounded. Lieutenant Bannehr had joined the battalion from the Inns of Court OTC in late 1915. He was admitted as a solicitor in July 1908 and was managing clerk with Macrell, Maton & Co of Cannon Street, London. In addition, Second Lieutenant J.F. Green, who arrived in France on 8 October 1916 and was attached to the 9th Durham Light Infantry, was also killed this day, as was Second Lieutenant A.L.L. Potts, who was also serving with the 9th Durham Light Infantry.

*Crosses erected on the Butte de Warlencourt after the war to commemorate the Durham Light Infantry attack on 5 November 1916.*

B and C Companies were allowed a few days' rest to recuperate before continuing with their work. The weather continued to wreak havoc with the communication trenches, causing them to collapse or flood, which resulted in the battalion spending the remainder of the month carrying out repairs to them. An additional hazard to be taken into consideration was the enemy, who shelled the trenches and their approaches constantly.

Change came on the 17th, when the division was relieved by the 1st Division, although the battalion continued to work in and about the trenches. Work went on continuously on communication trenches; the wet weather caused many of the sides to fall in, not to mention the damage done by enemy shellfire. The battalion was relieved of this duty by the 6th Welch Regiment (Pioneers) of the 1st Division and now took on the job of clearing roads as well as general work on camps and railways. The work on the roads consisted of cleaning the banks of mud from the side of the road, revetting and cutting drains. This shows that the battalion was not just fighting the Germans but also a constant battle against the weather and terrain.

The parents of Private Henry Hagel, D Company, received the following letter from his commander, Second Lieutenant P. Walker, dated 14 November 1916:

It is with regret that I have to inform you of the death of your son Harry this morning. He was in the trenches this morning when unfortunately a shell burst near him, and killed him together with his sergeant. Your son has been in my platoon ever since I came to it eight months ago, and consequently I saw quite a lot of him and knew him extremely well. He was always bright and happy and never grumbled no matter what the conditions were. He simply did his duty quietly and showed a splendid example to me who had not had as much experience as him.

The sergeant was Albert Davy, who had previously been awarded the Military Medal. Both Private Hagel and Sergeant Davey are commemorated on the Thiepval Memorial to the missing. Private Frank Brack, of Southwick, was also killed on 14 November and is buried in Caterpillar Valley Cemetery.

As the year was grinding to an end, so was the Battle of the Somme. The last action had been fought on 13 November at Beaumont Hamel, when the village of that name had been captured and other gains made, but at the usual heavy cost. The weather, deteriorating now due to winter, effectively put an end to any large-scale offensives, but it meant that the work of the Pioneers was essential in keeping open the communication trenches and ensuring the defences were in good order.

Although the battalion was employed on the Somme keeping roads open, digging trenches and assisting in the offensives of the division, not everyone in the battalion took part. Private Douglass had a different time on the Somme:

I was lying in the trenches with a South Shields lad that was in our battalion, Crick, Walter Crick. When Sergeant Adcock came up in the trenches, mind they were not proper trenches, they were just a cut in the ground really, you had to move about on your belly. And he tapped me on the shoulder; he tapped Crick on the shoulder and said, 'Make your way back to divisional headquarters.'

I said, 'Where's that?

He said, 'In Albert.'

'Albert! Bye that's a long way, how are we going to get out of this in daylight?'

'Aye you'll have to get yourselves back in daylight.'

Anyway, I could not tell you how we got back. We were on our hands and knees most of the time to get out of that position in daylight. He picked us out because we were the two survivors of the company; all the others were new men, reinforcements. Me and Crick were the two originals 7th, he was one of the first reinforcements and I was one of the first of the battalion. We came to an Australian camp and a sentry popped up. 'HALT, who goes there?'

Crick went marching on, saying to Hell with him.

I said 'Stop! These beggars are mad; they will shoot anything that moves.'

Mind they would. He told me, the sentry, 'You nearly got your brains blown out there, where you're looking for?'

I said, 'Albert.'

'You're a Hell of a way off Albert.'

'We have to get back to Albert; we've come from the front-line trenches.'

We got down through all them villages and all that battlefield right down to Albert. Reported to the RTO, that's the railway transport officer. He shoved us in billets. When we got there I think there were ten or twelve of us. We were scouts, me and Crick. There was us two from the 7th Durhams, there were two Borderers, two from the Northumberland Fusiliers and two from the Artillery; there were eight of us.

We were under divisional orders there. Still under shellfire you know, He could still shell Albert with the long-range guns, but it was a picnic to be out the front line. We were billeted on a woman, beside the railway station, called Madam Dufray, in the Rue De Jardin. She looked after us like a mother because her husband and sons were killed in the war. What our job was, we were notified when the troop trains were coming in with wounded and fresh troops to Albert Station. We had to collect them for our different divisions, fall them in for the 7th, 8th, 9th and Artillery. They used to bring all their own grub with them, tins of bully beef, tins of biscuits, tins of dates and raisins. When they get out of the train and lined up, 'How far is the front, mate?'

'Oh! A long way. Fall in we'll take you up.'

'We're not going to carry all this.'

'You'll want it mind afore you get there.'

'No we're not going to carry it.'

'Right no argument mate your funeral.'

Mind they did want it before they got there. We used to take it all to Madam Dufray, she had enough to set a superstore up. In the cellars, boxes of dates, boxes of raisins, all sorts. That's where I got that photo took that I have, the fella asked if I'd stand for a photo for him and he took the two of them. [These are the two pictures of Private Douglass in all his equipment after just returning from the trenches and when he had handed in his kit and was in his great coat.]

We were there a canny bit, just taking reinforcements up, new officers, officers straight for the front, that had never been over before. They had to do what we told them, it didn't matter what rank they had, we were under the RTO. When we set off

*Private S. Douglass, direct from the trenches 1916.*

*Private Douglass on rest after handing in his kit.*

with them, Cor Blimey, you should of heard them grumbling, you know what new men is, they have never seen now't.

When I was a scout I had the job of fetching German prisoners from a camp in Albert. There was a big German POW camp there, just outside of Albert. Albert was the railhead, when we got the Germans pushed so far up the Somme. All the troops used to come there and all the grub and munitions trains. I used to get a note off the RTO, me and Crick used to go up. The Jocks were on sentry at this big POW camp. We used to get about thirty Germans and march down to Albert, to the station to unload the trains and then march them back again. They didn't try to escape because if they had got back to Germany they would only have been sent up the line again.

They were a real good lot, I will say that, absolutely a happy jolly lot, there wasn't a wrong word off them. When we were marching them down, they used to whistle our songs, *Tipperary* and all that, to keep us in step, then all of a sudden they would stop and put us out of step. In their way having a bit of fun. A lot of them could speak English. There was no fear of them escaping, Crick was at the back and I was at the front, leading them. But when we were coming out the camp the Jocks used to say, 'When you get them out of here mate shoot the buggers will yer! Don't fetch them back. If you fetch them back we'll bloody well shoot you.'

We had some good days with the German prisoners while I was a scout. They used to work and all, empty the wagons, watching them and all the rest of it, mind they might of pinched a few rations on the quiet. They were quite a happy lot.

Private Surtees also remembered encountering German prisoners on the Somme:

We used to come out for walks, when on rest. The Germans used to have to look after the roads to keep them in good order. That was their job. They used to have a patch on the back of their coats, blue or red. We used to talk to them. There was one little fella, I asked where he come from, he said the Ruhr. He looked as if he was forty-five, he mightn't have been, but there he was repairing the roads, a whole regiment of them. We come to another one, my brother-in-law he got talking to him, a sullen looking bloke he was. He said, 'How are you going on with the war?'

'Oh! We are going to win,' he said.

We started laughing. They were losing. He was down in the mouth, he must have known but he was putting a brave face on it.

Although what Private Douglass went through may seem to be a cushy number there was also the downside to being on the Somme, as he related regarding burial details, which were gruesome affairs at times:

When you're out on rest you get all them sort of jobs – collecting the dead and that. You're not exactly free to do what you like. You get all sorts of jobs, repairing trenches, carrying stores and that. We were sent out to collect the dead. Anyway the tanks had just come onto the scene then, the Somme, that was it. We were sent out on a burial parade. There was such a large amount of men killed on the Somme. There was a great big trench around the side of the road and we were sent to collect and dump them all in. Just temporarily. You have two discs, one's green and the other one's red.

You leave the green one on the body and you collect the red one. That's so they know when they re-bury them they know who they are. But they were just huge graves, scores and scores of men of all regiments, chucked in and just covered up. If they were left there, there was a hell of a stench off them. We did that all day nearly. After the tanks we went up on the Somme.

Me and my mate were out on a burial parade, picking up the dead that were behind the lines after the Germans had gone back. We were not supposed to be in the line, but we were sent on a burial party. They had lain there in the water, goodness knows how long. When you picked them up, these were Germans mind, when you picked them up they used to fall apart because they were rotten, like anything gets when it's left in the open air and lying in water.

Private Douglass also remembered that when he and another soldier went to pick up a corpse, when they lifted it the arms and legs came away but the torso remained on the ground, it had been there for so long.

Work continued throughout the month of December on the Bazentin Road and High Wood

*Christmas card, 1916.*

Road, ensuring the drainage was adequate and moving the earth from the side. The narrow road was also widened to 23 feet. This was extremely heavy going, and the earth on the sides had to be thrown back 4 feet. Due to the continual repair of this road and other roads, there was a general shortage of road metal, which prevented lasting repairs. Although there was no truce this year at Christmas, it was observed as a holiday, dinner consisting of pork instead of turkey, followed by intercompany football matches both morning and afternoon. In the evening there was a concert, but it was interrupted by German shellfire, which left shrapnel holes in the roof. Then it was back to work as usual on Boxing Day, when the job of widening the Bazentin Road was finished.

The following is an extract from 50th Divisional papers:

The Corps Commander, Sir W. Pulteney, KCB, DSO, visited each brigade on 5 and 6 December and thanked them for the good work they had done since they arrived in the corps at the beginning of August. Not only did he thank them for the good work done in action, but also for the equally important work on roads and railways, which made offensive operations possible. He remarked that it was not until he had seen the areas of the other corps in the Fourth Army when acting as Army Commander that he realized fully what magnificent work had been done by the 50th Division.

The year ended with the division returning to the front line, relieving the 1st Division.

New Year 1917 commenced with a change in the weather; it started to snow, and this covered much of the desolation created by the war. It also meant a change in emphasis for the battalion. Work started on maintaining Pioneer Alley, Turk Lane and Factory Avenue and keeping them open, because after the snow came the thaw. The weather was typical for the time of year, bright days and exceedingly cold nights. The trenches were in a bad state due to the weather. Not only were all the rifle companies out at work each day but the Lewis gun detachment were also utilized on repairing overland tracks.

Things had changed in the rear area over the winter. The Fricourt area was now full of quartermaster stores and Bazentin-le-Petit had risen again to become a village of Nissen huts, which were very cold in the winter and exceedingly hot in summer. Hutted camps had been built as far forward as High Wood, but these were under German observation, which was not known at the time, until documents were captured later.

The battalion moved to the camp in Mametz Wood again. This time they found that the Germans had started to shell the valley with 5.9 shells and a long-range gun. Usually the attacks were at midnight and between three and four in the morning. The battalion lost some men during this period. One shell landed in the camp on 14 January, luckily proving to be a dud and no one was hurt. Unfortunately, on the 25th of the month, a shell from a 13.5-inch high velocity gun killed some Royal Engineers and also killed Private George Dixon, of Sunderland. According to the unpublished history of the battalion:

> Whether these casualties were caused by the long-range gun or a dud buried shell which suddenly came to life owing to a fire having been lighted over its resting place was never certain. Huge fragments of frozen earth were thrown up which seems to point to the latter as the true cause, moreover it occurred during the daytime when it was not usual for the area to be shelled.

On the first day of the New Year Captain W.R. Goodrick MC was killed in action, and on 8 January, Second Lieutenant C.S. Dalziel was killed as a result of shellfire. Private Surtees attended Lieutenant Dalziel's funeral, when they buried him with a top coat over him. Private Surtees described Lieutenant Dalziel as a fine, fair-headed lad. Captain Goodrick had been an assistant master at Catchgate Council School. He had also been a good hockey player, playing for Humbledon Club in Sunderland. Both of these officers are buried in Flat Iron Copse Cemetery.

After every action the dead had to be buried. On one occasion Private Patterson was asked by the padre to accompany him on such an expedition, as he related:

> I was on burial parties. I was behind Mametz Wood and the padre came up to me and said, 'Would you like to come along and help me read the burial service?'
> 'That's a big job.'
> I went round. Germans, our fellas and anybody else. When we were at about the end Jerry dropped some Jack Johnsons.
> 'If we don't get a move on somebody will be doing the burial service over us!'
> 'I would like a souvenir,' said the padre.

'Well have your pick.' There was a helmet. I picked it up.

'Do you want this, sir? There's still a bit of the man inside!' I said.

'No!' was the reply.

Anyhow he took a bayonet. It was a funny thing for a padre to take. We did quite a lot of burial services in one day. You felt sorry in one way because you could see they would only be temporary burial grounds, where we put them. We'd make a mound and put his hat on his rifle.

The padre buried seventy men that day. Another time he remembered a couple of incidents where men tempted fate and discussed their chances of survival:

There was a chap who wouldn't duck; they buried him just where he fell. There was another one; he was sitting talking about paradise and that in the line. He was shot; it went right between his teeth. He got up and let off such a shriek I got hold of him, I took him down to the dressing station.

There was another chap; I forget who it was now, a good way away. I was walking past, he was up on top and I could hear the sniper. I said, 'He's after you, get down man.'

He says, 'The officer says I got to stay.'

'Tell the officer to get up there then, come down out of it.'

I went along and about ten minutes after [came the call] 'Stretcher bearers'. They got him through his waist. I got him down to the doctor. He took a little spoon and put a little pill, he gave morphine. Just had to sit and wait of him dying. Half an hour later he'd gone. All for this stupid officer.

At times, with all the dead lying around, troops could become callous, as the following incident related by Private Surtees illustrates:

We were in Mametz Wood and just opposite; right over you could see the hills and the road went right up to different places. We took a bit of time to have a look around and we got on top of this hill. Oh you talk about skulls and German boots with shins in them. There were a couple of fellas, they picked up a skull and were pelting them. The Germans must have had a gun or battery up there; we must have blown a few to pieces.

This incident would not have been typical; it was probably one way for those soldiers to cope with the situation they had been placed in.

Shell shock was an ever-present problem. Depending on how the sufferer acted and who looked after him, he could possibly end up in front of a court martial. Private Patterson was able to help one member of the battalion after he had received a near miss by a shell:

If you had a fella standing in a trench being shelled all day and a bloke takes panic, you couldn't do nowt about it. I had a bloke and Jerry dropped a shell, I saw it, a gas shell. It dropped between his feet. 'Course it blew the cap off the end and out came the gas. Poor lad. I caught hold of him and I took him down to the clearing station. He said, 'We've had a few of these, you can't do nowt about it, his nerve's gone.' If he'd gone back with the MPs [Military Police] he'd have been a coward. That's why I reckon there were no cowards at all.

He also remembered those who showed bravado, and some who had lucky escapes:

I took a man down to be picked up; he was lying on a stretcher. A chap was standing there and as I bent down to look at him, this chap fell down with a bullet in him. If I hadn't bent down I would have got it. So we had to cart them two down. I opened him up [opened his tunic] and he had a hole just like a pencil, no blood.

To add to the inconvenience caused by the shellfire, the German air force was in the habit of flying over at night and machine-gunning the camps. This resulted in the order being given for no lights to be shown at night and no camp fires, which added to the miseries of the winter nights.

Relief came on 27 January, when the battalion was withdrawn for training and finally, at the end of the month, it moved to rest billets. Training was impaired due to the frost, which meant that only route marches were possible. On 10 February 1917, the battalion left the area for Hamel, in the Ancre valley, and then moved to a camp at Bois St Martin, on the Amiens-Péronne road.

The area the battalion now occupied and had to work in was almost a complete change from that which they had left on the Somme. The roads were good and some of the houses were in good repair, so they could be used for shelter.

Towards the middle of February, the battalion was once more employed on communication trenches, some of which were impassable, and the erection of prisoner of war cages and various buildings for the division. The area was taken over from the French and their communication trenches had been constructed differently to the way the British would have made them. They were deep but the sides had not been revetted, which had consequences when the weather changed. When the thaw set in, the communication trenches became very bad very quickly; they could not be used at all. They became one of those jobs that never ended. The front line was little better, which meant that the troops holding it had to stay put and rations could only be delivered overland.

It was during this time that information was received that at certain parts of the front the Germans were pulling back. One of the villages now occupied by the British was Serre, which was the scene of bitter fighting during the attack on 1 July. As a result the 50th Division was ordered to send out patrols to ascertain the situation on its front and to occupy any empty trenches left by the Germans. Unfortunately, on this sector of the front the Germans had not retired as yet and even raided the division on the right of the 50th.

An attack by III Corps was to be made in early March and the 50th Division was to co-operate by making a smoke and artillery demonstration. However, it was observed that the Germans were burning villages in their rear, which resulted in the attack being postponed. But the 50th were destined to take no further part in the scheme. Changes came on 5 March when the start of the divisional relief began and the battalion moved further south to Maricourt,

On Active Service,
*by James Hayes of
the battalion
machine gun section.*

Sketches of Army
Life, *by James Hays.*

Germans Practice Facial
Expressions, *by James Hayes.*

leaving behind the old battlefield. Three days were spent in cleaning up, removing the mud and dirt of the Somme from their equipment and rust from metalwork. Time was also spent in infantry training; a task that they still had to perform when needed. After the clean-up period A and D companies were ordered to Villers-Bretonneux, where they were to work for Commander Royal Engineers III Corps. The work allocated was the making of fascines in the Bois de Blagny and working on the railway siding at Blagny Station. This work progressed throughout the month with the other two companies working on improvements on camps and rifle ranges as well as carrying out company training. On the 25th of the month the two groups of companies exchanged places.

During this period casualties still occurred. Private Joshua Elliott received a gunshot wound in the abdomen on 2 March. The wound was serious and he died at 9.15 am on 19 March. He is buried at St Sever Cemetery Extension, Rouen.

On 17 March word came that the Germans opposite III Corps had begun their withdrawal to the Hindenburg Line, but the 50th Division was to take no part in its follow-up. They were now bound for the Arras front.

Gas Sentry, *by James Hayes.*

## Chapter 7

# The Battle of Arras

The battalion was on the move again at the end of the month, eventually ending up at Hauteville, in preparation for the 50th Division's part in the Battle of Arras, arriving there on 11 April. During the march north, the battalion was given the warming news that on 6 April the United States of America had declared war on the Germans. As is normal with infantry battalions, much attention was paid to march discipline and the condition of the men's feet. The following is an extract of Operations Order No. 5, dated 29 March 1917:

> Every boot must be dubbed and socks slightly soaped. No man will fall out without written permission from an officer. OC Coys will take steps to prepare chits in readiness. No water is to be drunk on the line of march without permission from an officer. Usual intervals will be maintained between Coys – 100 yards will be between every twelve wagons.

While the battalion was at Croisette, on 6 April Lieutenant Colonel Vaux and the other commanding officers of the division went to Arras to study the ground over which the battle was to be fought. It was on this visit that Lieutenant Colonel W. Carswell-Hunt, who was in

*B Company, Arras, 1917.*

*A Company, Arras, 1917.*

command of the 6th Durham Light Infantry, died suddenly of a heart attack. Lieutenant Colonel Carswell-Hunt was an original member of the 7th Battalion, having joined them in 1913, landing with them on 19 April 1915 and serving with them throughout until he received his promotion in March 1917.

The initial attack at Arras on 9 April was a success, with most of Vimy Ridge being captured by the Canadian Corps. The role of the 50th Division was to follow through the attacking troops once the front line had been pierced, and to keep the Germans on the move. After the initial success, slow, costly advances were made by the British troops as the offensive continued. This meant that the task the battalion was asked to do changed. Work commenced on 11 April on the road between Tillot and Wancourt. The weather did not help, for it snowed at night and rained during the day. However, the work continued for the greater part of two

*Guns moving forward.*

*The Lewis Gunners – known as The Pride. Those marked with an X were killed and those with a P were captured.*

weeks. Work was also started on building strongpoints on the captured ground, infantry shelters, and wiring the reserve and support lines.

The front line had been pushed past the village of Wancourt and lay to the east of it and of Héninel, the left flank of the division resting on the river Cojeul. Across the front of the division ran the Wancourt Tower Ridge, upon which stood an old windmill. This became the limit of the right flank, although the tower was destroyed on the night of 13/14 April.

An attack was planned for 13 April, with the 151st Brigade attacking Chérisy village on the Wancourt Tower Ridge, while other units of the 56th and 3rd divisions attacked on either flank. The other attacks were conditional on the capture of the ridge. The ground over which the attack was to take place was devoid of cover, and in addition the ridge was commanded by the village of Guémappe. As a result of this plan was modified. At 7.00 pm on the 13th, the 3rd Division attacked Guémappe but failed to take it. At 5.50 am on the 14th, the 151st Brigade attack started, with the 6th Durham Light Infantry leading. The attack broke through the German lines, but unfortunately the 56th Division's attack was not as successful, resulting in the 151st Brigade having to fall back to conform to the general line. Some of the 6th Durham Light Infantry had penetrated so far into German territory that they were cut off and never heard of again. The ownership of the tower (windmill) changed hands a number of times between the 15th and 17th, with the British finally retaining occupation. The tower was strategically important to both the Germans and the British as it commanded views of the British line and battery positions.

The division saw no more fighting until the 23rd, when the offensive was resumed. On this occasion the division had been allocated two tanks, which were to clear the exposed slopes of the ridge and also a railway cutting. The attack of the 149th Brigade commenced at 4.30 am. The flanks reached their first objective by 8.00 am, while the centre could not progress because of a small wood about midway between Guémappe and Cherisy. The tanks, which had completed their task, came to the assistance of the attacking troops and the advance continued. The wood was captured by 8.30 am. Unfortunately, the 15th Divisional attack, on the left, on Guémappe did not succeed and the 30th Division's attack on the right flank did not proceed as far as the 50th Division. Around midday the Germans counter-attacked, working around the left flank of the 149th Brigade and compelling them to retire to their original starting positions. The attack was resumed by the 151st Brigade at 7.00 pm and the first objective from the morning's attack was captured. Things became a bit shaky at 7.30 pm, when it was reported that the Germans had broken through the 30th Division. This resulted in the infantry of that division pulling back and the battery commanders also ordering their men back while taking the fittings from the guns. Fresh infantry was rushed forward and the situation was restored by the early hours of the next morning. The advance continued on the 24th. The 25th was a quiet day and the relief of the division began and was completed by the 27th. One of those wounded during this action was Private Ralph Henderson, who received a gunshot wound in the left hand.

The nature of the previous operations was unlike anything the battalion experienced on the Somme; this was open warfare, with the battalion closely following the advance. As already mentioned, their task was now to connect the captured ground to the British positions with communication trenches, restore the roads for the supply of the front line, and enable the Artillery to move forward and support the front. Two members of the battalion were wounded on 29 April, Private A.E. Hunter and Second Lieutenant J.W. Shield, the latter being hit by shrapnel.

Lieutenant Herbert, who had rejoined the battalion on the Somme, recounted what happened to him one evening when ordered to take his platoon to repair roads at Arras:

On the evening of 21 April 1917, I was detailed to take my platoon of men to repair a road (filling up shell holes) on the approaches to the supporting trenches of the front line. In the morning, an officer [Lieutenant Percival MacDonald, who had joined the battalion from Durham University Officer Training Corps. He originated from Newcastle upon Tyne and was twenty-eight when he was killed] had been killed at this spot. We had been in reserve near to the Arras front and the place we were making for was a point north of Monchy.

When we got to the place where the work was to be done, I got the platoon into dugout shelters and then, just before dark, my sergeant and I went outside to have a look round to see how best the work was to be done. On doing so, we must have been observed by the Germans, for a salvo of 5.9 shells came over and we were both hit. I learned what happened next much later when I arrived back at the reserve battalion at home. Sergeant Lambert was wounded in the lung and I in the hand, shoulder and left thigh. The men rushed to our assistance. I was taken to a first aid post, given emergency assistance and immediately despatched to 20 Casualty Clearing Station where (I was told later – I was unconscious for many hours) I was immediately operated on. The surgeon who operated on me did a remarkable job.

The road from Arras to Wancourt via Thilloy was important because it not only led to the front occupied by the 50th Division but also to that of the 3rd, 15th and, to some extent, the 29th divisions. Work on the road became more dangerous when the battalion was working on that part forward of Telegraph Hill, because it was from here that the road was under observation from the Germans at the Bois de Vert and from their observation balloons. The battalion worked not only on the main road but on its subsidiaries as well. The road forked, about midway to Wancourt, one part going to Wancourt and the other over the Wancourt Tower Ridge. These branches also had several other roads and tracks branching off them, all of which had to be maintained.

The road was devoid of cover and what made the German shelling particularly distasteful was that, instead of shelling certain areas, they randomly shelled all parts of the road. The battalion made progress with the repair of the roads and their reputation rose due to their steadiness under such circumstances.

Of particular grimness was the clearing of the way through Wancourt while the fighting was still in progress beyond the river Cojeul, which ran around the village, and the fact that the Germans were still in possession of Guémappe. The ordinary work of the Pioneers still had to be done, such as wiring and building shelters and strongpoints.

The battalion spent 26 April in billets in Arras. It was thought at one time that when the division was relieved the battalion would stay in the forward area under the Commander Royal Engineers VII Corps. However, the order was rescinded and on 27 April the battalion moved back by train to Coullemont for a rest. Part of the Operations Order for this move stipulated that during entraining and detraining there was to be no shouting or jumping in and out of the carriages!

There is an old adage of 'if it's not nailed down it be pinched'. A story by Private Patterson backs this up:

> When we were billeted in Arras, we were in a cavalry barracks and the window sills were high. I happened to look in and a Frenchman had been cooking with a big tin of mentholated wax. It was just stuck there. There was me and Frank. I said, 'Watch out Frank.' They were all tucking away inside and I whipped it [stole it]. Just what we wanted. You put it in a little tin and light it you could boil a can of tea. When we came back this Frenchman was looking out of the window. 'Angleterre big hands, Angleterre big hands.' 'What's the matter?' spoken in French.
>
> He didn't know we had it. He'd have only drawn another one from the stores. Handy stuff mentholated wax.

Private Patterson was pleased with his 'find' as cooking in the trenches could be dangerous, as he went on to he explain:

> You couldn't cook in the trenches, if you were lucky enough to have a little pan of tea, with the tea, sugar, milk all in together. There was always a little hole in the side of the trench and you pushed your little can in. You'd used to get a bit of wood to burn. That's all you could do in the trenches. One night we were in a dugout and it was pouring with rain, the roof was sloping, it was corrugated iron. It used to hit the back of it and run down but the floor sloped down with wood.

I said to my mate, 'Tide's in Jack.'

'Ah! Bale out again.'

We baled out. We had a little fire there, I said, 'I'll look for some wood,' a little charcoal fire. I went outside. All of a sudden Phewt, Phewt! He was firing on the cooker. We had a bit fun that night.

Private Surtees related that valuables found on bodies did not remain there for long and neither were they sent back down the line with the other personal effects of the deceased:

At Arras, there was a chap lying in a shell hole, with his gold rings on, they wouldn't be there long. You talk about laughing about the dead, another day we went out doing something and we said, 'Let's have a look along here.'

Here's a German officer lying on the top, I think he was an artilleryman. The first morning his clothes were alright, went past the next day somebody had took his boots off him. The next day someone had pinched his leggings and that's the last we saw of him. They would have been through his pockets. They used to get the watches, anyone would have done it. I didn't.

We saw the lads come back, down on the Somme, with watches on their arm and pocket watches and money. You're not supposed to do that, it's supposed to be put in a little bag to be sent off to their parents.

The battalion was billeted in huts and farms and spent the majority of May training, except for a couple of days when the division was ordered to the front to become part of a 'Corps de Chasse' under Lieutenant General Sir Ivor Maxse. The reason for this was, before the Battle of Arras came to an end it was decided on one last push at Bullecourt. The part to be played by the corps was to follow up any breakthrough by the attacking troops. The battalion arrived at Blairville, taking up billets in cellars. As the breakthrough did not materialize, the battalion moved back to Coullemont on 4 May.

Coullemont is a village set on a hill overlooking the river Grouches. This rest area was just what the troops needed, being set in a peaceful rural spot. Good relations were soon established with the local French population. The battalion was especially popular with the farmers in the area. The battalion lent them horses to work in their fields and the troops worked on the gardens around their billets. Because of this kindness the French Médaille Agricole was bestowed on Lieutenant Colonel Vaux.

Leave also became available, four-day passes being given to visit Paris and the small town of Doullens nearby. This leave did not count against any leave allocation for Blighty and so was doubly welcome. As always, all good things come to an end and on the 25th of the month the battalion was on the move again, this time to Couin, with one company being detached to work in the 150th Brigade area at Bayencourt. The battalion were inoculated, one company at a time. Those companies not being inoculated worked on the Couin-Caignaux road.

The company that was at Bayencourt returned to the battalion on 29 May. The next day the battalion started its moves again, initially to Fonquevillers and then, on the 31st, two companies and headquarters moved to Boyelles and the other two companies moved to

*Left to right: Captain Heslop RAMC, Colonel Vaux and Captain Broadley, with two young French girls and a pony at a camp near Flêtre, Belgium, May 1916. (DCRO/D/DLI 2/7/1/82)*

*Captain Broadley receiving a haircut from Private Emmerson, Scherpenberg, Belgium, May 1916. (DCRO/D/DLI 2/7/18/104)*

*On the farm: Captain Heslop RAMC and Colonel Vaux.*

*At rest on the farm.*

*Colonel Vaux with Captain Heslop RAMC and carriage on the farm.*

Beaurains. It is interesting to note that the Operations Orders for the moves of the battalion now contained references for a burial party.

Work commenced again on road repair and maintenance, continuing until 16 June. The following letter was received from Brigadier Tanner, Chief Engineer VII Corps:

> I should be glad if the good work done by the 7th Durham LI (Pioneers) could be brought to the notice of the GOC 50th Division.
>
> During the time this battalion has been employed under me on roads Lt Colonel Vaux has shown exceptional interest in its work, with the result that the battalion has done exceedingly well and executed work on the roads under their charge which will be of paramount value during the next winter.

On 17 June the battalion moved to Hénin shelters and relieved the 8th Royal Sussex Regiment (Pioneers) of the 18th Division. Work began on various trenches in the area, which continued well into July. The front that the division now occupied, after the relief of the 18th Division, extended from opposite Fontaine-lès-Croisilles on the left to the Arras-Cambrai road on the right, being divided into a two-brigade front.

Battalion headquarters and A and B companies remained at Hénin shelters during the summer. The other two companies were located in the old German dugouts at Neuville-Vitasse and camps in that area. As the Battle of Arras had come to an end, camps were being erected all over the rolling downs. There was little in the way of enemy shellfire. Battalion headquarters were shelled only once, near the end of their stay, and luckily there were no casualties.

The battalion worked not only on roads in the area but also the trenches. Some of the old German trenches were reclaimed and cleaned up and put into a usable state. They also provided shelter and comfort for the troops holding the line.

The Chief Engineer VII Corps still requested the services of fifty men of the battalion for work on road maintenance. Two companies, A and B, dug a new front line on 16 July between Dead Boche Sap and Byer Sap, joining these places together. This continued for the next few days, deepening and widening it, and joining it with other parts of the line. Other companies were employed on digging communication trenches and trench repairs.

The unpublished history of the battalion said about the digging that 'it was remarkable the speed with which the men dug themselves in. With a hundred men on a 300-yard stretch, by the time the last man had reached the position allotted to him, the first men on being visited were found to be well under cover.'

The divisional sector remained quiet during their tour, except for two trench raids, one of which was carried out by the 5th Durham Light Infantry with two companies of the 5th Yorkshire Regiment. The objective was a portion of the German trench, namely Rotten Row, in front of Fontaine-lès-Croisilles. The attack took place at 12.30 am on 26 June and was a success, with Rotten Row being captured as well as a number of the enemy being killed and captured. The role of D Company the 7th Battalion Durham Light Infantry was to dig a communication trench, joining the captured ground with the old front line, once the objective had been taken. The trench was completed under artillery and small arms fire. These were not the only hazards the company had to face as the British barrage also fell rather too close

*Field altar, 1917.*

at times. The result of the attack was that the Germans turned the artillery of two divisions onto the captured trench on 27 June and flattened it, after which they advanced over the bombarded ground and overwhelmed the surviving garrison. The battalion's casualties for this raid were Sergeant S. Thompson, and Privates G.C. Croom, P. McCabe and T.W. Taylor being killed. The battalion took no part in the second raid, on 14 September.

Throughout August and September, work continued on strengthening and improving the front line, the communication trenches generally and on roads. However, even though it was the height of summer, the work was hampered by wet weather; it proved to be so bad that on certain days no work could be done at all because of it. The work continued until 6 October, when the battalion moved into billets at Courcelles-le-Comte, where infantry training was again the order of the day, with squad drill and rifle practice. Training went on for just over a week, during which time a draft of 210 men was received. This indicated possible active operations in the near future. Lieutenant J.H.R. Massey was wounded by shrapnel on 2 September. This was his second wound, the first being another shrapnel wound received in April during the Battle of Arras.

Sergeant G. Thompson of the transport section remembered this about his time in the Arras sector:

> Our battalion went into the trenches and the transport made Boyelles their headquarters. We had all night work here, leading all sorts of material for the trenches. I remember one night our transport officer, Mr Walker, he belonged to Sunderland, went up with our convoy to a dump called Infantry Hill, some place too. He got off

*Left to right: D. Pescod, Tom Pegnan and William Allen.*

*A halt on the march.*

his horse and fastened it behind one of our wagons and started walking in front of the convoy. Poor chap he had not been in front more than five minutes when a shell burst right in front of him and blew him to pieces. We buried him near Boyelles, he was a fine fellow, everybody felt sorry for him, everybody had a good word for him.

Second Lieutenant Sydney Walker, who came from North Moor Farm, Silksworth, Sunderland, was killed on 15 August 1917. He had been commissioned in December 1915 and had served in France with the 9th Durham Light Infantry during October and November 1916.

Sergeant Thompson continued, relating some of the problems frequently facing his section:

Another time we were unloading our wagons at some dump. I was in charge of our wagons that night. I got all the wagons unloaded when I gave the order for the move on into a valley, when the Germans opens fire. I thought it was all up for us. They shelled at the front and the back of us, just as if they knew we were there. The horses were going mad with the shellfire. Every time one used to burst we thought our time had come. We stopped in that valley for one hour; it was no use making a rush for it as the shells came over quick and to the minute. However they eased up for a while. I took the opportunity and gave the order to gallop for it. Just as the last wagon was turning the bend to get on the straight road, a shell burst in his wagon and blew it to pieces. Funny part about it was neither the driver nor the horses were touched. I ran back to where he was. We went back a few hours later when things were quiet and brought what was left of it back.

*Second Lieutenant S. Walker's grave.*

One night while we were stationed at Boyelles some of our battalion came down to our lines to guide us up to where our battalion was in the trenches. Our wagons were already loaded with trench boards and ammunition and we set off as soon as it came in dark. Before we started off our officer asked the NCO in charge of the party if he knew the road alright. He said 'yes'.

We got into a sunken road where we had to go round one wagon at a time. So many men went with each wagon and as each wagon got onto this road we were fastened in. There was no road out of it. It was just like being in a valley. Well if the game 'wasn't on'. There was no room to turn our wagons round. We were stuck all through the night, 'til late hours of the morning. We had to unhook our horses out, unload all the wagons, pull the wagons so far up the sides of the valley and turn them round best way we could. I felt sorry for the NCO in charge, he had lost his bearings altogether. However, after a few hours hard work we got onto the right road only to go into some heavy shellfire.

That was one of our many troubles, hitting the right road. You might go up one road one night, next night there was no road, it would be all blown up with shelling.

On 18 October the battalion entrained at Bapaume and Miraumont for a move to the Ypres sector, where the Third Battle of Ypres had been going on since 31 July.

Private Robert Pearson wrote the following poem and sent it home:

*Tis the dead of night, no signs of a fight,*
*The rifles and the cannon nigh still,*
*In dream you thought of the battles you've fought,*
*And the Germans you've got to kill;*
*You dream of the Hun and his Jack Johnson gun,*
*And the gas they so often use,*
*Of the Kaiser's 'Hoch Himmer' of children and women,*
*Who have suffered from German abuse.*
*Then your thoughts go back to your first attack,*
*And the terrible times you went through,*
*Then another thought for others who fought*
*And fell for the Red, White and Blue.*
*When of Huns in their mass, by the help of the gas,*
*Have at times our lines tried to break,*
*The thought of our brave who are laid in their grave,*
*Keeps us watchful and ever awake,*
*'Tis to all of you to fight and be true,*
*To end this most awful of wars,*
*So we send a call to one and all*
*To come and respond for the Cause!*

*Chapter 8*

# The Third Battle of Ypres and Spring 1918

Initially the battalion were in tents in the La Cloche area and it was here that Captain W.F. Laing rejoined the battalion following his recovery from the wounds he received at the Battle of Arras. He again took up his appointment as adjutant. After two days the battalion marched to Proven, moving on again on 24 October to White Mill Camp at Elverdinghe. Here the way to the front was by two tracks, one by White Hope Corner and Boesinghe and the other by Dawson's Corner to the Yser Canal. These had been destroyed by enemy shellfire and rebuilt on the original site many times. This work was continued by the battalion with the aid of carrying parties supplied by the infantry, as well as working on the completion and repairing of a trench-board track known as Railway Street, which ran parallel to the Ypres to Staden railway.

*Captain and Adjutant Laing on the left and the battalion's American doctor on the right.*

Due to the constant shelling of both sides destroying the drainage system and the rain that had fallen since the start of the offensive in July, small streams burst their banks and the water occupied the valley floors. What were at one time streams only a few feet across had now grown up to 100 feet wide. To add to this the German positions were indistinguishable from the British. Towards the end of October the ground was pock-marked with a multitude of shell holes, and the trenches, being mainly battered, were waterlogged. The duckboards were covered in mud, as were what was left of the roads.

*Problems with a broken-down car.*

Movement off the tracks was impossible due to the mud and general state of the ground. White Mill Camp was in a bad condition. The tents the men occupied were ringed with sandbag walls and the floor level was 2 feet below ground level. The reason for this was for protection against enemy bombing raids, which took place day and night.

The division was also involved in the Second Battle of Passchendaele, which commenced on 26 October. One brigade, the 149th, made the attack on the division's front, with the 150th in support and the 151st in reserve. The Ypres to Staden railway formed the right flank of the divisional area, while the Forest of Houthulst, now the Belgian bomb disposal area for ordnance still found from the war, formed the left.

*In the trenches, 1917. (DCRO/D/DLI 2/7/18/225)*

*A group of officers sitting in a trench. (DCRO/D/DLI 2/7/18/212)*

During this time the enemy were active and the Lewis gun detachment took up positions in forward posts to deal with low-flying aircraft. The work on the road was not as straightforward as it seemed. There were constant interruptions from severe enemy shelling, the mud was bad and everything had to be carried over long distances. Despite all this, the work done on the road was of enormous benefit to the infantry. It was also while doing this work that the battalion suffered a number of casualties from gas and it was not just on the road that they were shelled; the Germans also shelled the camp, making rest impossible.

On 28 October, A and B companies moved into Red Rose Camp, just to the east of the Yser Canal. This camp was nearer their place of work. Unfortunately, it was badly sited, for it was shelled and bombed constantly, which resulted in the men getting no rest. As a result the two companies were moved back to Hall Camp at Boesinghe. C Company was given the task of draining the Breenbeke, near Langemarck. This was an unpopular assignment as it was on the German counter-barrage line.

During the night of 31 October/1 November a large enemy air raid took place, with German aircraft dropping from 150 to 200 bombs on the camp and divisional area. The divisional transport lines were also hit, with the result that thirteen lorries were set on fire. This lit up the area, providing very good aiming marks for the Germans. During the raid Captain T.F. Forster was killed, and Captain H. Stewart and Lieutenant Ridoutt (who subsequently died of his wounds on 19 February 1919 at St Thomas's Hospital, London) and eleven other men, were wounded. Captain Stewart was wounded in the right arm. Lieutenant Ridoutt had been educated at Portsmouth Grammar School and later at University College, Durham. He had been gazetted to the 7th Durham Light Infantry on 15 October 1915 and landed in France on 22 November 1916. The unpublished history of the battalion has this to say of the bombing raid: 'Colonel Vaux had an extremely narrow escape, reaching the shelter of a dugout as he was passing by brigade headquarters at the very moment a bomb burst on the road some 4 or 5 yards away.'

This bombing raid left an impression in the minds of many of the men of the battalion. Private Douglass distinctly remembered:

> We were on church parade at Elverdinghe, just after we went out. We had come out on rest, into a town called Elverdinghe, it's before you come to Poperinghe, the big town. We were having church parade on the Sunday morning. We were living in huts then and it was payday as well. We were going to get paid that day, five Francs we

*Lieutenant W. Ridoutt and section.*

used to get paid. The whole company was on parade. All the transport was standing; all the horses were tied, neck and neck all the way up and down the lines. All of a sudden, two or three planes came over, started dropping bombs. The place went up. The horses squealed; He killed a lot of horses.

Four of us dived into a cellar of a house. I never touched the steps. It went on for an hour or two that bombardment. He hit the house a direct hit and buried us all. We just had room to put all the bricks out the stairway, because there were steps down. We had to pile them up so we could scrape through a little hole. We just had enough room to pile all them bricks to get the four of us out. We were trembling like Hell, we couldn't stand still. We had a lucky escape there. When we were out, the shambles, there was hardly anyone left standing, any amount of wounded and dead.

I don't know whether or not we were kidding at the time or whether or not we were really singing that Hymn, *All things bright and beautiful comes from Heaven above*.

He came, about three or four planes, and He wrecked the blooming place, there wasn't a horse left standing. There was no money found because it was payday and Captain Forster was killed and I don't know who got the money.

Private Patterson also had memories of the Germans dropping bombs from aircraft while at Ypres in 1917:

I went to Passchendaele; I had a lucky escape there. A moonlight night it was as bright as day. A German Gotha, you could hear them a long way away. I said, 'Quick, find a spot.' We just managed to get to a little break in the ground [and] dropped down there. The bomb went in and didn't go off. Then he went across and dropped on the transport lines and attacking the motor transport. The rest of them went off. Oh! The horses, there were a lot of horses killed. The chap in the lorry on the road, it lifted it up and threw it on top of the other. We had a Hell of a time. This wasn't a nightly occurrence. They used to go to different parts, bombing.

Private Surtees described the bombing as more frightening than the shelling because the bombs practically came straight down. During this attack, he and a lance corporal had a narrow escape when a bomb fell near them. Luckily it didn't explode, but buried itself into the soft ground.

Corporal George Thompson described how difficult conditions were for transport in this sector and what it was like to be bombed:

Our battalion went into the trenches repairing them and on to road work. Our transport had to lead bricks and timber up to where our battalion was working.

The roads were in an awful state. Our horse lines had to be removed about every three days as the ground was so muddy.

With having so much rain the roads got into an awful state and as the mud got soft, it started to run anywhere it could.

Having got back from the trenches at this part of the line we would get our horses fed and see to ourselves. We would no sooner get started to eat what was for us, boiled meat and spuds, the usual … when all of a sudden, you would hear the whistle go. The Germans were over bombing. Lights out, if you had any. It was awful.

I took cover behind a large tree. The aeroplanes were flying low and I could see where they were dropping. I worked my way around the tree. Next morning I looked at that tree, you should have seen the holes in it with shell splinters off the bombs. While I was behind that tree, our sergeant was not far away from me. He shouts, 'Oh I am hit!'

As I run to get hold of him, I run right into a pond. Nearly drowned myself, it was deep in the middle. I got over to where our sergeant was lying and we got him away to hospital.

There were other dangers facing the transport section as well as shelling, as mentioned by Corporal Thompson:

We were coming back from the trenches, having taken up rations and ammunition for our battalion. The Germans opened out with heavy shellfire, when our sergeant gave the order to gallop. Going down open roads, you have not much chance on horses. Rifle fire, heavy shells and lights going up from the trenches made you feel very uncomfortable. However, we got off the road and came into a large wood. Here there were field batteries, firing as hard as they could.

There were telephone wires lying all over the ground and we got into a right fix here. The wires got fastened to our horses' shoes, round our wagon's wheels. We were in a right mix-up. We had to stop and cut as much as possible, to get our horses' feet clear of all the wire. Luckily no one got killed over it. Shells were bursting on both sides of us, it was impossible for our horses to walk; otherwise we would have went further on before we stopped.

After a lot of trouble, which nearly cost us our lives, we got clear and made our return journey, all our work was done in the dark, at this part of the front.

Private Patterson was also batman to Lieutenant Ridoutt, who had unfortunately been wounded on 31 October and subsequently died of his wounds in England. Lieutenant Ridoutt used to play the church organ and Private Patterson always remembered the time he had to help:

I was an officer's orderly one time. We were passing a church and he said, 'I'll just go in and see if I can use the organ.' He went in, I got at the back. I had to pedal with my feet. I was pumping away with my feet and I had a rest, the organ stopped. He said, 'Come on, come on.' He was a nice chap though.

My duties [as batman] if you go into a billet I had to see his bed was right and everything ready for the next day when we had to parade. There was an order came out that officers had to carry the same as infantry as regards pack. He told me when he came back, 'Patterson you've just about broke my back. What did you put all them things in for?'

'We get them. You should have them.'

The QM had a pillow in his pack.

143

The work continued on Railway Street during November, the battalion suffering the hazards of enemy shelling as well as a lack of materials for the repairs. Work was also carried out on the improvement of their camp, one company per day being detailed for this work. The battalion worked under the technical direction of 183rd Company Royal Engineers. In addition to this, work was carried out in the forward areas and on the main Pilkem to Langemarck-Poelcapelle road. Part of the briefing received from Major H.E.B. Hickling, of the 183rd Company Royal Engineers stated that 'the road sectors vary in unpleasantness'.

Work started at 6.00 am until 10.30 am. Rifles and other arms were not carried on these working parties. As the work was unpleasant, the company that remained in camp each day became the relief company, as each company worked for three days before being rested.

Private Patterson related that it was easy to lose one's way in the trenches and what aids they used to ensure they took the right turn:

> It was easy to get lost in the trenches, because there was that many trenches. There was a part, night time when you went on a working party, one branched that way and one branched that way. On the other side a dead German had been buried but his head was sticking out. We used to come along at night time, 'There he is, opposite to him.' His little prickly hair when you touched him we knew then it was straight opposite. That's how we found it. You could get lost.

Private Douglass was once again made a battalion scout and again his duties were to bring up reinforcements. On one occasion he unfortunately had lost his way while leading replacements to the battalion in the devastation of the salient, as he remembered:

> We got on the wrong road; we had to pass a place called Hell Fire Corner. Of course our battalion is being shifted about and we had to find them. I stopped at Hell Fire Corner, where you had to dash past, two at a time at the double, from a trench on one side, over the road, to a trench on the other. There was any amount of dead horses and all sorts lying around there, you were right under German observation. I just got talking to a blooming military policeman I was asking him the way. He was standing there and he was just going to answer me, when a little hole appeared in his brow and the back of his head blew off. I went down into the trench. It was a sniper from somewhere. They nearly panicked, they were new fellas. I kicked them down the trench, they never got off their hands and knees them buggers.

Although the division had been relieved the Pioneers had remained behind to carry on with their vital work. However, on 30 November the battalion prepared to rejoin the division in the Éperleques area. The battalion was billeted at Ganspette, where it rested and caught up on training, route marches being carried out as well as small jobs for the division. St Omer was near to Ganspette and leave was allowed for visits to the town. On 12 December the battalion moved back to Brandhoek, with the transport going to Hopoutre.

The division now took over the Passchendaele sector, with a greater frontage than they had previously held. The road from Ypres up to the railway crossing, also known as Devil's Crossing, was in decent condition. In addition to this there were also three other tracks, made

*Trench scene with Colonel Vaux.*

from trench boards, which were available to the troops, namely RAMC, Judah and H tracks.

The Third Battle of Ypres had come to an end with the capture of Passchendaele in November 1917 and things were settling down for the winter. The ground was just the same; a sea of mud and impassable off the tracks and roads. The battalion went into Sunderland Camp, which was east of the canal. The tents themselves were originally pitched close together, and in order to alleviate the possibilities of casualties, the troops were ordered to repitch them further apart. On 14 December the battalion commenced work in the Passchendaele sector.

The Lewis gun detachment relieved the six guns of the 18th Middlesex Regiment (Pioneers) employed on anti-aircraft work. Two men were placed with each gun in the forward area and were relieved after forty-eight hours. The rest of the battalion carried on working on roads, using beech wood slabs and sleepers to extend the roads. Work was progressing slowly on extending the Mule Track, which ran from the Devil's Crossing, along the bottom of the railway embankment to Zonnebeke Station. This was due to enemy shellfire and the lack of material, the wooden slabs being scarce. The track eventually reached the Seine area and it was here that a dump of RE material was constructed. Christmas 1917 saw no ceasefire; it was a case of everything as normal. The battalion spent its third Christmas Day in France and Flanders at Brandhoek. Church parades were held during the morning, no work being carried out. Once again the weather was starting to interfere with the work; frost was causing problems with the erection of Nissen huts.

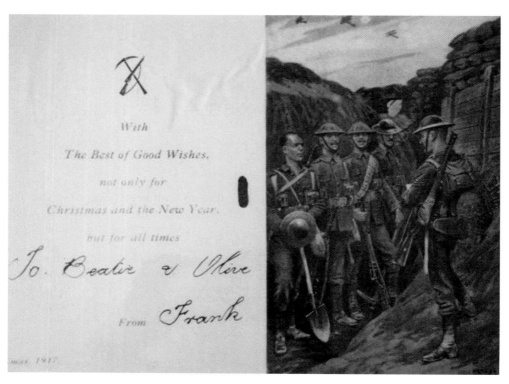

*Battalion Christmas card, sent by Frank Surtees.*

Christmastime still had its tragedies and suffering, as Corporal Thompson related:

> One Christmas, when our transport was stationed at Vlamatinghe, not far away from Ypres. We had got some Christmas pudding sent out from England, by some very kind people. There was a small one for each man. We were given each man one, when our farrier had just gone into his hut when a shell burst and blew him to pieces, poor chap. He was an awful sight. We buried him near Ypres.

Work was also carried out on light railways, especially the one running from Brandhoek, past Ypres and almost up to the dump in the Seine area. At times the trucks of the light railway were used to convey men to the front, especially if it was a working party that needed to be near the front line quickly. One particularly unpleasant task was carried out by a party of men under Lieutenant J.E. Scott. They were engaged in clearing pillboxes in the forward area, the work proceeding slowly due to the state of the boxes. Their original occupants were still in residence and had to be removed and buried.

On 29 December, Major A.H.B. Birchall MC left the battalion to attend a six-month senior officers' course at Aldershot. As a result, Captain G.D.R. Dobson was promoted to major and appointed as second in command.

# Chapter 9

# 1918 and the Spring Offensive

Just like Christmas, there was no truce between the two warring parties at New Year; the only incident of note on New Year's Eve was the firing of a number of coloured flares by the Germans at midnight, possibly as a celebration, but no infantry assault followed, nor any artillery barrage.

With the collapse of the Russian front in November 1917 it became apparent to the Allied high command that the Germans would be moving their forces to the Western Front for a knockout blow against the Allies, who were exhausted after the offensives of the earlier years and especially before the Americans arrived in strength. To meet this threat, work progressed on strengthening and deepening the lines of defence. The Allies had approximately three months to strengthen their defensive works before the conditions of ground and weather would allow the Germans to launch their offensive.

January saw the continuation of the work from December for the battalion, except this time with additional help. For the first three days of the month the battalion had 180 Belgians attached to it for the purpose of road building.

On the 4th of the month the battalion and the 18th (Pioneers) Battalion Middlesex Regiment exchanged their various duties. The Middlesex Regiment also relieved the Lewis gun detachment on anti-aircraft duties. Work started the next day, again on road construction, this time on the Plank Road from Devil's Crossing through to the Seine area, and on levelling the ground ready for the laying of sleepers. However, on 6 January the 50th Division was relieved by the 38th Division and went out to rest. Unfortunately, the Pioneers remained for two further weeks working on the wiring. As well as increasing the wiring on existing positions the battalion was involved in making new machine-gun posts and clearing out pillboxes. Work was still interrupted by the weather, and on some days no work was done at all. Orders were received for the battalion to rejoin the division and move to the Tilques area, the transport arriving on 20 January and the companies a day later. A and B companies and headquarters were billeted in Gondardenne, C Company at Fresinghem and D Company in Esquerdes. The next couple of days were spent on inspections and replacing deficiencies in kit and equipment, with the rest of the time engaging in light training. Towards the end of the month the battalion was back working in the forward area on road clearance, improving the light railway at the Seine Siding, wiring of the Crest Line, burying cable, and reclaiming pillboxes. A letter had been received by the commanding officer from Lieutenant Colonel G.F. Evans RE, CRE 33rd Division expressing his appreciation of the good work done on the army battle zone by the officers and men of the 7th Battalion while working for him.

On the Western Front the overall outlook was proving to be fluid, with the situation changing constantly. Sir Douglas Haig had been ordered to take over an additional 28 miles

*A ruined mill near the front.*

of the French front and by the end of January this had been completed. This part of the line was not in as good a state of defence as the other parts of the British front. The Germans had been moving troops from the Russian front since the previous November, following the armistice on the Eastern Front. By March they had moved no less than twenty-eight divisions, together with a large number of guns, and it was obvious that something was afoot.

February saw more of the same work, with the additional duty of burying cables, while under the supervision of the divisional signals section. The burying of cables was important work because the deeper they were buried, the safer they were from being damaged by enemy shelling. The onerous task of clearing out pillboxes was now given to Lieutenant J.P. Knight. On 12 February the battalion lost Lieutenant A.V. Dickinson, who was wounded, being subsequently discharged due to his wounds in September 1918. Accidents happen in wartime as well as in peacetime. On 13 February Sergeant James Down of Monkwearmouth, Sunderland, suffered a fatal accident when he received a fractured leg and a compound fractured skull. He is buried in Nine Elms Cemetery.

The battalion was ordered to the Tilques area on 22 February. Lieutenant S. Probert was in charge of the advance party, which took over the billets formerly occupied by the 18th Middlesex Regiment. The battalion went into GHQ reserve from noon on the 22nd, but was on forty-eight hours' notice to move. Infantry training and pioneering training was undertaken until 8 March, when C Company moved to Apoul Station to load all 151st Brigade transport.

It was becoming apparent to GHQ that the expected German offensive would not be long in coming. There had been signs of enemy troop build-up and reports from spies of troop movements. This information had been passed down to the various units by the Intelligence Department. As a result, work progressed apace and as many precautions were taken as possible. It was also at this time that the British Army was facing a manpower problem. Most of the divisions were short of men following the fighting at Ypres the previous year. Politics came into play and Prime Minister Lloyd George was keeping back more than 100,000 men in the United Kingdom. He was deliberately starving Field Marshal Haig of these reinforcements in the hope that this would prevent him wasting them in another offensive similar to the Somme or Passchendaele. This policy resulted in a reorganization of the army in France. Although no divisions were disbanded during January and February, brigades were reduced from four infantry battalions to three. The surplus battalions were either reallocated or disbanded and the men moved to other units or the battalion itself being moved to another division. No Regular or Territorial battalion was broken up, only service battalions were disbanded. The battalions chosen from the 50th Division were the 7th Northumberland Fusiliers, which moved to the 42nd Division, the 9th Durham Light Infantry, which moved to the 62nd Division, and 5th Border Regiment, which moved to the 66th Division. Both the 5th Border Regiment and 9th Durham Light Infantry were converted into Pioneer battalions.

The reorganization at a lower level had an adverse affect on the workings of the battalion because time had to be taken out to implement the new establishment. It was reported in the war diary on 24 February that, 'The battalion has been formed in accordance with new war establishment.' The battalion was now organized into 'headquarters' and 'details', and three companies instead of four.

On 9 March the battalion entrained for Longueau and then proceeded by route marches

*Colonel Vaux holding an orders group, Hebnel.*

to the Péronne sector, part of the area that had recently been taken over from the French and consequently the defences were not as strong as other parts of the British line. Training continued, platoon attacks were practised and time taken for the companies to go to the baths for a good wash and clean their clothes. One platoon of C Company was detached and went to Harbonnières to work for the Commander Royal Engineers.

Tensions were starting to rise and for three days the battalion practiced 'Attack' at platoon level. The battalion moved to Tertry on the 16th, and on the 17th remained in camp awaiting instructions. On 18 March, work commenced on spending the next couple of days on digging small defensive posts along ridges west of Tertry.

On 21 March, the Germans launched their long-awaited offensive with a violent bombardment of explosive and gas shells, with at least sixty-four divisions assembled along the whole of the front line and battle zones of the Fifth and Third armies. The two British armies, on the other hand, comprised thirty-four understrength and partially trained divisions.

The weather was also on the side of the Germans; a thick white fog masked their advancing troops. The fog also hindered the British artillery, which could not see the SOS signals being sent up by the front-line troops, so they had to fire on pre-registered positions. The 50th Division received orders as early as 4.30 am from Fifth Army headquarters, to be ready to move at twelve hours' notice.

The battalion stood to arms at 4.30 am. They were about to face one of their sternest tests: the Third and Fifth armies now faced about three million Germans. A warning telegram had been received from divisional headquarters informing the battalion to expect an attack on the 21st. As no further orders had been received by 9.00 am, the companies went to work on strongpoints. At 9.00 pm, the infantry of the division passed through Tertry to reinforce the front line. The infantry were rushed forward, leaving their transport and supplies behind, which meant that many of them were hungry the next day. Although the Germans continued with a heavy bombardment, the next day was quiet for the battalion and at midday they were recalled from their work. Things changed at 2.00 pm, when orders were received to move to Cartigny and to await further instructions. When they arrived they found everything was quiet, with no shelling taking place in the village, although rifle and machine-gun fire could be heard in the distance. The situation at the front could be assessed by the number of wounded passing through the village.

Private Patterson remembered the opening of the offensive:

In 1918 on the Somme the Germans were putting up a terrific bombardment; we were 20 miles away and we could hear it. We had to sleep with our boots on. When I saw the nurses coming down with steel helmets on I knew that was that.

The situation was very fluid. The Germans' tactics were to infiltrate between the various units of the British Army, seeking out weak points and bypassing areas of resistance, which would be dealt with by follow-up troops. Consequently, at 9.00 am on the 23rd, orders were received to move immediately to Le Mesnil. On arrival work was begun on digging a defensive line from Le Mesnil to Athies, to which all units of the division fell back until further orders arrived to retire. During this time the battalion transport were ordered back over the Somme to Belloy.

As the enemy were still advancing and the infantry was in front of the battalion, the GSO

1 (General Staff Officer Grade 1, who held the rank of Lieutenant Colonel) gave the order to retire as soon as the divisional infantry had reached the Athies-Le Mesnil position. The country was open in front of the battalion and the Germans did not initially follow the retirement. When the infantry were clear of their fighting positions they changed into columns for the rest of the march back. However, after a while the mist cleared and this enabled the Germans to harass the British. The move was completed by 11.30 am, when the line running across the north-eastern entrance of Le Mesnil was occupied by the 8th Durham Light Infantry on the right, the 6th Battalion on the left and the 5th Durham Light Infantry in reserve. Once the infantry had taken up their positions the retirement of the 7th was commenced. Unfortunately, as a consequence, the battalion left all their packs, which had been neatly stacked in the village centre.

Once across the Somme, the battalion took a short rest at Villers-Carbonnel, which was now in ruins, there being only a painted sign to indicate where they were. The moves were not without danger as low flying enemy aircraft were machine-gunning the roads. The battalion retaliated with their own rifles and Lewis guns and succeeded in bringing one machine down and driving the rest off.

Just before the move to Belloy, Major G.D.R. Dobson and three men were wounded and Privates 4/8311 Matthew Smith, from South Shields, and 79035 Walter Wombwell were both killed by high explosive shells. Major Dobson suffered a gunshot wound to the chest.

At 8.00 am on Sunday, 24 March, the battalion was ordered to line the canal at Éterpigny, filling a gap between the 66th Division on the left and 8th Division on the right. The position was taken up by 3.00 pm. The Germans were quiet but the battalion was harassed by shells from the British howitzers falling short. The 8th Division had been allocated the job of destroying the bridges over the Somme Canal. With the wide canal to its front the battalion felt its position was safe. However, daybreak on the 25th brought a shock. During the night the battalion on the right had been relieved but the new battalion had overlooked the post holding a bridge that was not totally destroyed – a situation the Germans were quick to exploit. They set up a machine gun in the village, which fired into the battalion's positions, and attempts to locate the gun failed.

Large numbers of the enemy had also crossed the bridge. This concentration of enemy troops now made location of Captain Thompson's company, which was on the right, untenable. Orders were given to withdraw to the ridge behind the canal in front of Barleux, where they met the 5th Durham Light Infantry coming down the hill to deliver a counter-attack. During the morning, 150 men were sent to reinforce the 5th Durham Light Infantry.

The 5th Durham Light Infantry took up a position in an old trench that was well wired. To their left was part of the 7th Durham Light Infantry and to their right was another platoon of the battalion, and after them, no other British troops. Their flank was in the air, exposed to enemy infiltration. The enemy advanced in twos and threes and regrouped into larger formations before advancing again. In this way the Germans were able to get round the flanks of both of the battalions. Orders were received by the 5th Durham Light Infantry to 'hang on to the death', whereas the 7th Durhams' troops had been ordered to retire. The company commander of the 7th Durhams offered to stay but luckily orders were received for all troops to withdraw.

At 7.30 pm, orders were to retire to Estrées, which was reached shortly after midnight,

*A ruined town near the front.*

and positions were taken up to the north of the village. It was during this period that the battalion had to withdraw across the fields because the roads were packed with vehicles of all types.

The position of the 50th Division at this time was as follows: The 150th and 151st brigades, less the 5th Durham Light Infantry, had been lent to the 8th Division. The remainder of the division was under the command of Brigadier General Riddell, 149th Brigade. In front of Estrées and in touch with the 8th Division on the right was 7th Durham Light Infantry. The 5th Battalion then continued the line north whence the 149th Brigade held the line north of Assevillers, joining up with the 66th Division.

The enemy continued to advance in large numbers and were making progress in the 66th Divisional sector, which, as stated, was on the flank of the 50th Division. Orders were again received to withdraw to the Rosières-Vauvillers-Proyart line and by 10.00 am the retirement had commenced. By 2.00 pm, all the units were in position. The 5th and 7th battalions Durham Light Infantry acted as rearguard to the 149th Brigade. One of those incidents that happen in the fog of war took place. During the 26th, one of the battalions of the division received provisional orders to retire, and unfortunately acted immediately upon them. This resulted in a gap in the line being formed. The Germans seizing their opportunity pressed on, capturing Vauvillers, and at one time it appeared they might even break through.

General Riddell acted quickly. A and B companies of the battalion received orders to make a counter-attack on Framerville, a village that stands on a broad spur running towards the Somme, while the 5th Northumberland Fusiliers attacked to the left of the village. The attack itself was successful, the companies forcing their way through the village twice at the point of the bayonet, but they were unable to hold on to their gains due to the commanding positions held by the enemy, who were well supported by machine guns. The result was that the battalion withdrew to the south of the village and took up a position in a sunken road, a further withdrawal taking place at midnight. The Germans made no further advance from this position during the day. During this time the battalion lost three officers (Lieutenants J.P. Knight and H.J. Little, and Second Lieutenant K. Tindle) and eight men killed. Second Lieutenant Kirton Tindle, who had been educated at Durham School, had been in charge of a platoon, holding a trench near Framerville. He saw some Germans who had surrendered and on advancing to take them prisoner was fired on by a hidden machine gun and was not seen alive again.

*Second Lieutenant Kirton Tindle, killed in action 26 March 1918.*

Private G.W. Wrigglesworth wrote of the following incident, concerning Framerville, in his memoirs: 'I remember one of my pals getting a wounded chap on his back to try and get him away but as soon as he had him lifted on his back another Boche put another bullet in him and killed him outright.'

The 27th dawned with the immediate battlefield in front of the battalion covered in a heavy mist. Under cover of this the Germans attacked Rosières, engaging the 6th and 8th battalions Durham Light Infantry, while at the same time advancing from Raincourt. The heavy fighting that was taking place on the right of the battalion, and word having been received that Proyart on the left had fallen to the Germans, orders to retire to Bayonvillers and Guillaucourt were issued. As the enemy had been repulsed orders were given towards nightfall to advance and occupy the sunken road running from Rosières to Harbonnières and later at night the battalion advanced further to positions on Vauvillers Ridge, which was done against little or no opposition.

At 5.00 am on Thursday, 28 March, the battalion was relieved and moved into support, and later still moved further back to Caix, this being the divisional concentration area. However, troops on both flanks had retired, thus inadvertently making the battalion's position critical. But the 7th Durhams held on until 3.30

*Private G. W. Wrigglesworth (seated).*

pm, when they were ordered to take up new positions on a ridge to the west of Caix. Relief was again on the way in the form of the French, who took over a portion of the front, which allowed the battalion to withdraw at 6.00 pm. Headquarters, details, B and C companies went to Moreuil, while A Company went to Boves. This was the first opportunity for the battalion to enjoy a real sleep since the start of the German offensive on the 21st. An unusual incident took place on Friday, 29 March when at about 1.30 am a man came to headquarters and said that all troops had to clear out of the village as the Germans were quite near and in force. This later turned out to be untrue, being the work of a spy. A similar incident took place a couple of days later at Villers-Bretonneux, where all the transport of the division was located.

At Moreuil the remnants of the battalion, amounting to about sixty men under Captain Dickson, along with other units of the division, were once again called upon to enter the fighting near the crossroads at Dèmuin. All other oddments of the division were collected at Boves and then marched down to Sains-en-Amiénois, where on 30 March attempts were made to gather together the dispersed members of the division, prior to its pending relief – a relief that did not happen.

As is the nature of this type of warfare, where men fight often in individual trenches or with a couple of other comrades, when orders to retire are received by the battalion, they do not always filter down to everyone. As a result, some are left behind to either become prisoners or rejoin the battalion at a later date. Some brave souls knowingly stayed behind to cover the retirement of their comrades, sure in the knowledge that they faced an uncertain future.

In the course of the retirement, members of the battalion attached themselves to units of the 20th, 39th, 60th and 61st divisions, to name but a few, so mixed up was the situation, but most eventually rejoined the battalion.

During the turbulent days of the retreat the resupply of ammunition and finding the battalion was a constant problem for members of the transport section. Corporal Thompson described how it was done:

> We had to take ammunition up on pack mules. I was sent up in charge of ours. This was a rotten job as we had to get as near to our battalion as possible. The Germans were still advancing and we were under heavy rifle fire at times. On some parts of the line the Germans were ahead of us. All we could do was to dump it at different places so our battalion could pick it up as they were retreating. We opened the boxes already for them. Away we would go and do the same thing further back.
>
> I met one of our CSMs [company sergeant major] who had just came back off leave. He asked me how far away was our battalion. I said they won't be long before they are retreating through this place. He and a private out of one of our companies went up to try and find their companies. Next time I went up with ammunition the poor sergeant major got a right one through the head and was killed on the spot. They buried him just outside Harbonnières.

The only company sergeant major killed during the retreat was 275004 Company Sergeant Major Robert William Wardropper DCM. He had joined the battalion on 12 April 1907 and had worked as a riveter before the war. An officer wrote of him: 'His loss was a great blow to us, as he was always a cheery and ideal warrant officer.' He left behind a wife and three children.

As far as the 7th Durham Light Infantry were concerned the fighting in the March offensive was over. On 30 March it was pulled back with the rest of the 50th Division, eventually arriving at Bernay, near Crécy, where they were billeted in farms.

With the battalion being withdrawn from the front line, they looked forward to a period of rest and relaxation and on 4 April they boarded lorries, thirty-two men in each, on the main road between Abbeville and Montreuil, for their move north. The lorries took them through Montreuil, which was the headquarters of the British Expeditionary Force (BEF). Unfortunately there was no time to stop and the lorries pressed on, turning onto the Boulogne Road, which raised the hopes of the troops of a stay near the coast. Their hopes were short-lived as the convoy turned east and eventually arrived at Beuvry, on the south-eastern outskirts of Béthune, being billeted in Le Quesnoy, in the neighbourhood of Béthune. The 50th Division now became part of the First Army.

During the retreat the evacuation of the wounded broke down because of the speed of the advance of the Germans. Private Patterson, a stretcher bearer in B Company, told what happened:

> Anybody who got wounded, there wasn't any stretcher bearers, well they had had it. Best we could do was bandage them. If they were badly wounded you could only leave them in the end, you couldn't get the ambulances up because they were retreated also. They were taken prisoner, but we saw them alright before we left them.

There was also a place for humanity, as Private Patterson continued:

> When the big retreat was on, in March, the refugees, I felt sorry for them. There wasn't much looting. What I did, there was a shop; he'd hopped it that quick he'd left all his birds in the cages inside the shop. The door was open and I opened ever door of the cages. I let all the birds out. That's the only looting I did. I've never ate so many chickens in all my life.

Private Douglass also took part in the March retreat, standing firm, then retiring before the Germans completed any potential encirclement:

> Before the push we were pulled out and we were sleeping in tents behind the lines. They had shoved tents up, camouflaged tents, and built sandbags right round the walls of the tents. But they were all full of mud, over your shoe tops. That's the conditions we had to sleep in. Blankets were soaked, but there were about twenty men in a tent, but you couldn't lie down and sleep, you used to put the blanket down and curl up, like ducks all sitting round the pole. We pulled back into a billet; that was before the retreat started. When we were going up into the trenches we passed the Yankee camp. They were the first Yankees out [here at the front] we'd seen, a new division. All like cowboys with their cowboy hats on. They looked smart, there must have been thousands of them, a whole battalion, a whole division, we passed on the way up to the line. This was the last year of the war they came in. It looked great because all their packs were dead straight in a line, in front of their tents. They were under canvas. It was a picture to see them, all fresh troops. Further on they had an airfield and all their planes were lined up.
>
> We got to the front line and held it for a bit before the Germans started to push us back with his big offensive. We had to come all the way back to where we'd passed

these Yankees. These Yanks were supposed to be in support of us. We never came up to them yet. They had left all their packs, planes were laying, there were no Yanks, they had all gone.

'Course He was shelling, the planes were going up a height, getting burnt. There was a Hell of a lot of fires then. I don't know what happened, if they were pulled out quick. I've never known an army leave its packs before like that and hop it. They might have been shoved into an emergency gap somewhere that we didn't know about, but that's the way it was and that's the way we saw it. We called them every damned name after that. They had never been in action as far as we knew. But we didn't know what was happening on the whole battlefront, but that's the way it was left, the same as when we went up, packs lying all over as if they had scrambled off.

As we were falling back He was shelling. We used to stop and hold him. The orders were, 'You don't fall back anymore; you hold him here.' Then the order would come to fall back. You began to wonder what the Hell they were playing at. What really was happening was He was belting round on the flanks and He would have captured all of us in the centre, you see. We could have held him in the centre but the flanks were falling back. If He had gotten round us He would have encircled us, so with them falling back we had to fall back. We fell back. When He came in sight we gave him a burst of rifle fire and machine-gun fire and all that. We did that for about twelve days, falling back and falling back all the time. He was stopped eventually, but of course like everything else we the infantry we're in the front line we don't know what's going on. We were just doing what we were told.

Maybe the Yanks fell back for the same reason they had not had time to get their equipment up. And besides that, as we were falling back you cannot use the roads because He was up in his aeroplanes dropping darts on you. The roads were [also] full of evacuees, going down, women and children, bits of carts, handcarts. Handcarts all with their possessions. Poor devils. He was dropping all these darts. We were going in two lines down each side, one on the right, one on the left, dropping these darts. It sounded like rain at first we wondered why he did not drop bombs, but they caused terrible, terrible havoc them darts. Any amount of people killed with them. He was also setting fire to the villages in front, all the villages you had to pass through, they were all blazing, flames from each side. You had to dive through them, with all that ammunition on you had to go through them; it was no use all bunching to get round each side of them. That was what He wanted. We went through them with scorched uniforms, many a time, dashing through there. You could barely get your breath afore he was halted in that offensive.

It was now a time for reflection and to reorganize and make good the equipment lost during the past week. Time was allowed to go sightseeing in Béthune, visiting the various shops and other attractions it had to offer. On 6 April the battalion moved to the Estaires area, being billeted at Robemetz, which lies between Merville and Neuf-Berquin.

The day of 9 April was a sad one for the battalion for it was on this day that it said goodbye to Lieutenant Colonel Vaux, who relinquished command on grounds of ill health. The unpublished history of the battalion has this to say on the departure of Colonel Vaux:

It was only in the September of 1911 that he succeeded to the command of the battalion so his term of four years in the appointment had not expired when war was declared in 1914.

Knowing him for the earnest soldier he was one can realize with what energy he threw himself into the training during the months of preparation in England, and the pride with which he took his 'Boys', they were never anything else to him but that, overseas in April 1915.

Understanding and sympathetic, forceful but never imperious, he gained his men's confidence and secured their obedience.

'If they are going to get you boys they will, so why worry,' was his constant advice, and he lived up to it.

*Colonel Vaux.*

Three years, save a few days, almost continually in the line is a remarkable record for a commanding officer of a battalion. He was not content after the change was made from an Infantry to a Pioneer battalion, that his companies should be detached for duty with the Infantry brigades of the division during some operation but he saw for himself how things fared with them.

As a collector of 'Souvenirs' he was perhaps without equal in the Expeditionary Force and his 'Boys' going on leave carried home for him many treasures to England.

When he had set his heart upon some relic, weight and size made but little difference. Coming one day into the 151st Infantry Brigade headquarters he told of how he had chanced upon an old weather vane lying in the mud outside which had fallen from its place on the roof of the farm. 'You would have passed it by,' he said to the staff captain.

Perhaps the farewell of the Maoris to King George V when as Prince of Wales he visited them in 1901 expresses more happily than any other words could the feelings of all when he said Goodbye: 'Though our eyes see you no more the love of our hearts goes with you to the distant land.'

Shortly afterwards he was invalided to England, placed upon the Retired List, and later appointed honorary colonel of the battalion he had served so well.

Major A.H. Birchall MC, having completed his senior officer course, returned to the battalion to assume command. Captain W.F. Laing remained as adjutant, with Captain W.M. Morant, who had returned from his appointment as assistant provost marshal, as assistant adjutant. The company commanders at this time were Captain R.A. Dickson, Captain MacIntyre, Captain A.T.R. Hudson and Captain F.C. Tilbrook.

*A pen and ink drawing of Colonel Vaux with his shepherd's crook.*

The front north of La Bassée Canal had been stripped to meet the demands of the offensive on the Somme during March. All in all, ten divisions were withdrawn from Flanders. The division's immediate front line was held by the 2nd Portuguese Division, which had been in the line longer than had originally been planned because of the offensives on the Somme. Their morale had suffered because of their extended front-line service. Consequently it was low, and it had been decided to withdraw them in the near future. However, what was not known was that the Germans were planning their second great attack in this neighbourhood. In the event of a German attack, the Portuguese had been told that they were to hold only the forward line, while British troops would be sent to the battle zone. Prior to this the Portuguese had similarly undergone some reorganization; the 2nd Division now comprised four brigades. Unfortunately, according to the *British Official History: Military Operations*, 'the four-brigade division numbered only 21,000, with a fighting strength of 17,000, and was short of 139 officers and just under 6,000 men.' It was the job of the 50th Division to relieve the Portuguese on the night of 9/10 April.

The German offensive opened at 5.30 am on 9 April, with a heavy bombardment of the front line and battle zones. The Portuguese fell back in disarray, which resulted in the resting British divisions to their rear being rushed up to fill any gaps and halt the Germans. By midday the Germans were in what had been the rear positions of the Portuguese line and had fanned out north and south to attack the flanks of the 40th and 55th divisions, respectively. The fight was taken up by the 151st Brigade of the division and the 7th Durham Light Infantry were placed under its orders.

This day the battalion's job was to keep the communication routes open. B Company was in Merville and C Company in Estaires removing debris from fallen houses off the roads, both towns having been heavily shelled. The offensive continued throughout the next day and A Company was sent forward to reinforce the 6th Durham Light Infantry along the western bank of the river Lawe, just south of the railway bridge, where it was in contact with the 51st Division, then over open ground to the canal and then along its northern bank until it reached the Estaires-Chapelle Duvelle road. During this time the remainder of the battalion stood to arms in reserve.

The day of 11 April was one of action; both B and C Companies were initially engaged in digging a line of posts along the main Neuf Berquin-Estaires road and in front of Merville. The enemy kept up the pressure and all companies of the battalion were in close contact with the Germans. B and C companies were holding bridgeheads at Merville onto which the 6th Battalion retired, while A Company was still along the canal bank. By 2.45 pm the Germans had gained a foothold in Chapelle Dunville. A party of 100 men, organized as a makeshift company made up from the battalion Details, was ordered by Brigadier General Martin to make a counter-attack. This was initially successful, but as the Germans were still advancing on both flanks there was no alternative but to withdraw to the canal to the west of Chapelle Duville at Robemetz. By nightfall the line had been further withdrawn and was now established north-west of Neuf Berquin. During this day the battalion lost Lieutenants A.E. Hopson and J.E. Tetley (during the counter-attack on Chapelle Dunville) killed as well as 13 other ranks, including 275428 Company Sergeant Major Thomas Coleman from Sunderland, the only man of the battalion to be awarded both the Distinguished Conduct Medal and the Military Medal. Also among those killed was Private Frederick Smith Mackenzie of C Company, who had worked as a printer's moulder at Messrs Lynn & Co, Sunderland. He had joined the battalion on 10 May 1914 and was one of the first reinforcements to reach the battalion in July 1915. Unfortunately, he died on the road to Russell Farm, of wounds received at Merville the same day, and was buried at Russell Farm. He now lies in Aval Wood Military

Cemetery. It had taken four hours to carry him on a stretcher to the dressing station, where he was pronounced dead on arrival.

Another of those curious incidents that happens during wars took place at this time. During the afternoon of 11 April one of the battalion's transport limbers was returning from Robemetz with a load of empty boxes after delivering small arms ammunition when a shell burst close to it, killing one of the horses. The other horses were brought back to the transport lines but the limber had to be abandoned due to the German advances. It was found weeks later, still standing there, when the Germans retired in the face of pressure from the First Army.

Fighting continued during the night around Merville. The battalions of the division were now in a much weakened condition and as a result a gap of 500 yards developed on the right flank. The 51st Division tried to fill it but were unsuccessful and the Germans exploited the situation. The situation became so critical that the divisional commander ordered the town to be evacuated, which was accomplished by 1.00 am on 12 April. A new line was formed by the remains of the battalions, together with the 2nd Royal Fusiliers (29th Division) along the river Bourre to the north-west, where bridgeheads were established. The Germans kept up pressure on the right flank, where by midday they had occupied the village of Le Sart, not far from the Fôret de Neippe. The right flank had been turned and forced to withdraw. The left flank, which had been reinforced by two companies of the Irish Guards, beat off the enemy attacks. The line, lying astride the La Motte-Merville road, was now held mainly by men from units of the 50th and 51st divisions, the 2nd Royal Fusiliers of the 29th Division, Irish Guards, together with other details. Every available man was pushed into the line. This was at the time when Field Marshal Haig was writing his famous Special Order of the Day, which was issued on 13 April, part of which read, 'With our backs to the wall, and believing in the justice of our cause, each one of us must fight on to the end.'

Although the division had started to be relieved on 12 April by 5th Division, which had been brought back from Italy, the full relief was not completed until 3.00 am on 13 April. The battalion itself was relieved by the Grenadier Guards on 12 April at 9.00 pm. Collecting at La Motte, on the north-western side of the forest, before moving off, the battalion were subsequently billeted in the outbuildings of the chateau. The field cookers awaited the battalion with a hot meal, which was much appreciated. The men, being very fatigued, were soon asleep after they had eaten. Life was far from quiet. During the night enemy aircraft kept passing overhead but luckily they did not drop any bombs. At approximately 5.00 am on the morning of the 13th, the Germans put a heavy bombardment down on the chateau, shattering huts and bivouacs, and causing a great number of casualties, with thirty-five men being killed and a number wounded. Escape from the shelling had been impossible.

The unpublished history of the battalion records this from Colonel Birchall:

On no other occasion had I seen so many casualties in such a short space of time but as the area was small and congested that can be more easily understood than can the order which placed such a number of men in so prominent a place. It was understood that the shells were British, fired from British guns which the Germans had taken from the Portuguese. If that were so then the Boche must have experienced many bad moments when the British Artillery sought to teach them that war was not all beer and skittles.

The wounded were removed to the basement of the chateau at La Motte. High praise was given to the drivers of the motor lorries, who risked everything to collect the wounded to take them to the dressing station while the shelling was still going on.

After the affair at the chateau, the battalion was withdrawn further back, where it resumed its role as divisional Pioneers by spending the next three days digging new trenches and wiring the lines against further German aggression.

An amusing incident is recorded in the unpublished history:

> While the battalion was digging the new line west of the Forêt de Nieppe, and on the watch for any breakthrough by the enemy, not far behind them stood a large Expeditionary Force canteen. Here the staff, of the canteen, not of the division, were it was understood destroying at the back of the canteen stores lest they fell into the hands of the Germans. As things turned out the precaution proved needless but what rankled in the minds of those who knew of it was that at the counter end they were still insisting on charging for supplies to the poor devils who had for days, and still stood, between them and the Boche.

The fighting endured by the battalion had been heavy, especially due to the nature of the ground, which was flat and exposed, giving good fields of fire for the German riflemen and machine-gunners. Casualties were heavy amongst the company commanders with Captains A.T.R. Hudson, W.M. Morant and F.C. Tilbrook being killed, as well as Lieutenants J.C. Tetley (D Company) and F.W.R. Nesbitt.

Captain Morant had been educated at Durham School, one of three officers of the battalion who had been educated at the school and were killed during the war. He was a qualified solicitor who before the war worked on the staff of Sir Charles H. Matthews, Bart KCB, Director of Public Prosecutions, at the Home Office. He was killed on his twenty-sixth birthday.

The story of Private Charles William Petfield, a native of Hull, is a tragic one, although probably not unique. He was attested for the Army on 5 September 1917 and mobilized on the 6th. After his training he left for France on 5 April 1918, arriving on the 6th. He then joined the battalion on 11 April, during the fighting around Merville, and was killed in action on 13 April, one of the many casualties suffered during the battle. He was just eighteen when he died. At this period of the war, with the Germans on the offensive, it was usually not very long before new arrivals were killed, wounded or taken prisoner.

*Captain W.M. Morant, killed in action 11 April 1918.*

The fighting that the division had taken part in lasted for four days and the enemy advanced only 4 miles. This was against a division composed of tired men from the March offensives and 19-year-old replacements – men such as Private Petfield, with little artillery support.

Private Douglass took part in this action, going to the aid of a wounded Scotsman, until he himself was wounded in the leg and rescued by men of the Artillery, as he explained:

I was falling back; Scottish regiments were with us, we were all just hurrying back. The Germans were pushing us as hard as they could. All of a sudden one of the Scottish fellows fell down with a Hell of a gash in his thigh. I knew he would bleed to death in a minute or two so I stopped and bandaged him up, which is against the rules, you are not supposed to stop for the wounded, but he would not have lasted five minutes. So I put a tourniquet on. My rifle was lying beside me and he said, 'Look out; here's a German on top of you.'

I just looked up and he was a few yards away, so I just picked up the rifle. I didn't have time to point it so I clouted him in the face and nearly tore his face off and he dropped beside me. I started to tighten the tourniquet again and he said, 'Here's two more behind you.'

So I picked the rifle up. They were a bit further apart and I shot them two beggars, just in the last stride. Then I finished the tourniquet with an entrenching tool till it was tight, then I bandaged it up and left him.

He said, 'You might as well give yourself up; they are coming all around you.'

I said, 'What! With these fellas lying down. No fears, I know what I'll get if I did.'

'You'll never make it,' he said.

So I dived into a trench and wormed my way down as fast as I could, there were shots flying all over. I got away back with some other stragglers till we got to a line that was held with fresh troops.

In the first place they wouldn't be bothered with you; I was only one, they would only be taking one prisoner. They were chasing us back. We were falling back as fast as we could, we couldn't get a stand. If they caught a man where he'd killed three Germans, they were not going to be bothered with him to take him back. The other lads were all further down, I could see them.

We were pulled behind the Portuguese front then and we only got a week's rest there when He [the Germans] attacked the Portuguese. They were caught on the hop because they were retreating to us as we were rushing up to the line. They were falling back; we were rushing up to stem them. Half of them had no shoes or boots on; they had been caught on the hop. You're not supposed to take your boots and things off in the front-line trenches. And we were really shooting the Portuguese because they had the same damned coloured uniform as the Germans, field grey, till they started shouting.

Then there was another time I was sent by my officer out of the trench with a message. I don't know what was on it; he just came and said, 'Get this through to battalion headquarters, Douglass.'

I left, but the observation balloon must have seen me leave the front-line trench, go into supports, leave the supports into the reserve and go down the communication trench. The Germans up in the observation balloon would know I was carrying a message, I suppose. Anyway, I didn't know anymore until a blooming aeroplane came buzzing around. He dropped a bomb just in front of me, all the soil came over the top of me and I lay there and he circled round. I thought he might drop another one while I'm sitting (I was in the trench all the time mind, leaning back). So I gets a bit further down, he dropped another and it buried me again. So I thought I had better play dead this time, see if he goes away. I lay there, I could not tell you how long I lay there and he was still circling and circling round, and I made another dive for it and he dropped another and then he was away. But he was well out of mark with the third bomb because our anti-aircraft guns were starting to shift him then. I got the message to headquarters. I don't know to this day what was in the message, but it was urgent.

We went forward to make contact with the Germans first and we held them. There was a canal behind us, in front there was a space in the road and He was trying to get this machine gun across. Well we kept popping them off all the time. We were in a bit of a ditch that had been formed. When I got hit in the side it was a ricochet because we were in part of a trench, it tore my mate John Evans' lug [ear] off. The bullet went right through his lug and it entered my leg and the fella this side, I forget his name now, he was only a little fella, he went down, the top of his head lifted off like a lid. He must have just put his head up above that bit ground. They had a machine gun. Right across there and it lifted off like a lid, and the daft corporal there, I forget his name now, he says, 'See if he wants bandaging there.'

'He has no heed [head] on man,' I replied

Behind us was a canal and I couldn't stand with the pain. I told them that I'm going to try and get back now. There was no bridges across the canal. I thought well we're going to retreat just now.

We knew we were going to retreat, we could not hold them much longer. I was hopping on one leg and dragging the other and just jumped into the canal, never thinking how I was going to get out the other side, I could swim in those days. I had to go down the canal and find a break. I'm not kidding, I don't know how I got out of the canal, there was a break and I got out there. I was limping and falling down and limping. We were retreating and the Artillery were pulling their guns out. There were two of them that stopped their team, they had a limber on the back that they carried their ammunition in. Two of them got off the driving seat, picked up and threw me in and told me to hold on.

I clung on 'cos they were pulling the guns out as well and I bounced up and down in that limber 'cos the roads was all full of holes, of course it couldn't tipple. And that's the way they got me down to a dressing station.

When I got down there, there were scores and scores of wounded to be attended to. He came and looked at me, the doctor.

I said, 'Here, I'm hit here.'

He cuts the trousers. He says, 'This will hurt, just clench your teeth, bite something.' He pulled the bullet out; I nearly jumped off that bloody table. He gave me it as a souvenir.

They bandaged me up and I was away down to the field dressing station, the hospital.

There is an interesting postscript regarding the Scotsman that Private Douglass helped. In the 1960s Private Douglass received the following letter:

Comrade.
By a million to one chance I happened on your letter in an English local paper and your name and regiment, which I have never forgot since that day you saved my life on the battlefield with a field dressing and a trenching tool handle. When I asked what mob you were in all I got was, 'No names, no pack drill'. Quite the clam weren't you? 'Til at last you told me 7 DLI. I said lucky number and you came back with, 'Yes quite lucky, there's none of us left.' Hardly I dare say you have forgot all this, not me. I still see you with a grin on your face as you smashed that Jerries [sic] face to a pulp with your rifle butt and shot the other two creeping up on you and I thought you hadn't a cat in Hell's chance of getting out alive. You were either mad or you have a marvellous sense of humour. Well now we know, we both survived. Please don't get mad at this present; it's a noose for your neck. I hope no one pulls it too tight. I am just passing through, no time to visit you but we'll meet again for sure either in H or H [Heaven or Hell]. So quoting your last words to me, 'No names, no pack drill'. So long hero, your comrade in arms ex.
A. & S.H.

The Scotsman had bought a scarf and sent it to the *Sunderland Echo*, with the above covering letter, to be sent on to Private Douglass, which he duly received and treasured for many years. He never knew the name of the Scotsman.

The transport also had its problems during the Battle of the Lys. Corporal Thompson described what happened when he delivered rations and went to investigate cries from a building:

I remember going through Merville. We could hardly get through for those poor French people. Our first stop was at a place called Locke. Here I remember there was a very large wood or forest. Here I saw those Portuguese Infantry running away through this forest; some of them had no boots on. Those were allowed to get away to safety. Our troops had to make a stand for it.

About this time our battalion was spread all over, some here and some there. We had to take some ammunition up to them. It was a long road, just outside Merville, and a forest on both sides of this road. On one side the Germans were in this forest. We did not know this until we got up. Our officer which we had, while our captain was on leave, said that he had been up to see if he could see any of our battalion and said he could not see them. So he told me to go up in charge of a limber wagon with some rations and ammunition. He gave me the direction but that was all. So I started off with the driver of the wagon to find the battalion.

I was mounted and on our way up we came across the guide who was looking for us. He asked if we had any rations for them and I said yes. So I said jump up into the wagon and we crossed over open country to get there sooner. The Germans were shelling awful and rifle bullets and machine guns were whipping past us. I remember the driver saying, 'Corporal I don't think we will get out of this.' We went up a narrow road and here at the other side of this road, there was our battalion, all along the hedges of the road.

The guide shouted for someone to come and get the rations. They were not long before they emptied our wagon. The road that we had to go back on was all blown up. So I said, 'Follow me, Harry.' He belonged to South Shields.

'Alright,' he said. We jumped over a little stream and it brought us near to a farmhouse. The shells were coming over worse now and just as we were nearing this farm house I heard someone shouting.

I said, 'Did you hear that, Harry?' He said, 'yes'. I said, 'We will have to be careful, there may be Germans.'

The voice told me it was some Englishman. So nearer I got and to my surprise it was our own machine-gun sergeant. Poor fellow, he was all shot down his back. He had been caught with a machine gun I think.

I shouted to the driver to come over and he was lying on an old bed, just in the passageway of the house. We lifted him up and he started to shout, 'Don't leave me.'

This poor fellow must have been left there to die I think. That will show you how far we were in front of our battalion at this spot.

We got him into our wagon and started off for our new lines, which were in Locke. We managed to get him across the open country alright 'til we came to four cross roads. I thought we would have never got back to this road. Shells bursting around us and just as we were getting onto the main road four shells burst in front of us. The shock turned the horses right round. I felt all sorts hit my horse. After a second I said, 'Are you all right, Harry?' 'I think so.'

I turned his horses round for home and full stretch and gallop. The horses knew what it meant.

We got to where our transport was resting, just outside of Locke. I reported to our officer and he asked who was in our wagon and I told him. He told me to take him to hospital at Hazebrouck.

When we got to Hazebrouck they were all leaving the town as the Germans were shelling and advancing quick. The place was in uproar. I saw a field ambulance and I put the sergeant in and off he went.

Corporal Thompson also remembered another unfortunate incident at Merville:

One day, as we were retreating through a place called Merville, I was just going to the back of our column to see everything correct, when a shell burst just in front of one of our wagons and blew horses and driver to pieces. It was awful. Poor chap had only just got those horses that morning as the driver was away. Just luck you see.

This was the end of the battalion's part in the second German offensive of the year. During this offensive the Germans had committed forty-two divisions, thirty-three being fresh and the other nine having fought in the March battles. Against this the British could only employ twenty-five divisions, eight of which were fresh.

Two moves were to take place, firstly to a village called Mametz, near Béthune, where once again inspections and kit deficiencies were made good or requisitions put in for replacements. On 20 April the battalion was inspected by the divisional commander, Major General H.C. Jackson DSO, who thanked everyone for the work they had done during the last two battles and said how proud he was to have such a Pioneer battalion with the division.

The battalion had suffered heavily since the commencement of the German offensives in March, not only in killed and wounded but also in prisoners. As a result, the battalion was brought up to strength with young lads and men transferred in from other corps. This was the same for the whole division. The next few weeks were taken up with training, ranging from physical exercise, musketry, gas drills to practising attacks both at company level as well as at battalion level. It was not all work and no play; sports were built into the programmes.

At 5.30 am on 26 April the battalion marched to Pernes and from there, as part of 149th Infantry Brigade Group, boarded trains for the move south. This was a long journey, finally arriving at Fère-en-Tardenois on the 27th and moving to billets at Vézilly. This area had seen a lot of heavy fighting in the early years of the war but had now become quiet. The 50th Division, along with the 8th, 21st and 25th divisions, which formed the IX Corps, now came under the command of General Duchêne of the French Army. On 5 May they took over a sector of the front line facing the Chemin des Dames, with the river Aisne to their rear. These trenches were the furthest south any British units had occupied.

The battalion spent five or six days at Vézilly, which made a surprising change from the villages of Belgium and Northern France. The local inhabitants were friendly and enthusiastic about the arrival of British troops. On 6 May the battalion reached the Centre d'Evreux in the Forêt de Beau Marais, near the Craonne (Californie) Plateau. The transport was stationed at Concevreux, a village on the Aisne canal on the south side of the Aisne département. The dugouts at the Centre d'Evreux were quite large, big enough to hold a whole battalion, and were fitted out with electric lights and electric fans for ventilation. These had been constructed for the French offensive of 1917.

After settling in, a platoon of A Company was sent to a Royal Engineers' dump and workshop at Beaurepaire on 7 May, whilst another platoon of that company was sent to work on the railway at Le Sapinière.

The accommodation at the Centre d'Evreux was luxurious by comparison to many others the battalion had occupied before; therefore, it came as no surprise to the troops that a move was on the cards. On 8 May two platoons of B Company were despatched to Poste Command Brest and the other two platoons to Champs Asile to work on roads. The next day the remaining two platoons of A Company were moved to Craonne to work on the trenches and dugouts. At the same time, C Company was attached to the 151st Infantry Brigade to work on the line. Headquarters, now being alone, moved on the 11th nearer to Monaco Dump, which was south-west of the Centre d'Evreux.

The Forêt de Beau Marais lay in the centre of the divisional front. On the left flank was the Craonne Plateau, described as a huge hog-backed hill, along which ran the Chemin de Dames. Also on the left flank was the river Ailette. The right flank consisted of a low-lying plain with conical hills, called buttes, rising out of it. At some parts of the line no-man's-land was more than a mile wide. The division was much reduced in strength due to the recent battles. As a consequence all three brigades were holding the front. The 149th were on the right, with the 151st in the centre, holding the Forêt de Beau Marais, and the 150th on the left, on the Craonne Plateau and Chemin de Dames. To the south were the 8th and 21st divisions, with the 25th in reserve and the French to the north.

The trenches held by the 151st Brigade were in front of the forest. In the forest itself there were many other supporting trenches and strongpoints. Unfortunately, these did not have a good field of fire and no observation greater than a few yards. The strongpoints ended up being used during the battle mainly for last stands by small groups of men. With hindsight the loss of these men could possibly have been avoided if these strongpoints had not been there and the men been allowed to retire to more organized and easily defensible positions behind the forest. Initially the brigade had one battalion in the front line, one in close support and the third, at Chaudardes, in reserve. After a few days the dispositions were changed around, with two battalions in the front line and the third still in reserve at Chaudardes.

The 8th Battalion Durham Light Infantry was weak in numbers. The reinforcements it received to bring it back up to strength were men mainly from the Army Service Corps and Inland Waterways Transport, who had little or no infantry training. Because of this lack of expertise these men were left out of the line to continue their training at the 50th Divisional School. This deficiency was made up by the attachment of C Company 7th Durham Light Infantry, who were assigned to Poste Command Hoche and Ouvrage Toulon.

The days passed quietly, but on the evening of 25 May the 8th Battalion Durham Light Infantry undertook a raid on the German trenches with the purpose of obtaining a prisoner to find out which unit was holding the front opposite the battalion. The raid succeeded in its objective and a wounded Polish corporal belonging to the 4th Company 444th Infantry Regiment, 231st Division was captured. He gave the enemy order of battle as he knew it, how the front line was held and much other useful information.

Two French prisoners of war who had managed to escape from the Germans made it across no-man's-land and into the lines held by the division and reported a build-up of enemy troops behind the front. As well as this, aerial reconnaissance stated that they had seen a large number of German tanks.

In the event of an emergency the bridges over the Aisne would prove to be a bottleneck. Repeated requests had been made to pull some of the troops back to the south side of the river, but they had all been refused by the French commander. Ominous signs of a German build-up in preparation for an offensive started to show. The unpublished history of the battalion has this to say:

When the sector was first taken over brigade headquarters was established in Poste Command Hoche. After a few days here they were ordered by the division to move about a thousand yards further to the south-west to Centre d'Evreux, the reason given being, 'If the enemy were to attack here you would be involved in the fighting immediately in your present position and unable to control the battalions under your command.'

'I hope they are not going to attack here,' said the brigade commander.

The second hint of such a possibility was contained also in a message from the division, this having reference to the Defence Scheme – in every sector there was always such a scheme prepared to meet the emergency of an attack by the enemy –

'In the event of your being attacked no reinforcements need be expected east of the river Aisne.'

The task now was to prepare for any enemy action. Dumps of small arms ammunition, bombs and iron rations were made throughout the divisional area. This was also a routine precaution, especially as the stores taken over by the British were French and, therefore, the ammunition was of no use in their rifles. To add to this the battalion reserves had also been run down owing to the recent offensives and the move away from the normal British bases.

During the evening of 25 May, brigade headquarters ordered all units to 'Adopt defensive precautions'. Everyone started to get ready for what lay ahead. Extra ammunition and bombs were drawn and the battle position was occupied.

The next day saw some movement of the companies of the battalion: A Company joined the 150th Infantry Brigade, C Company moved forward and took positions on Lamoureux Hill with B Company 8th Durham Light Infantry, while two platoons of B Company 7th Durham Light Infantry moved into strongpoints. The remaining two platoons of B Company were ordered to ensure that the roads were clear for the transport and artillery.

At approximately 11.00 am, divisional headquarters received word that an attack was imminent the next day. The remainder of the day remained quiet, with hardly any shots being fired, but at 7.00 pm the French 75s opened up on the German positions. The 50th Divisional Artillery opened fire an hour later on roads behind the German line. All this time the German guns remained silent. The silence was ominous. Then, at 1.00 am on the morning of 27 May, a great light flared up all along the German front. This was the signal for the start of the bombardment. The bombardment went on for three hours, with both gas and high explosive shells, in large quantities. Batteries, communication centres, roads, machine-gun posts and brigade headquarters were all targeted, as well as the lines of trenches. It was not long before communication between the various units was lost. The only way they could contact each other was by runner, and not all of them made it. Infantry casualties were very heavy, with most of the machine guns and artillery being knocked out.

The men of the transport section stood on nearby hills and watched the bombardment and the grooms took their officers' charges over the river in case they were needed.

The bombardment was so intense that all communication with brigade headquarters was virtually cut; it could take up to three and a half hours for the runners to cover the 800 yards.

The German infantry assault commenced at 4.30 am, with twenty-eight divisions on a 35-mile front, supported by tanks. By this time quite a number of the British batteries had been knocked out. The front line had been flattened and those who remained on Lamoureux Hill were cut off from the rest of the 8th Durhams. Captain R.H. Wharrier, 8th Durham Light Infantry, discussed the situation with his remaining officers and decided to fight it out to the end. No one escaped.

According to the unpublished history of the battalion:

Soon after 5.00 am, a party of the 7th Battalion from near brigade headquarters, together with about forty machine-gunners, reached C Company of the 8th Battalion, which had almost been annihilated, and these moved along the embankment of the broad gauge railway near to the Ouvrage de Chemin de Fer, where the machine and

Lewis guns found unusual targets in the large number of Germans who endeavoured to pass through the wire, held on desperately till much reduced by shellfire they were surrounded and only three or four escaped.

The German artillery kept shelling the British positions although their own troops were in the vicinity. One lucky shell fell on the brigade headquarters of the 151st Infantry Brigade and killed General Martin and wounded General Riddell of 149th Infantry Brigade, while General Rees, 150th Brigade was captured. This same shell killed and wounded a number of the German infantry, whose survivors retired for a short while, allowing the remaining personnel of the three brigade headquarters to escape, only two officers being unhurt.

The German infantry was able to creep up to the British positions almost without being noticed due to the noise and smoke from the bombardment, combined with a ground mist, and they were almost on top of the defenders before being observed. The Germans poured into the forest from the north in ever-increasing numbers. Those of the British who retreated and broke cover out of the south side of the forest found that a German aeroplane was waiting there to fire at them as they crossed the open fields to Chaudardes and the bridges over the Aisne. It was similar to being flushed out on a grouse shoot.

Lieutenant Colonel Birchall, with Major Gould of the 8th Durham Light Infantry, collected together a number of stragglers at the headquarters of the 7th Durham Light Infantry and decided to hold a trench 300 yards in front of Cuiry-lès-Chaudardes. This group made a stand until surrounded by the Germans, who attacked from behind, coming from the direction of Beaurieux. The British succeeded in fighting their way out and crossed the Aisne and established a position south of the Aisne Canal on high ground. By 8.00 am the Germans had succeeded in capturing Pontavert, together with its bridges over the Aisne.

The Germans had broken through the French on the division's left flank and succeeded in entering the village of Beaurieux, passing behind the front held by the three infantry brigades and taking positions between them and the river Aisne. The divisional forward headquarters was situated in this village, some of the staff and attached orderlies being captured. Apparently, Corporal A. Marsh, of divisional headquarters, was last seen defending himself with a carving knife against a German. He was eventually taken prisoner and spent the rest of the war in a POW camp. Finding that the headquarters was about to be overrun, Major W. McCracken destroyed the division's papers. Unfortunately, this action delayed his departure and he too was subsequently captured.

During the morning, German artillery fire had slackened. This was because the gains made by their infantry had forced their artillery to move forward to fresh positions so that they could provide the necessary support. The Germans advanced in two columns, converging on Maizy. The bridge at this location had not been fully destroyed.

The Aisne Canal position was held around Concevreux. The east of the village was held by some Northumberland Fusiliers and the village by troops from the 5th, 6th, 7th and 8th Durham Light Infantry and to the west by troops of the 25th Division. Due to the losses the remnants of the division were organized into a composite 149/151 Brigade. The 150th Brigade, which was on the extreme left of the British line, had by this time been surrounded, cut off and then ceased to exist. Only the transport and quartermaster's staff got away.

The position held on the Aisne Canal, although a strong one, was weakly manned and, as happened before, the Germans outflanked the British, forcing them to retire to an old trench system south of Concevreux, which held out until 5.00 pm. Similarly, the Germans outflanked this position, the division and other troops, which forced them to withdraw to a hill north of Ventelay.

During the fighting on the Lys in April, the Germans had advanced 4 miles in four days. Here, between 4.30 am and the evening, they had advanced 12 miles.

Not only were the fighting elements of the division formed into a composite unit, the transport sections of the various units were also amalgamated together. On the night of 27/28 May, a composite convoy set out with rations and small arms ammunition for the division. By good guesswork they found them at Jonchery. Also, towards the evening of the 27th, reinforcements arrived, made up of officers and men returning from leave, courses and hospital. Divisional headquarters organized these men and sent them forward as appropriate.

Losses were heavy this day, with three officers killed (Captain R. Dickson DCM and Lieutenants S. Probert and J.E. Scott) and twenty-three other ranks killed, as well as a great number wounded and taken prisoner. Lieutenant Probert had been reported missing, but after the war his death was confirmed by Private Root, who had witnessed the event and confirmed that he had been killed. Apparently, Lieutenant Probert had been in the middle of the road when he was shot through the head by a German officer. The incident occurred near Craonne. Captain Dickson had been a publican at the Colliery Inn, Burnhope, County Durham. He had been commissioned from 1/8th Royal Scots in 1915.

Second Lieutenant E.B.F. Athy was one of the officers taken prisoner on 27 May. He was captured at No. 37 Casualty Clearing Station, which was near Frimes, when it was overrun. He had been wounded, with a gunshot wound to the left forearm, which had to be amputated. Also among the prisoners taken on the 27th was Captain H.H. Joseph, a schoolmaster from Chester, and Captain W.F. Laing, who had enlisted as a private in the battalion on 5 September 1914, was commissioned on 15 March 1915 and was wounded on 11 April 1917. He went on to be awarded the Military Cross. All in all, twelve officers were taken prisoner on 27 May. Lieutenant F. Graham was also among the wounded that day, as was Lieutenant Peter Walker, who suffered a gunshot wound to the left shoulder. He was a schoolmaster from Durham.

The casualties for the 50th Division amounted to 227 officers and 4,879 other ranks killed, wounded or captured. Most of the casualties occurred on 27 May, when the majority of the infantry were surrounded and either died at their posts or were forced to surrender.

The speed of the German advance meant that a lot of men were taken by surprise and made prisoner. Arthur Speight, who went to France with the battalion in April 1915, was later attached to divisional headquarters as a draughtsman with the G Branch. He worked alongside Corporal A.J. Schaeffer (5th Northumberland Fusiliers) and a man named Garton, who came from the Beverley area. Divisional headquarters were situated in Beaurieux Chateau; their drawing office was in a summerhouse at the bottom of the garden. When the bombardment started, on the 27th they decided to remain in their accommodation, protected by a concrete floor over where they lay. Arthur Speight described the German shells falling in a most haphazard and disconcerting manner. This was about 1.30 am. They later turned out to be mostly gas shells, which forced them to wear respirators. At about 7.00 am, they were visited by Captain Milne, the intelligence officer, who informed them that the plateau had been lost and they should remain where they were until he sent word. The three of them started packing ready for a move, taking things like tobacco, matches and iron rations. Sergeant Speight took up the story of their adventures, when they realised that they had been forgotten:

During this time we could see a number of fellows in khaki wandering down the road to Maizy, where there was a good iron bridge over the river Aisne. Shells of a small type kept dropping amongst them. I had not heard or seen shells quite so small as these before and was rather curious but not altogether happy about them.

When all was ready I took two tin dispatch cases of papers and maps up to the dugout and shouted down to the inhabitants, if any. There was no answer, so I went below and found the place deserted. On all the woodwork/tables, etc., there were small candles burning, in length about ¼-inch, evidently to burn the place out. Here I left my boxes of maps in the hope that Fritz would not get them. I returned again to the fresh air and hearing a clatter of horses' hoofs turned and saw one of the French Gendarmes who were attached to the division, coming along at full gallop with sword drawn and a rather grim look on his face. I howled out, '*Holla Jacques! comment ca va?*' He waved his sword, pointed up the road and shouted, '*Allez! Les Boches!*' I *allez-ed* and made my way down the street in the direction of the HQ chateau. I suddenly became aware of sudden buzzing noises, accompanied by sharp cracks, rifle bullets. This was rather too much for my shaky nerves so I made for the chateau without any more ado.

As I entered the door a bullet hit the door post with a resounding crack so I did a swift side-step to the right, and behind the wall. The rooms lately occupied by the clerks and other people were empty, the room occupied by the general and the staff officers was in turmoil, the furniture etc. being all piled up in the centre of the room and crowned with an overturned and flaming oil lamp. Not caring to endanger my valuable carcase any more I left via the French windows and wandered down the garden to the summerhouse. Here I spread the joyful tidings that we had been left stranded and we got our kit together, loaded our rifles and sallied forth.

On arriving at an open space in the garden we were suddenly fired on by a low-flying aeroplane with a red body and dazzle-painted planes. We disappeared into the bushes again until he cleared off, then got going once more. Now, there was a farm at the roadside and from here a drainage trench ran down towards the road to Maizy. As this looked like a good spot from which to make a dash for the bridge, we set off for the farm. I was first, Tony second and Garton last. When I reach the road I was astounded on looking along towards the village to see dozens of Germans standing at the crossroads. This was a blow and no mistake. Luckily they all seemed to be gazing in the opposite direction from where I happened to be seated in the ditch so I hopped quickly over the road behind the farm. I signalled to Tony to hurry and he and Garton joined me. Those beastly little shells began to drop a short distance from us so we got into the aforementioned trench and made our way along it at a good pace. As we got to the end we remembered that where the trench joined the road, the road was slightly 'sunk' – being in a cutting about 4 feet deep. On coming to the road I peeped round into the cutting then beat a rapid retreat up the trench again. There were only about sixty Germans in the cutting! Tony always had a fairly good vocabulary and he certainly said some strange things! We held a short council of war and decided that we couldn't put any show against sixty and thought we would do well to clear off further up the trench to seek another way out. However, Fritz stopped all argument by coming in on top of us with pointed rifles and waving bombs and shouts out, 'Hands auf! Englander'. I had often thought that in a case like this I should be scared to death but, strange to say, fear didn't seem to come into the picture at all. Disappointment seemed to be the great thing. Here we were captured without a chance of hitting back. We had the satisfaction, however, of knowing that our hands did not go up! They went into our trouser pockets instead. Fritz then began to show us things. We were kicked, thumped, jabbed in the ribs with rifle butts and generally made to feel that we were, to say the least of it, superfluous! We were forcibly propelled onto the road and made to carry machine guns forward towards the bridge. In a short while we were hustled back to the cutting, where other fellows had also been collected. With this lot we were marched up towards our former home, passing large parties of Germans coming down the hill. Suddenly there was a scatter as some lad in the British line with a strict sense of duty opened up with a Lewis gun. The bullets travelled up the village street and caused quite a commotion.

Well away back we went, the procession growing larger in proportion to the distance from the front line. It was strange to see the ADMS [Assistant Director Medical Services] and his band of RAMC [Royal Army Medical Corps] looking after wounded men at the roadside. As we got towards the trenches we were given a job of work – to fill in shell holes so as to allow the passage of transport. While we were busy I noticed several officers coming down the road under a guard and recognizing a certain Captain Bennett I handed over to him my silver cigarette case on the assumption that he might be able to keep it. Certainly I would soon have had to say goodbye to it. As yet we had not been searched. (This cigarette case was returned to me after the war – Captain Bennett lives in Sunderland.) The work we found lasted until about 8.00 pm, when we were again formed up and marched further eastwards.

That was the end of Arthur Speight's war. He was marched away to a prisoner of war camp and remained there for the duration, along with thousands of others.

For some, being captured came out of the blue. Private Wrigglesworth and his party were surrounded when they were told to run for their lives, as he took up the tale:

but it was too late. A machine gun was already on us, we had four wounded and one killed. I had a bullet through my puttee, but never touched my leg. An order came down to take equipment off. So we all did and to put all our arms in the trench. Well for a minute I did not realize I was a prisoner, but a few minutes later I realized when I had to carry a heavy machine gun for the Boche.

Attacks on Jonchery were renewed at 10.00 am on 28 May. The pressure was such that the 8th and 25th divisions were forced back by 11.30 am to a line held by Colonel Kirkup, and men of the 8th Durham Light Infantry on a hill to the south, and the Germans occupied the village. Attempts to evict the British from this hill failed, but the situation changed in the late afternoon when the Germans occupied hills to the north-east of Vaudreuil, thus allowing the Germans to bring more guns to bear on the position. It was now decided to withdraw yet again, to a position a mile and a half north-east of Savigny.

Here the men of the 50th Division, comprising about seventy all ranks, together with men of the 8th Division, repelled all German attacks. Only once did the Germans succeed in occupying part of the division's front and an immediate counter-attack restored the position. A company from a French regiment came up on the left flank during the evening. On 29 May two officers and sixty men of the 7th Durham Light Infantry, made up of details from divisional headquarters, reinforced the 74th Infantry Brigade.

*Drawing of Private Fred McKenzie's grave by Private Wrigglesworth.*

The German advance continued throughout the 29th and 30th. While this was going on the transport had been ordered to cross the Marne at Châtillon and then to move to Igny. At Châtillon the transport had to wait around to cross the bridge. On the other side of the river, French reserves were arriving and they had priority to use the bridge and move to the front, therefore the transport took five hours to move a hundred yards. The situation was eased by the discovery of a pontoon bridge 2 miles up the river at Reine. On the 30th, the transport succeeded in reaching Igny, and on the 31st moved to Aulnizeux.

According to Private Joe Robson, one of the tricks the troops employed to fool the Germans when the trench was thinly manned was for a couple of men to rapid fire, then run about 6 yards down the trench and open fire again. Thus they tried to give the impression that the trench was occupied in numbers.

Private Patterson remembered this about the Aisne retirement:

We went to the Chemin des Dames; when you look at it it's like a woman lying on her back. This was the last year of the war. We came down and a bloke said, 'If Jerry breaks through on either right or left of you, you cannot get out, you're caught.' That's just what he did. About sixty men and one officer came back.

When we were in the retreat aircraft used to fire on the roads. I spotted three coming along. I went across and there was an officer standing against a wall. He says, 'Don't you fire at them.'

I thought that's funny. 'Do you hear what he said?' I said to my mate.

A bit down the road I said, 'We're a clot at times, that's a Jerry, dressed as a British officer.'

He told us, 'Don't you fire at them.' If I'd known he was a Jerry I'd have fired at him, because there was quite a few of them behind the lines. The three of them used to come along and fire at women and children, anybody on the road. Shoot them down. He must have been a spy. We had to keep pushing on.

There were times when the British turned and gave the advancing Germans a bloody nose, followed by incidents of lucky escapes. Private Patterson continued:

We caught them when we retired in a village where we'd been billeted and we knew there was a certain way he'd come through onto, like a football field. We knew the Jerries would come through that way. We waited for him on one side. We didn't half give him a sorting.

They were nearly on top of us, we were nearly captured once. There was a police sergeant on a horse; he said, 'Don't go up there.'

'What for?' I asked.

'Jerry's just up the road and you'll be walking straight into him,' was the reply.

Back we went. We came to a bridge across the Marne, the engineers were standing ready to blow. 'Come on, if you don't hurry up you'll have to swim for it.' We got across. They blew the bridge. Jerry didn't worry about that, he just came down. When he got to the riverside he walked on the other side of the river. He was walking along, he could have crossed anywhere.

Private Surtees also remembered his time on the Aisne and how he escaped during the battle:

It was supposed to be a good rest, which it was. We were down there for about three weeks or a month. Glorious weather. We had a nice time; we used to go into the canal for swimming. We use to jump in; you had to jump in straight away because it was too deep to walk in. We come back on the Sunday night, we had been out and the word got around that there was a big attack coming on.

Now this was the biggest bombardment I had seen. We were on the edge of it. It was short, one o'clock in the morning it started, terrific, but it was short, short and sweet you might as well say. I've seen a few bombardments; it was like a million stars. But he took all our fellas prisoner, near the entire army, the battalions were small, they were not built up to strength.

We were just on the banks of the Aisne, in a little dugout. We got through somehow and thought we would give it half an hour, see what happens and we'll go back. Some went back and got their things. We had to go out, get our wagon and put our bits of things on and he wasn't far behind. My pal, who's my brother-in-law now, said let's get out. There was wire to stop him if he came, but it was on the wrong side for us, well we got through and down onto the banks of the Aisne. Away we came, across the river Aisne and Aisne Canal and everywhere he was following wherever we went. We put into a place at night, it was full of kids about sixteen to eighteen, up stairs. We just went straight up and clattered down and went straight to sleep. They were crying, they were away from home and that. We came out. I don't know where they had gone. We got on the road again the next day.

When we went back we saw all the damage. We did not know what had happened to the battalion. We saw the quartermaster as we were coming out; he asked if anyone had seen his son. His son was an officer in our lot. No we hadn't seen him, he was worried to death, poor fellow, but I think he would be a prisoner.

Among those captured on 27 May was 81120 Sergeant Fred Hunter. After his release in November he wrote home to say that he had not had any letters from home. He went on to say that when he was captured he had been held behind the German lines, working there for a week until he went sick because of his knee, when he was lucky enough to be sent to hospital. He had been captured with 64833 Private G.R. Clarkson.

Corporal Thompson described how the initial surprise of the bombardment turned into a mad dash to get the transport away:

One night we were returning to our camp, a few of us that was off duty, this night in particular. We reached our camp and turned in to our dugouts. This would be on to midnight. When all of a sudden there was a roar of gunfire. It seemed funny as it had seemed quiet for weeks.

I went to the top of the hill. To my surprise it was nothing else but a mass of shells bursting for miles around. It was terrible to look at.

Up comes a despatch rider to give us orders to get all ready for moving as things seem to be getting worse. Our captain gave orders, everybody to harness up, and to get onto the main road ready to make a gallop for it. By this time our first and second lines of trenches had been captured. Half of our battalion were taken prisoners, by now, it was getting towards morning.

We moved out of that camp to an unknown destination. We had no sooner got over the top of this hill, the Germans were at the bottom, my orders were to stop and see everybody got away alright. I was the last one to leave our camp. I waited on the main road. When they had gone I jumped on to my horse and made a dash for it.

I was riding hard over the hill and could see our transport in the distance, when over comes German aeroplanes dropping bombs and putting their machine guns onto us. I reached our transport and reported to our captain and he asked if everybody got away. I said yes.

So on and on we went day after day, night after night, wondering what was going to happen to us.

One day I thought we were captured. There was a large field on the side of the main road and our captain said to me, 'Corporal, I think we will cross that field and we will hit the main road sooner.'

It was alright looking at it but when we had got so far over, one of our wagons sank into the ground as it was that soft. Well what a game we had on. We had to get as many horses out of the other wagons before we could get it out. By this time the Germans were not far away. We had just got onto the main road when up comes a mounted police officer and said, 'You are lucky, they are not far away and get a move on.' We did put a move on, full gallop down the road to catch up with our transport.

After the March and April offensives, the authorities in England started to look for men to send to France as reinforcements. Private Joe Robson, who had been gassed in May 1915 and had spent a couple of months at the 3rd Western General Hospital, Cardiff, before being returned to light duties in England, was one of those selected for return to the battalion. After he landed his camp was attacked by German aeroplanes. Luckily, the only casualties were the tents. He rejoined the battalion just prior to the Aisne offensive, as he explained:

In 1918 we were picked out for drafts to go to France. The battalion was at half strength; it had already been in one big battle. They said they were going to send us to the south of France for a rest, between Rheims and Soisson. We were right between the two. We had two Gurkhas to each company. They were treacherous fellas, they had a knife like a sickle, no rifles just a haversack and that knife. They used to go over at night into the German trenches, catch the sentries, cut their throats and bring their ears back with earrings in and fingers with rings on in his haversack.

We used to go on raids, sometimes half a dozen of our chaps used to go over with one Gurkha to fetch one man back, a prisoner to get information to see what they were, who was in front. We sent two Gurkhas over one night to make a raid to fetch a prisoner back, not to kill him, to get information, see who was in front of us. We did not have any idea because it was that quiet. So anyway they came back with a 6-foot chap. They got to know it was the 6th Division Prussian Guards in front of us, who had not been in action since 1914. This was April. So we were up against something, they were all massed in front of us and we were only at half strength. It went on another week quiet like that. Then one morning about 27 May the heavens opened, a terrible bombardment started. Shells dropping all over. Dugouts were blown up, lads were getting killed. They were blowing the place to bits around us. We didn't know how to get out. We had our clothes off, just our pants on but we soon got our coats on, picked up our rifles and ammunition. When we got outside we saw the tanks and everything coming towards us. We just had to run for it. As we were retreating our Engineers were blowing the bridges up, checking the Germans a bit.

As you were retreating they were coming after you; one had a machine gun on his shoulder and another was running behind him firing it. The bullets were hitting the trees. We had to duck and run and if you got hit, you got hit. That was it. You just had to run on, bullets were flying all over, shells bursting.

Private Robson was wounded and nearly captured:

There were no branches left on the trees in the woods, just the trunks standing up. We used to pick a tree that was standing at an angle and we used to put laths across it so we could walk up it and your mate used to be at the bottom with telephone earphones on and a tapper and you used to be up there watching the front. There were German observation balloons, they were watching our lines, we were watching theirs. If you saw any movement you told your mate down below and he would phone back and tell them.

We were like that one time when an attack started and I was blown off a tree. They started to fire and I told Neddy they have opened fire on the right flank. We used to say four o'clock, one o'clock etc. You used to know exactly which part.

'Two o'clock Neddy,' I said. 'They have opened fire, there are shells bursting about 200 yards in front here.'

So he notified them at the back, next thing we knew, our lot opened fire as well and there was a right ding dong battle going on. Shells were flying all over the shop. Anyway I knew nothing about it until the tree shook and I came over with it. I don't remember anything after that 'til I got back behind the lines. How I got back I don't know, I must have been dragged back. They took my mate prisoner.

Private Robson was eventually evacuated back to the UK and once again he was sent to the 3rd Western General Hospital in Cardiff. Again his mother could not afford to visit him as she used to work for herself, cleaning at the Empire Theatre, Sunderland. Luckily his foreman from shipbuilders Osborne, Graham & Co, Joe Simpson, had a sister who was a matron in one of the nearby hospitals. He sent word to her to ask if she would visit Joe. She did this and used to take him out in his chair for visits. Private Robson always believed that it was she who brought him back to life.

It was during the battles of the early part of 1918 that Lance Corporal A. Smeaton won his Military Medal, while performing his duties as a battalion stretcher bearer. The award appeared in *The London Gazette* in August.

The early battles of 1918, with their rapid retirements, meant that reports to headquarters would only be made when time allowed, and they also led to the loss of a lot of the records. All of this caused confusion with the late notification of casualties and consequently grief to the families. One such case surrounded Lance Corporal Thomas Willings, of Sunderland, who had joined the battalion on 5 February 1915. His parents had received no notification of his death on 25 March 1918 and in May they wrote the following to the authorities requesting information:

> Having no word from my son L/Corporal T. Willings 1/7 Battalion DLI 275951 for about seven weeks I would be much obliged if you could give us any information of his whereabouts as soon as possible as we are anxious for news of him.

*Stretcher bearers.*

The sad news of his death was then passed on to them.

At Vert-la-Gravelle, the division formed a composite battalion, using any man they could find. Men continued to drift in throughout this period and were assigned to this battalion. It seemed that there were only 103 officers and men present with the division who had survived since the initial assault on 27 May.

The move to Alnizeux on 1 June and the commencement of training saw the end of the battle for the battalion. Another move followed on 9 June to Mondement and training. The battalion was eventually reunited with the two officers and sixty men of the Composite Battalion on 19 June.

The recent battles had left a number of divisions substantially under strength and it was not possible with the amount of manpower available to bring them all back up to strength. At the beginning of June it was decided that those exhausted divisions would be broken up and the men used to reinforce other divisions on the active list. The 50th Division, which had been very badly knocked about and had lost heavily, was one of those divisions to go. It was not reformed until later in 1918, and by then it had lost its Territorial connections, being composed of units brought back from overseas theatres like Palestine. On the 20th the battalion left the 50th Division and joined the 8th Division, exchanging its unicorn head divisional sign for that of a red square within a white one. The other infantry battalions of the old 50th Division were reduced to cadre strength, the surplus men being sent to other battalions.

On the 21st, the battalion was on the move again, ending up on 22 June at the village of Allenay. Training continued here and on the 28th the stores of the 22nd Durham Light Infantry were taken over. The 7th and 22nd battalions were no strangers to each other as they had fought alongside at St Quentin during the March retreat.

# Chapter 10

# Advance to Armistice

Throughout most of July 1918 the battalion spent its time training the reinforcements and reorganizing, as did the rest of the division, with combined training in the mornings and specialist lectures in the afternoons. At the same time, night exercises and route marches took place. After all that they had been through it was back to training, and particular care of the health and comfort of the troops was of paramount importance. The job to rebuild the battalion and division was well under way. The units of the division were not far from the sea and every opportunity was taken for sea bathing, the weather being glorious. Other activities took place, such as a divisional boxing tournament, which was won by 1st Worcesters, and on 13 and 14 July a divisional horse show was held.

The amalgamation of the 7th and 22nd Battalions Durham Light Infantry took place on 3 July at Allenay, when the 22nd Durham Light Infantry, after an honourable career, ceased to exist. Temporary Lieutenant Colonel B.C. James DSO, Devonshire Regiment, took over the command of the battalion from Acting Lieutenant Colonel A.H. Birchall MC, who was posted as the second in command of the 1/5th Duke of Cornwall's Light Infantry. The company commanders were as follows:

| | |
|---|---|
| A Company | Captain Iliff |
| B Company | Captain Hurford |
| C Company | Captain Reay |
| | Captain T.W. Howey was appointed adjutant. |

Corporal Thompson described in his memoirs how the transport sections of the two battalions amalgamated and the differences involved with moving to a Regular Army division:

> We found ourselves in a village called Mondement. Here our battalion mustered together. I think there was only 200 of us left. At this place our division was broken up, as it had been reduced so much.
>
> The old 50th Division was no more; we were put into the 8th Division, where all the polishing went on. Everything had to be polished on our wagons. They made us polish everything that could

*Portrait photograph of Private Douglass, showing the Infantry Pioneer collar badges and battalion patch on his left arm.*

polish. You did not get much time to spare, when you came down the line for a rest, all wagons, harnesses and horses had to be spick and span and they saw that you did it.

Being only about 200 of us, we got extra rations and a few parcels, such as cakes, that had been sent out to our fallen comrades. While I was at Mondement I was told I had got the Military Medal for getting rations up to our battalion through heavy shellfire on many occasions and saving that sergeant's life at Merville. I got the medal on 21 May 1919.

Their transport was sent down to the base and some of their officers and some of ours. There was a big change. Their commanding officer took command; our RSM [regimental sergeant major] was sent down to the base, our transport sergeant also. I was made sergeant. We were a new battalion. A new headquarters staff as well. The new CO Col James, he was a fine soldier and treated us very well indeed.

Our transport sergeant, I heard later, he had got a job down the base guarding German prisoners. He was on the old side a bit; however, he was my best pal and was well liked by all that knew him. That was Sergeant Tweedle.

When we got our transport made up to full strength, our CO used to come down to the sea shore with us and have a bathe. We had races on the beach as well. We used to have a bathe, then take our horses in as far as we dare to.

I remember there was a lot of our men taken to hospital while we were at Ault. That awful disease spread among the troops, the flu. There were large numbers dying with it. I myself was laid up with it for a fortnight.

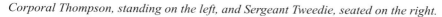

*Corporal Thompson, standing on the left, and Sergeant Tweedie, seated on the right.*

During this time the morale, efficiency and health of the men improved immeasurably, the time spent near the sea being considered more of a holiday. However, while the battalion was refitting events were moving at the front. The Germans had attacked on both sides of Rheims and the British sent eight divisions to help the French. On 9 July the division was placed in GHQ reserve and put on twenty-four hours' notice to move, either by train or bus. Orders were received that the division was to move to the First Army area, the artillery leaving first on 14 July, followed by the rest of the division over the next few days. The division came under the orders of Lieutenant General Sir Aylmer Hunter-Weston, commander of the VIII Corps.

There then followed a number of moves, first by train on the 20th to Tincques, arriving on the 21st, where inspections and further movement preparations were carried out, and then by motor bus to Cellar Camp at Neuville St Vasst, on 23 July, relieving the 17th Northumberland Fusiliers (Pioneers). Part of the operation order for the move included instructions for the Regimental Police to be in charge of and responsible for the custody of prisoners. B Company was to form a guard immediately on arrival at the new location.

The divisional relief was completed by 23 July, on which date Major General Heneker assumed command of the sector. The battalion had never served in this sector before, although it lay just to the north of Arras. The work here was improving the trenches in front of Farbus and around Vimy village and running those northwards to Givenchy. These trenches were known as the 'Brown Line'. The various working parties reported that the area was 'more like Blighty than the war' and that they were prepared to stay there for the duration. The dream continued for a few more weeks until 27 July. Work now started on a new line, a thousand yards in advance of the right of the Brown Line, while work was continued during the nights on the Brown Line itself.

It was noted now that the Germans had shot their bolt; a lot of the territory lost during the May and June battles around Rheims had been regained, as well as there being advances around Amiens. It seemed that each day brought fresh advances for the Allies.

On 3 August the battalion received the code 'Test Actions', which was part of the 8th Division's defensive scheme in case of emergency. The signal was received at 8.53 pm and by 9.15 pm all ranks were assembled and ready to move, with the exception of three platoons out on working parties and a party of one officer and twenty-one other ranks out on railway maintenance. Messengers were sent out to recall these parties and by 12.59 pm all had reported back. Shortly afterwards, the battalion stood down and normal duties were resumed.

Work continued during August on improving the communication trenches to the front line, general wiring and salvage work. The Germans had shown no signs of making any rearward moves in this sector. Any men from those areas that were quiet and not actively engaged with the Germans were wanted for the offensives elsewhere. On 13 August the division was ordered to 'side step' south, taking over the sector covering Oppy and Willerval. This now meant that the division had all three of its brigades in the front line, which necessarily increased the work of the battalion. August saw a lot of activity with gas shells and gas projectors, by both sides, the Germans especially using mustard gas. The *History of the Eighth Division in War, 1914-18* (published 1926), has this to say:

Many of these casualties were caused by liquid being evaporated by the sun on the day following the bombardment. Warned by this lesson, stringent orders were issued by the divisional commander that gassed areas must be immediately evacuated by all troops and no return to them permitted, until the gas officers and NCOs had pronounced them safe for occupation. As a result of this order, although gas shelling by the enemy continued on the divisional front and was from time to time very heavy, few further casualties were suffered from this cause.

Private Stan Douglass described his first encounter with mustard gas:

We were out digging on the top behind our lines; anyway we were running wire out when He started to bombard us. We were ducking and falling down; none of the shells were going off. They were just going plop, plop, plop.

I just happened to remark to someone that 'We must have friends in Germany; they are sending all dud shells over here.' But what it really was, was mustard gas; it was the first contact we had had with mustard gas. I got a great big blister on my neck, which nearly drove me mad, all the lads got blisters on their arms and faces and we were falling about until stretcher bearers came and picked us up and took us back. I did not get into hospital for that because it was only on my neck. It got bandaged, a great bandage. I don't know what was on the bandage to take the swelling down and the burn.

During the week ending 17 August, War Savings Certificates were sold throughout the division. The battalion bought 543, which was more than half the total bought by the rest of the division and the commanding officer expressed his appreciation in Battalion Orders. It was announced on 25 August that the French Croix de Guerre had been awarded to Lieutenant Colonel James DSO, Devonshire Regiment attached 7th Durham Light Infantry.

Towards the end of the month Second Lieutenant Squance was appointed battalion Lewis gun officer on account of Second Lieutenant Smart going to hospital. On 29 August, Captain W.L. Percival RAMC arrived to take up the post of battalion medical officer. It was at the end of the month that the companies and forward headquarters moved to take up billets in a railway embankment, between Long Wood and Bailleul Station. Bailleul was just a ruined village on the Arras-Lille road, near Oppy, not to be confused with the large town south of Ypres. The rear HQ remained at Cellar Camp.

There was a change of command on 2 September, with Lieutenant Colonel B.C. James DSO handing over the reins of the battalion when he returned to the UK to Major J.P. Turcan MC.

Urgent work was done throughout September to clear out communication trenches and effect road repairs in and around Bailleul. The work was interrupted by gas shells landing in the area, which inflicted slight casualties. Work was also carried out on the Bailleul-Oppy road as well as the Bailleul-Gavrelle road. Working parties were supplied to the Royal Engineers for general repair work and to assist on a light railway. The work of the battalion was recognized by the divisional Commander Royal Engineers, who wrote to express his gratitude for the hard work done.

On 6 September, the divisional commander inspected all the transport within the division and the battalion won third place in the competition. Later during the month a set of new musical instruments arrived from England, so a new battalion band was formed, the original having stayed with the 50th Division.

The battalion suffered further casualties on 12 September, when Second Lieutenant W.R Forrest was killed along with Privates Sydney Cockburn and Wilfred Ward. Second Lieutenant Forrest had enlisted as a private in the Coldstream Guards before being commissioned into the 7th Durhams.

Advances were being made at Ypres, with the Allies now at Roulers and, in the south, Péronne had been recaptured, although in front of the 8th Division the Germans still stood fast.

October 1918 started off much the same as September, with work on roads and general maintenance of trenches. Battalion headquarters moved to Blangy Trench on 3 October. By the 10th, quite an area had been taken from the Germans and as a result the battalion moved yet again on the 12th, to Fresnes, to work on the roads. Fresnes lay halfway between Arras and Douai, on the main road, and the battalion settled into Gloucester Wood. However, things started to change, for on 18 October the Germans commenced their retirement on the front of the 8th Division and the battalion moved to Esquerchin, which lay in a valley north-east of Douai, again to work on the roads. The 8th Division formed part of the First Army; they now moved in a north-easterly direction, with the Fourth Army on the right and the Second on the left. The Germans were now being hassled in their retirement. It was not the orderly withdrawal they had hoped for, and large quantities of stores were being left behind. In their haste to retire some of the road junctions that they had prepared for demolition had been forgotten and the mines not primed. This was beneficial to the divisional forward movement as it saved a lot of work as well as lives. The advance was dependent upon good roads and connection with the railway at the rear. The area the division had to advance over had been heavily shelled over the years of trench warfare, and the roads and railways ceased to exist in some places. The road upon which the division depended for their maintenance ran from Gavrelle to Fresnes-lès-Montauban to Douai, and a great deal of work was needed to make this passable for lorries and other vehicles.

The battalion followed up on the retreating Germans, repairing the roads where the enemy had mined them in order that the transport and guns could keep up with the advance. The transport and artillery themselves were having an adverse affect on the condition of the roads due to their weight and constant use, and this necessitated quite a bit of maintenance. The German measures were not as thorough as those carried out in the retreat of March 1917, although they did leave behind a number of delayed action mines, which were meant to cause havoc. These were of a relatively simple construction, made by passing a wire through a container filled with acid. At one end of the wire was a weight. When the acid had eaten its way through the wire, it fell and detonated the explosive. Some of these mines created quite large craters and unfortunately there was a lack of material available to fill them, which could result in serious delays. To help in moving stores forward certain transport and all tanks and guns were now directed to move through adjoining fields. This was the start of an advance that would not finish until the Armistice in November.

The *History of the Eighth Division in War, 1914-18* has this to say about booby traps:

Timber embedded in roads and tracks and connected to a mine which exploded if the timber was either raised or depressed was a favourite device. Fresh ruses were discovered every day and as each came to light appropriate warnings were issued to all ranks. The extent of the danger can be gauged by the fact that by 27 October the 185th Tunnelling Company, of whom a party under Capt G. Howatson was attached to the division, had removed no less than 1,395 mines and booby traps in the divisional area.

The first thing to be overcome, as mentioned above, was the devastation of the old no-man's-land. This is described in the unpublished history of the battalion:

> Interminable lines of wire entanglements, the gaps in these sometimes marked by the figures still lying in front of them. Dreadful hollows where the age-blackened barb wire still shewed amongst the rank undergrowth, derelict trenches with years' old impediments of war, trenches lately held and foul, battery positions some with still their guns – guns that in some cases had been well served by the dead gunners lying beside them amidst piles of empty cases; they had died hard these men.

Once through Lens, which was a wreck, and over the plain of Lens, the terrain was much easier. Local inhabitants were still occupying their homes; many had hidden in their cellars during the German retreat. As they retired the Germans also destroyed the bridges over the canals and rivers and it was part of the battalion's role to see they were repaired as soon as possible so that the advance did not slow or falter. Reports of the sound of German transport moving through Douai were reported to divisional headquarters and on 18 October British troops entered to take possession of the town. Although the Germans had taken everything of value and destroyed the rest, including the cathedral's organ, the buildings themselves were left intact. It was reported that mines had been put in place but had been subsequently withdrawn.

By the 19th, the battalion had reached Auby, north of Douai, and Marchiennes, in the valley of the river Scarpe, the next day. Owing to logistical problems the division did not advance on the 20th. The roads were also crowded with civilians, whom the Germans had released. The advance resumed on 21 October. A change of work occurred on the 27th, when bridge building over a canal at Chemin-du-Mont-des-Bruyères was the order of the day. Things appeared to be quiet for the battalion during the advance, but headquarters was shelled on the 25th, causing slight casualties. The only man listed as dying on this day was Corporal Norman Ord, of Hetton-le-Hole.

The unpublished history of the battalion has this to say of the work at this time:

> Lest anyone should imagine from this that the work of the battalion had been carried on under conditions of safety a long way behind the actual fighting it must be made clear that often it was the work of a Pioneer battalion which enabled an attack to be developed or supported for there were points, such as a canal, where infantry alone in small numbers had been able to cross and means had to be established whereby large numbers, guns and limbers, could pass over, and that quickly.
>
> Nor could such work always be carried out under cover of darkness, and too, though the infantry might have effected a crossing here and there, the enemy still held other positions with machine guns.

There was the necessity for a previous reconnaissance of a road or destroyed canal or river crossing and this, where the enemy was still in and about the vicinity, was an exciting experience.

At times work on some temporary bridge or causeway went on with the guns close up behind firing over the parties and enemy shells intended for the guns fell instead amongst the men as they struggled with heavy timbers or girders.

Yet when the task was ended the labour and the sweat were forgotten as the guns came slithering down the bank, crossed, strained up the far side and with a lurch vanished beyond its crest. Sometimes there were accidents but generally the work done stood the test.

It must still be remembered that the battalion was an infantry Pioneer battalion and as such could be called upon at any time to assume the normal role of line infantry. The Germans did not retire altogether; they left behind pockets of resistance, which had to be dealt with – a sole machine-gunner, a patrol, or a small group manning a strongpoint. There were also stragglers, who had been cut off, trying to return to their own lines, especially at night. Private Douglass remembered an incident when he was moving through German trenches:

There was another time I was going through a trench, this was when Jerry was retiring. I was going through this trench, one that I should not have been in, with my rifle on my shoulder. I had a Mills bomb in my hand with no pin in it. We'd been throwing Mills bombs down into the big dugouts just to close them. Thinking all the Germans had disappeared, and them that was in was all dead. I think it was the Hindenburg Line or something like that. This German pops out with his bayonet, he saw the Mills bomb in my hand, he just dropped his rifle and put his hands up. I think I would have been daft enough to blow the two of us to pieces that day, the state I was in. Anyway, that Mills bomb in my hand saved my life there.

The Germans carried out a scorched earth policy to the best of their ability during the retreat. Private Patterson had this to say about the closing months of the war:

When we advanced we were careful of booby traps. If you were walking across a field and you see a board across a footpath, step over it, you knew what it was. Oh yes there were booby traps all over. I felt sorry for the old people who were left behind, nobody to look after them.

In a village there was a butcher's shop. There was a big lump of meat and the cooks took charge of that. We had a feed there. We went into another shop; the French used to wear little shirts, short collared shirts, our blokes took them for their lousy ones.

There was a little village and there was this house. I went in. He had shells down in the cellar ready fused and upstairs were tins of bully beef. He'd punctured them all. He'd knocked a hole in them. I think we could have eaten them but you daren't risk being poisoned.

The last farmhouse I went in, when we were chasing him back, I was the leader of the party. I said, 'It's quiet, isn't it?'

They had pinched all his cattle. There was a double door. I told someone to keep that end, some of them round that end and I'd go in the door. The old farmer sitting with his wife, I told them I'm sorry I had to knock it in and I asked him how long the Germans had been. He said they went the day before. I asked if they had treated them alright. He pulled up his vest to reveal a scar, they had cut him, they had operated for appendicitis or something, there was a great big scar. I said, 'Tarrah.' I shook hands and he was kissing my hand. The lads enjoyed that. He was pleased to see the British; he knew he was free then. I said, '*Allemand fini, Allemand fini.*' They had taken all the cattle and everything and left them nowt.

Booby traps feature in a lot of veterans' memoirs. Corporal Thompson remembered:

The Germans did not leave everything alright; as they were retreating they left some fine traps for us. One day as we were making our next move to a place called Douai, a battery of guns were going into action. When they were just about to pass a four road end, when all of a sudden the whole team of horses, men and guns were blown up with their booby trap, which had been laid by the Germans. It was an awful sight. Another great trick they left behind them. You would be looking for some wood, to make a shelter for the night. I saw one poor chap go and pick up a new piece of wood, about 14 feet long and about 2 feet in breath. As soon as he touched it he was blown up. Some of our men lost their lives by going into German dugouts. As soon as they touched this certain thing, up they would go, blown to pieces. They left some awful traps.

Not long after this there came up from the base a special battalion to locate all these traps. They found some not very far away from us.

Even in the water wells, they tossed as much rubbish down them as they could; dead bodies even were in the wells.

During our advance, the Germans left heaps of dead lying all over the place. Dead horses and broken wagons scattered all over the place.

As the advance increased so did the number of prisoners taken, and more Germans were now willing to surrender. The scene was changing. The men now saw lights in windows at night, which a few months previously would have been unthinkable and meant that the Germans had retired from that area. However, this did not mean that the Germans had ceased all warlike activities. Roads and towns were still shelled and bombs dropped from aircraft. Corporal Thompson and his section had a near miss from enemy aeroplanes; luckily no one was injured:

We never seemed to get any rest at all at this place. One morning we were going to water our horses when suddenly a German aeroplane flew over us very low. It was a misty morning, never expecting to see a plane. They turned round and put their machine guns onto us. I shouted to all drivers to spread out into different directions. By doing this they missed the whole lot of us.

Private Douglass remembered three affairs in which he was involved, one tragic, one lucky and one thoughtful:

During our advance we came to a canal, there was a big railway and a big signal box, like we've got in this country. We were bogged down there and I saw this fellow bobbing up and down in the signal box. I thought he was a German observer. I drew a line on him and shot the bugger. When he jumped up I saw I had shot the old Frenchie or Belgian or whatever he was, he was the signalman.

Then we were going up a street there and I didn't think about any Germans being there, and one jumped out of a doorway. Of course I had my bayonet fixed, [I hit him] right in the chest with my bayonet. He up with his rifle and I fell flat on my back, he had cracked me on the head and broke my collar bone. But what had happened was, I would have gotten him first only I hit him with the bayonet, he had a bullet-proof vest on underneath. Because when the ambulance lads picked me up and wondered what had happened they looked at him and he was dead. He had a bullet-proof vest, steel vest on him. That knocked me off balance, 'course he just clubbed me with his rifle. It hit me steel helmet with a Hell of a bang and broke me collar bone and I was whipped off that field 'til that was mended in hospital. I don't know how many days I was away from the line at that time. I got back again and in the advance to the Rhine. …

I'll tell you how desperate we looked, we passed through a village. Me and Hobson, we were clamming for a drink. The Germans had held this village all through the war practically and we knocked on a door. A woman answered it. They had been under German occupation. She took one look at us and she tried to close the door. Hobson, he was a big 6-footer belonging to Shields, got his foot in and was cursing her; she wouldn't understand what he was saying like. We wanted a drink of water. We had to fairly push her in for a drink of water. She kept looking up the stairs.

I said, 'There might be a Jerry up there Ned.'

'*Allemande. Allemande*,' he said.

'No. No. No!'

She shouted and there were three daughters came down, three bits of lasses in their teens. She thought we were after her daughters I think. She gave us a drink, mind she was very unwilling. We kept telling her, '*Angleterre* soldier, *Angleterre* soldier.'

But I said to Hobson later on, 'Mind Ned, when you look at it the poor old woman must have got a Hell of a fright, never seen now't like us before in her life.'

Aye, I says, 'You begger, they wouldn't give you a drink of water and you're fighting for their country.'

But I could understand her later on, the fright she would get when she opened the door and saw us 'cos we were covered in mud. After that we went away and a day or two later Hobson says, 'You know, Stan, that woman had damned good rights to be terrified. When we look at each other covered in other people's blood and mud. She had good right to be terrified, she wouldn't know if we were men or animals. I thought it was Germans hiding first when she was scared of us. We may have been the first British troops she had seen really.'

Another time, during the final advance, Private Douglass remembered that the battalion was being held up by a German machine gun:

The Germans had a machine gun that was sweeping round and we were going up on our bellies and we had a lot of casualties with him. I got into a position to pick them off. I was a marksman and Sergeant Mottram, he knew I was a marksman because I'd been on sniping business. This machine gun kept us down; we couldn't lift our heads up. I worked my way around on my belly 'til I got to the side. I picked two of them off but the gun still went. There was another fella, he was only young, I could see and he was scared stiff, but he kept that gun going. I thought it was a brave thing for the lad. He was terrified, you could see by his face, yet he would not leave go of that gun, he kept at it. So I got further round and I got a bead on him and I shot him through the shoulder. I could have put a bullet through his head, easy. Sergeant Mottram played merry Hell, when he got up to me.

He says, 'You just wounded that man you know Douglass, you're not going to take him back to get out of it.'

'I didn't intend to take him back to get out of it. I think he was a blooming brave lad. He was scared to death and yet he wouldn't stop.'

I often wonder if that lad got out of the war.

Towards the latter part of the month things started to become easier for the battalion, with one company each day being rested, while the others worked on the roads and practised bridge building.

During the battalion's time in England and overseas it had been inspected by King George V and various field marshals and generals, with all the resulting spit and polish. However, Private Douglass remembered an altogether different inspection, by royalty:

We went right up to this place where we brayed [pushed] Him back. I cannot remember the names now. We were pulled out of the line; we were stopped because He [the Germans] was at the canal. We could not get any further until they got bridges across. We were in billets, there were about twenty of us in a barn and we got orders to fall in. We just fell in outside and this joker came along. Mind we were covered in mud and all sorts, we had not been stopped quarter of an hour. We hadn't had time to get our valises off. We were up to the eyes in mud and blood. I cannot describe what a soldier looks like after he's been through all that, he's like something now't on earth. Your face is all covered in mud, your hands are all mud, clothes are all torn.

This fella came along. We thought he was just a general, but when he had gone they said that that was King Albert [of the Belgians]. He shook hands with me, and the next fella and the next and patted the next on the shoulder, he went along the line. We heard it was King Albert after that. There were tears in his eyes, mind, the sight of us must have fetched him to tears, but we looked a motley crew. I couldn't describe what we looked like. We looked anything but soldiers. Aye they said it was King Albert, just took my hand, you could see he was full, he hardly spoke.

November saw the advance continue, with the battalion reaching Rosult on the 4th and Vred on the 5th. The division was relieved on the night of 4/5 November and four days of training and inspections followed before the battalion moved off on the 9th to Bousignies and the next day it crossed the border to Bernissart in Belgium.

A booklet issued by the First Army described the record of the division over the previous three weeks: 'By the 25th the 8th Division had come a distance of 30 miles in a straight line since October 7, capturing thirty-five towns and many villages, freeing large numbers of civilians, capturing immense quantities of material, and inflicting heavy loss on the enemy.

There were additional hazards to be faced during the advance, as Private Douglass related:

We advanced right up to the border; we were passing through villages which the Germans had occupied for years all through the war. We got stopped at the canal. He blew the bridges, we could not get across. We were shoved into billet there. All the shops had been evacuated, all the Belgians too. The Belgians had been taken back into Germany I expect, none of them had come this way towards us.

It was there that we nearly got shot for looting. The jewellers had a great big cannon in, it was gold coloured. I don't know if it was gold or not but it was a lovely replica of an old cannon. There were three of us, we climbed into the fruiter's shop next door, 'course it was all closed up with shutters and things. Bob Baxter, he stepped onto a tray of eye glasses. It was all quiet you know, and it made a Hell of a crash. On all the doors there were signs, 'Looters will be shot on sight'. Anyway we got out of there. I had a box of lovely earrings and the cannon. The cannon was too heavy, when you're on the move, you roll your blankets up in bundles of ten or twelve and the transport takes them. Well I just put it in a blanket and rolled it up and I lost it all together after that, but I got the earrings home.

Weather-wise, 11 November 1918 was a bleak day. The troops had been informed that hostilities would end at 11.00 am. Many were glad that the waiting was now over and looked forward to what lay ahead. Life in the Army still went on though and during this day they marched to Harchies, which was heavy work due to the rainy weather.

The Armistice came as a bit of a surprise to Private Surtees and his mates, as he related:

It was foggy, cold and damp. It was in the November, we were sleeping in a barn upstairs. We came out to see the battery go by. We didn't know the Armistice was coming until eight or nine o'clock. There was a battery going up and their officer, he was a nice chap, says, 'Well boys you're finished at eleven o'clock. The war's finished.'

You heard the field guns up to eleven o'clock then all of a sudden it went dead.

George Thompson looked back on this day with happiness, as he described:

On that Glorious day we were just entering Tournai, when we heard that great news. Oh it was right enough, our captain said. Just then a French captain posted it up on a board. See all the French people jumping with joy and not forgetting ourselves. I don't know that anybody slept that night, both in France and England.

Bye we did shake hands with each other that day. We did say we were going to see old England again. I shall not forget that day, 11 November.

Back home in Sunderland, for those who had served in the battalion, been wounded and subsequently discharged, there also were celebrations. Corporal J. Allan, who had been wounded and later discharged to work in the shipyards, remembered that work continued normally until eleven o'clock, when the buzzers and hooters sounded to mark the Armistice. Everyone stopped work and went home to join in the various celebrations, which had been quickly arranged. One eyewitness in Sunderland remembered that tramcars stopped running and shops and offices closed, with customers and shop assistants joining in the celebrations. There was dancing in the streets. But thoughts still turned to those who had lost loved ones.

For the battalion, a move to Hautrages followed on the 12th. They remained there for the next four days, spending their time on drill, inspections and short route marches, and the band entertained the civil population. Much had to be done for the civilians, especially those whose homes had been destroyed and were living behind the Allied lines. From here the battalion moved, by bus, to the infantry barracks at Tournai, where they remained until the middle of December. During this time the battalion helped returning British prisoners of war, who were making their own way back from camps in Germany. Private Surtees noted that they wore 'a sort of yellowy uniform'. Sport and recreational training were the order of the day to keep the men amused. While at Tournai, King George V visited the troops and the battalion was on parade. This was the second time during the war the battalion or a part of it had paraded before the king.

Sergeant Thompson enjoyed his time at Tournai, even if it did involve some spit and polish:

When I was at Tournai I enjoyed myself, I think everybody did. Well our duty at Tournai was just to go for rations and keep our horses fit.

*The battalion band in Belgium, 1919.*

We got orders that our general was coming to inspect us. So we got everything as correct as possible. Our transport was paraded in front of our own CO before our general inspected it, and he said we looked fine. I remember well the day when our general came to see us. He said, 'I'm proud of you all.' This was when he was inspecting us at Tournai Barracks.

Yes, he had a good right to be proud of us. I think it was marvellous to see so many old faces come right through that Great War without a scratch.

Before we left Tournai each man received a slip of paper and on it was written:

FROM
Lieutenant General Sir Hunter Weston
TO
Major General W. Heneker CB, DSO
Officers, WOs, NCOs and men of the 8th Division

I congratulate you heartily on being selected, to take part in the triumphal advance to the Rhine.

Much though I regret that thereby the division will be severed from my command. I consider myself to be fortunate to have you under my command, for so long. Both during the difficult and dreary days in the Passchendaele Salient, when you stuck it out so well on the Vimy Ridge and in the last Glorious Advance by which you have succeeded in finishing the war, on the very spot where some of you received your baptism of fire in our first great battle. The discipline, self-sacrifice and devotion to duty which have been the main factors in your success in the war, will I am sure be displayed by you throughout the trying period of demobilization and will be carried by you into your civil life, in peace. In the hands of men such as you who have been through the stern realities of war, and have thereby acquired a broad outlook on life, the future of England and of the Empire, is safe. In bidding you all farewell I desire to place on record my appreciation of the splendid work that you have done and of the initiative and endurance that you have displayed. I congratulate you on your splendid achievements in this war and I wish you each and all both those who continue in the Army and those who return to civil life, the very best of health, happiness and prosperity.

FROM
Hunter Weston

Meanwhile, back in Sunderland, the battalion colours, which had been laid up in Hendon (St Paul's) Parish Church, were received by Lieutenant Colonel Vaux CMG, DSO from the Reverend J.B. Purvis at a ceremony on 16 December. The Colour Party consisted of Lieutenants T.C. Squance and H. Cross, Sergeants W.A. Coupland and S. Crosby and Corporal H. Jacoby. Only Lieutenant Cross was not an original member of the battalion that had landed in France in April 1915. The parade formed up at 12.45 pm at the Garrison Field under the

*Parading the colours,
Sunderland, 1919.*

*Being presented
with the colours,
Sunderland, 1919.*

*Receiving the
colours from
Bishopwearmouth
Church, 1919.*

command of Major Cuthbert Vaux. It was headed by the band of the 3rd Sherwood Foresters and comprised men of the battalion let out from hospital for the occasion and also those who had been repatriated and discharged – nearly 300, in all – and marched through the town to the church. Lieutenant Colonel Vaux was delayed owing to a problem on the railway to the extent that he did not arrive at the church until after the service had commenced. His appearance, though, was loudly applauded by the congregation. The Colour Party rejoined the battalion in Belgium on 20 December.

From 17 to 19 December, the battalion was on the move again, this time to Irchonwelz and district, with headquarters and C Company being billeted at Villers-Saint-Amand, A Company at Ath and B Company at Irchonwelz. Christmas Day was spent quietly, with no work being done. Any work done now was of the nature of general training and sport.

Demobilization was proceeding quickly, with various categories of men such as mine workers being amongst the first to return to their civilian lives. In order to help the men readjust to civilian employment educational classes on a wide range of subjects were given by the officers and other suitably qualified personnel. There came a time when the numbers remaining in the battalion meant that little in the way of training could be done. The football team lost in the final rounds of the Divisional Commander's Bowl because some of its best players had already left for England.

While he was at Ath, Sergeant Thompson related how danger had not altogether disappeared. It was also at this time that Sergeant Thompson received his orders for home and demobilization:

Our duty was just to go and bring rations from the railhead and take them to our QM stores. So we had an easy job. I remember one night while we were at Ath, we thought the Germans had broke through again. Not far from our billet there was the railway station, such as it was. One night there was some truck loads of shells put onto a siding for the night. About midnight, somehow or another, one of these trucks exploded and you should have heard the noise. We all thought that another war had begun. There was a few wounded over this, we heard next morning.

I was out in the village of Ath, when one of our headquarters runners came up to me and said, 'Sergeant, you have to report at the orderly room at once.'

There were altogether three of us from the Transport.

So the three of us got into one of our wagons, which was going that way. We had a right escape. There was a railway crossing which we had to cross over. There was no gates on [it] or anybody there to warn us of the trains coming. The gates that had been on had been blown off. So just as we were turning the bend, to get to the crossing, there was an old house which stopped you from seeing down the line. It was a misty night to start with, and just as we got to the crossing, up comes an express. It passed us like a flash of lighting.

I nearly pulled the driver off the seat, as I was behind him in the wagon. Well we could not speak to each other for a while. 'Well,' I said, 'that was a bit lucky, fancy going for your papers and nearly getting killed into the bargain.'

We got to the orderly room. We got our papers, had a good shake of hands and left for our billet, as we had to pack our kit.

[Next day] When we got to the station, there was a large number of our division coming home. To our surprise, when the train did come in, it was an English train, all third class coaches. They must have sent those trains over for our troops to come home in as we had never seen any before. There was eight of us got into one carriage. [At Boulogne] We got some rations, a wash and a quick march down to the docks. When we got there the ship was just coming in and her name was the SS *Perth*.

From the ship coming in and going out, it took two hours. So they cast off the ropes and we steamed out of the harbour just to go right into a fog. We sailed on until we came out of the fog and the sailors said we were now going up the Thames and we would land at Tilbury Dock. To our surprise, when we got to Tilbury they kept us on board ship all night, 'til 8.00 am next morning. When we got onto the quayside, before proceeding onto the train, each man received rations for the next stage of our journey.

So after a long ride, it took a few hours to reach Ripon. We marched up to the camp and there we spent the night. Next morning came and we went through different things handing different parts of our kit in different places 'til you had no kit left at all. There were heaps of kit and rifles, just as men had put them down. After we had done that, the next thing was to get all clean clothes and a bath.

Next evening came and all of us were put into different groups and marched down to the station and then we left Ripon for Sunderland and for good this time.

So we were now free men after serving over four years, it seemed like eight to us, in the worst war in history.

It was 6 January when I left the battalion at Ath.

The battalion was further weakened during March when drafts of officers and men were sent to 2/6th Durham Light Infantry. The three companies were now combined into one, being designated as HQ Company as the battalion was now at cadre strength. On 16 March, four officers left to join the 9th Durham Light Infantry, for service with the Army of Occupation.

Due to the decrease in numbers the men were employed on cleaning and the guarding of mobilization stores, ready for the order to proceed back to the UK. To keep the men occupied during their leisure time dances and concerts were organized within the division. The war diary's last entry is for 31 May, because the cadre 7th Durham Light Infantry returned to Sunderland, under the command of Lieutenant Colonel Birchall, arriving on 20 June, the train pulling into Sunderland Station shortly after 1.30 pm. They were greeted by Lieutenant Colonel Vaux before proceeding to the town hall for a civic reception.

Other tributes followed over the coming months and those of two of the divisional commanders were printed in the *Sunderland Echo* in June 1919. Major General Sir P.S. Wilkinson KCMG, CB, who commanded the division shortly after its arrival in France up to March 1918, had this to say of the battalion:

To be suddenly called upon to undertake new duties of a technical and arduous nature in the middle of a great war might well prove a difficult task to the best troops. When the 7th Battalion Durham Light Infantry were ordered to convert themselves into pioneers they attacked the problem with a wholehearted earnestness that brought its own reward and in a surprisingly short time became, in the opinion of the division, the best pioneers in the Army. A division is critical in these matters, and its praise is not lightly given.

The heavy batteries will remember the road repairing carried out under heavy shellfire that enabled their guns to advance from Arras to Tilloy in April 1917. The divisional artillery can recall many occasions when they were enabled to get forward on tracks hastily made by the pioneers under shelling which never ceased, and which enabled them to give close support to their infantry in successive stages of the attack.

The repair of the road from Bazentin-le-Petit to High Wood was a notable example of this heroic work of pioneers, particularly in stationary warfare, is connected with the infantry, and to record what the battalions owe to the pioneers will require many pages. The following are a few examples:- the digging and revetting of main communication trenches like Foster Avenue; the still more difficult though shorter communication trenches in front of Eaucourt l'Abbaye; the building and keeping in repair of the train lines by which the forward troops were fed and supplied both on the Somme and at Ypres; and the linking up of the Flers lines under heavy rifle and machine-gun fire and bombs was perhaps the most supreme task of what the pioneers could do and willingly did to assist their comrades.

It might be mentioned that so much difficult work would in some way affect the value of the battalion as a purely fighting unit, but Colonel Vaux made a point of keeping the rifle shooting and bayonet training up to a high standard, and no battalion could have fought with more gallantry and stubbornness than the pioneers in March 1918.

This tribute was followed by one from Major General H.C. Jackson, who succeeded Major General Wilkinson as divisional commander and had this to say of the battalion:

When I took over command of the 50th (Northumbrian) Division on 23 March 1918, it was already engaged on a wide front, the 7th Durham Light Infantry taking their full share in the fighting. Two days later, the battalion was sent back to prepare a new position. I then had an opportunity of judging their capabilities as pioneers. This

*Silk postcard for the battalion after they became Pioneers.*

position they afterwards manned and fought most gallantly. When at last the division was relieved I had a chance of meeting the battalion at rest, and was much struck with the fact that they were such a happy family, with their gallant CO, Lieut Colonel E. Vaux, CMG, DSO, as their father. Their period of rest was short, the division being brought up to strength and rest to Flanders, where it arrived in time to stem the second big German attack, which commenced on 9 April. It was just about this time that Lieut Colonel Vaux left them, but the fighting spirit which he had instilled into them was still there, and again they performed in a magnificent way their dual task as fighting soldiers and pioneers.

The division was withdrawn, having suffered very severe casualties, and were sent to the French zone, and took over trenches on the Chemin des Dames. On 27 May, the division for the third time had to bear the brunt of the German attack. The pioneers were living close to their work, and were at once involved … pioneers can fight, but it was at great cost, and the numbers withdrawn after the fighting were few. Owing to the heavy casualties it was decided not to make up the division, and the 7th DLI were transferred in June to absorb the Pioneer Battalion of the 8th Division.

To my great regret the battalion therefore left the Northumbrian Division, with which it had been associated so long and so gloriously.

# Chapter 11

# 2/7th Durham Light Infantry

Mention should now be made of the role and contribution of the second line battalion. On 15 September 1914, the original battalion along with the rest of the Territorial Force was invited to volunteer for service abroad. Those battalions that did were then ordered to recruit to 25 per cent over establishment.

The 7th Durham Light Infantry soon found the required percentage for foreign service and started to recruit the additional men to form the reserve battalion. Many who were medically unfit or had other commitments that at the time prevented them serving overseas were joined by men who had previously served with the battalion and who had left before war broke out and rejoined. The second line battalion was distinguished from the first battalion by the figure 2/ before it. As a result, the 2/7th Durham Light Infantry were formed on 16 September 1914 at Sunderland. Early in 1915, the second line battalions of the Durham Light Infantry Brigade were formed into their own brigade at Leam Camp, Heworth. Their responsibility was for the defence of the coast from Seaham to Newcastle upon Tyne. The brigade was renumbered in August 1915 as the 190th Brigade and the 2/Northumbrian Division became the 63rd Division. This division never saw action and its number was given to the Royal Navy, who formed the 63rd Royal Naval Division, which served with distinction in France and Belgium.

During most of the war years this battalion moved around the UK and helped train and supply reinforcements for the front-line battalions. However, in October 1918 it received its chance to serve abroad, being selected to form part of the Allied forces at Murmansk and Archangel.

When the order to form part of this force arrived the battalion was stationed in Colchester. It subsequently entrained at 7.00 pm on 5 October for Glasgow, where it embarked on HMT *Goentoer* the next day. The ship put to sea on the evening of 8 October, sailing round the Mull of Kintyre and passing the Faroe Islands, arriving at Archangel on 23 October at 1.30 pm and berthing at Bakaritza Dock No. 23.

It was at this time that Spanish Flu was raging throughout Europe and one petty officer on board died during the voyage. Private A.G. Tasker, B Company, died of pneumonia on the day the battalion arrived in Russia.

The next day seven officers and 244 other ranks, commanded by Major T.C.B. Holland, disembarked to undertake duties to guard stores at Bakaritza, taking over from the Americans and White Russians. An additional eight officers and 232 other ranks under Captain R.A. Swan disembarked and crossed the river to Constantine Barracks, Solombola, where they took over duties from the French. On the 25th, a further two officers and 100 men, under Captain L. Raynes, moved to the detention barracks at Archangel. Battalion headquarters established itself at the Bar Hotel, Archangel.

The strength of the battalion at the end of the month was seventeen officers and 576 other ranks, under the command of Lieutenant Colonel W.J. Bowker CMG, DSO. In addition to this figure there were four deaths from pneumonia, four more men had been evacuated back to hospital in England and seven were in hospital in Russia.

The troops were fairly comfortably billeted, with electric lights and radiators in their huts. Water was a problem as it had to be brought from the river in barrels. As well as language problems the members of the battalion soon found the prices of various articles to be expensive and some other commodities very hard to come by. At a café it cost three roubles for a cup of coffee, or two for a bottle of beer, when the exchange rate was 5d (2p) for one rouble. The YMCA hut did provide cheaper entertainment.

In November battalion headquarters moved to Bakaritza and on the 2nd of the month Major Holland was attached to the Dvina Force, at Berenetz. A curious incident happened on the 13th to 277744 Private A. Wagstaff, A Company, who was shot in the left arm while on guard at the docks. He claimed a man had tried, unsuccessfully, to take his rifle from him. Life at this time was not all guard duty. On 23 November a raid on the village of Glukui was carried out by 100 men under Captain F.G. Laurie MC, who were in search of arms and stolen government stores. Sadly, not much was found. Towards the end of the month the weather began to get colder and Lieutenant W.J. Colborne suffered frostbite to both ears. The war diary states that 'fur hats, leather jerkins, white canvas (Shackleton) boots, thick long stockings, index finger gloves, heavy mitts and heavy mufflers' were issued to all ranks. Due to the weather conditions, the troops were awarded 6d extra, which they called 'Arctic Pay'. 'It is dangerous to stand still for even a couple of minutes. The small hairs inside the nostrils freeze, and when breathing the cold air can be felt very keenly on its passage to the lungs. ... Everyone you see out in the open is a copy of Father Christmas. Fur caps and mufflers are covered in rime and beards and moustaches are in a like condition,' wrote a soldier of the battalion.

An incident occurred on 11 December when the 1st Archangel Regiment mutinied. The alarm was received by the Detention Barracks and Customs House detachments at 1.50 pm and by the Bakaritza detachment at about 2.00 pm. All guards were doubled. The mutiny was suppressed and the Solombola detachment was given the job of guarding the ammunition dump and the twenty-three ringleaders. The remainder of the detachment escorted 500 Russians to Sobornia Quay, where they were embarked on an icebreaker.

Just before Christmas parcels arrived from the Overseas Club, whose funds were from contributions of teachers and scholars from all around the Empire. The parcels containing tobacco, pipes, chocolate and the like were issued to the troops, and each contained a postcard with the name of the school that had donated it. These postcards were suitably replied to in the kindest of ways, with many heartfelt thanks. Christmas Day was celebrated in style. In a letter to the *Sunderland Echo* a member of the battalion described how Christmas 1918 was celebrated:

On Christmas Day reveille was at the usual time, 6.30. Breakfast at 7.30 followed. It consisted of porridge, bacon and sausage. At 10.30 there was a church parade, the service being held in the grounds of the British Consul. The party returned at 12.15. Dinner was timed for 12.45. Beef, potatoes, cabbage, turnips, Christmas pudding and sauce, well combined to make a really good dinner. Each man had also a bottle of beer or stout with his dinner. After this meal cigars and sweets were issued. Tea consisted of pears and custard, biscuits, bread and butter and jam. The concert in the evening was a huge success. For supper each man had a meat sandwich. We finished up with *Auld Lang Syne*. All lights out was at 11.00 pm instead of the usual ten o'clock. So ended our first Christmas Day in cold Northern Russia.

The New Year brought a spate of arson attacks at Bakaritza. On 5 January a water filling shed at the docks was partially destroyed and at 7.15 pm a more serious fire swept through two barrack rooms, destroying them. They had been occupied by the RASC. Due to difficulty getting the fire engines to the scene, it was not until 10.00 pm that the fire was brought under control. Another broke out on 15 January, destroying a shed containing the Royal Engineers' stores, which consisted of the electric lighting plant and miles of cables, as well as other stores. During the early hours of 22 January a slight fire occurred in B Barracks, Hut 11, at Bakaritza, no damage being done, while another on the 23rd gutted the sergeants' mess and dining hut of the 82nd Casualty Clearing Station.

The only point of interest in February was another raid on Solombola and surrounding villages, where nothing of interest was found.

Private Walter G. Miller, No. 1 Platoon, A Company, writing home had this to say about the rations:

> The food we get is sufficient but such a sameness about it. For breakfast biscuits (hard as iron) or bread occasionally and bacon – dinner stew and beans or peas and tea biscuits or bread and margarine and jam – sometimes soup for supper. We cannot get drinking water and I often feel awfully thirsty.

A change of command took place on 3 March when Lieutenant Colonel W.J. Bowker left for England and handed over to Lieutenant Colonel T.C.B. Holland.

On 8 March, Lieutenant C. Dickson, CSM, F. Neesam, DCM, and Sergeant J. Colman were detached to special duty with Russian troops who were to join up with the Siberian Force. By 21 March, a junction was made on the Pechora River. The war diary's entry for 23 April reads as follows:

> It was reported that a party of Russians with one British sergeant which had left Archangel on 8 March had arrived on this date at Usolsk, north of Perm, after covering 1,440 miles. This is probably Sergeant J. Colman of this unit who left with the party and Lieutenant C. Dickson and CSM F. Neesam DCM.

Another alarm was raised by an American bugler at Smolny at 1.50 am on 27 March. It was discovered that a hut shared by the Americans and Durhams was on fire. The fire spread so rapidly that all the canteen stores, food stores and cooking equipment was lost. The other hut occupied by the Durhams was saved. In all, two huts were destroyed. Luckily, no one was killed but Major R.A. Swan suffered injuries to his right hand and forearm.

A change in the weather and the arrival of icebreakers meant that by the beginning of May the harbour at Bakaritza was opened. Another change of command took place on 23

*The divisional concert party. Private Frank Surtees played in the band.*

May, when Major Swan replaced Lieutenant Colonel Holland, who had left for the UK. At the end of the month, battalion headquarters also moved to Smolny.

June saw the beginning of the end for the 2/7th Durham Light Infantry in Russia. The three men, Lieutenant C. Dickson, CSM, F. Neesam, DCM, and Sergeant J. Colman, returned to Archangel on 22 June, after their detached duty.

On 6 June, Captain W.G. Shaw RAMC and Lieutenant C. Pateman were evacuated sick to the UK on HMHS *Kalyan*. They were followed by the first draft of demobilized men, comprising 100 men under Lieutenant Foulis on the 17th, with a further three drafts leaving by the end of July. Captain J.H. Bowman had acted as courts martial officer to the force from 11 July. Captain F.J. Thomas, who had acted as base quartermaster since February, returned to the UK on 28 July.

The last entry in the war diary was written on 29 August 1919:

In view of the early departure of the bulk of the battalion, a farewell concert was given by the Battalion Concert Party in the YMCA Hut Smolny. ... The concert was followed by a farewell supper to the men, and nearly all remaining in N. Russia were present. At this time there were only four officers and 226 other ranks remaining who came out originally with the battalion.

*Third-line Durham Light Infantry Brigade signallers.*

The base commandant, who attended the concert, spoke highly of the work done by the battalion. He congratulated them on the way they had carried out their duties, remarking on the fact that owing to shortage of troops, they had often remained on duty for forty-eight hours without complaint, in freezing temperatures. The battalion returned to the UK shortly afterwards.

During the war and its time in Russia, the battalion, suffered twenty-six deaths, ten of which were in Russia, mostly from pneumonia and influenza.

# Chapter 12

# Reformation to Disbandment

Like all other Territorial Force battalions, at the end of the war the 7th Durham Light Infantry was demobilized and ceased to exist. However, in 1920 plans were put in place for the Territorial Force to be reformed. Consequently, in the middle of February three regular warrant officers were posted to the unit and Captain W.F. Laing was appointed acting adjutant and OC (Officer Commanding).

Things started to move pretty fast from then on, with the first recruits arriving on 3 March. Captain Laing did not remain adjutant for long because in March the War Office appointed Captain A.S. Smeltzer, DSO, MC as adjutant, whilst the quartermaster was Captain and Quartermaster F.J. Thomas. Lieutenant Colonel A.H. Birchall, MC, who had commanded the battalion in the latter stages of the war, was once again appointed Commanding Officer, with Major W.F. Laing his second in command being appointed on 1 July 1920.

The first camp took place at Scarborough from 25 July to 8 August, with fourteen officers and 180 other ranks attending. It was a wet camp, but the time was devoted to internal organization of battalion duties and platoon work.

*Group photograph taken at camp.*

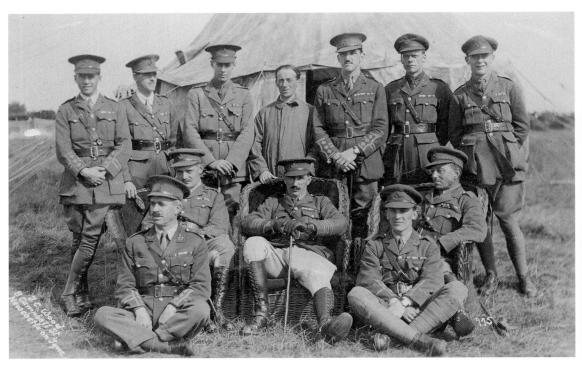

*Scarborough 1920. Back row: Captains P. Hickey, W.H. Liebrecht, T.C. Squance, J.P.B. Grey, J.A. Bell, J.C.R. Pacy, Lieutenant A.V. Dickinson. Front row: Captain L. Laing, Lieutenant Colonel A.H. Birchall and Captain A.S. Keates. Seated on the ground: Captain F.J. Thomas and Lieutenant G. Nixon. (DCTO/D/DLI 2/7/18/45)*

One of the high points of the year came in November, when a memorial to the fallen of the battalion was unveiled by the mayor (Councillor W. Raine) at the drill hall in Livingstone Road, Sunderland.

It had been decided to hold a recruiting week, for the week ending 16 April 1921. However, due to the political situation and industrial unrest in the country at this time, a Royal Proclamation was issued on 9 April 1921 that called for local citizens to join a Defence Force, for a period of ninety days. Under the terms of its engagement the Territorials were not to be used for civil disturbances, although members of the Territorial Force were invited to leave the force and join the Defence Force and any service with them would count towards fulfilling their Territorial obligations. Almost all the officers and ninety other ranks quickly enlisted. Within five days this nucleus became a full battalion of twenty-eight officers and 680 other ranks, which were organised into companies and stationed at Whitburn. Their duties were to guard the Docks and other important installations, including the oil stores on the Tyne. Lieutenant Colonel Birchall, MC was appointed the Commanding Officer and second in command was Major W.F. Laing, MC. The Defence Force dispersed from 3 to 7 July 1921.

Due to the need to form the Defence Force, recruiting for the 7th Durhams practically ceased. Camp still went ahead from 15 to 29 August, on the coast at Whitburn, just north of Sunderland, with fourteen officers and 400 men attending. During the training, time was taken to lay wreaths at the war memorial at Whitburn Village and at the memorial at Christ Church, on the battalion's return march back to Sunderland. The permanent staff instructors (PSI) with the battalion at this time were Regimental Sergeant Major Drew and Sergeants Brown and Phillips.

September 1921 saw the Territorial Force becoming the Territorial Army. A Royal Proclamation disembodied the Territorial Force, which formally ended the mobilization of the Territorial Force, which had started when the United Kingdom became involved in the Great War on 4 August 1914. Army Orders 166 and 332, of 1921, provided that officers not selected for the reconstructed Territorial Force or the Territorial Force Reserve should cease to hold their commissions as from 30 September 1921, or a later date according to the emergencies of the service.

The old colours of the 7th Battalion Durham Light Infantry were handed into the keeping of the Bishopwearmouth Parish Church on Sunday, 30 April 1922. This was the first occasion on which the officers wore swords (these having been discontinued during the war and handed in to the stores). Changes continued to affect the battalion. A new

*Ypres, 1922.*

*Battalion officers, 1922.*

establishment was authorized for infantry battalions and published at the end of April. Instead of four companies, they would now consist of Headquarters Wing and four companies. The HQ Wing would comprise band, bugles, machine gun platoon, signallers and others specialists. Each company would consist of 118 other ranks and the HQ Wing 165. The number of officers in the companies was reduced from five to three. This brought the establishment of the battalion to 637 other ranks – its highest since the war.

Annual camp this year was at Catterick, from 30 July to 13 August, with sixteen officers and 581 other ranks attending. It was during this camp that the battalion won the Brigade Football Cup. Costs always featured in army life and with budgetary constraints imposed on all units Catterick was chosen over Scarborough because it would be less expensive to transport the battalion there and the hire of the ground would be obviate. Catterick had improved a great deal since the war; it now had a theatre, officers' club and sports grounds.

The battalion subscribed £50 towards the Memorial Chapel in Durham Cathedral. It was proposed that the chapel would hold all colours and trophies now in the cathedral. The Sunderland War Memorial in Burdon Road was unveiled on 26 December 1922. The battalion presence consisted of one officer and fifteen men at the base, the band and bugles and four officers and forty men. The unveiling was by the Honorary Colonel of the Battalion after the dedication by the Bishop of Durham.

The battalion started 1923 virtually up to full strength, only being short of four officers to reach establishment. The permanent staff instructors (PSIs) were Captain F.J. Thomas, Adjutant, who had served in Russia, Regimental Sergeant Major W.R. Drew and Sergeants H. Cranston and J. Entwhistle. Promotion boards for NCOs (non-commissioned officers) were held for the first time since the war. Camp was again at Catterick during the third and fourth weeks of June, and those who were eligible received their bounties there.

*Burdon Road war memorial, Sunderland.*

The battalion was represented on two major remembrance ceremonies during 1923. The first was the dedication of the Durham Light Infantry Chapel at Durham Cathedral and the second was the first Armistice parade at the new war memorial at Burdon Road, Sunderland. Large crowds turned out for the unveiling of the war memorial, with people gathering early and

*The grave of Bandmaster Close, who died in 1923.*

*B Company at camp at Ripon in 1924.*

Burdon Road being full as soon as the tramcar service was halted. A commanding officer normally only commanded for four years. Lieutenant Colonel Birchall had completed this period but was granted a two-year extension in 1924 and promoted to Brevet Colonel. Captain and Quartermaster McBeath was awarded the Territorial Decoration for the completion of twenty years' service.

This year also saw the battalion colours and drums emblazoned with the regimental pre-war honour scrolls for the first time as well as those awarded for the Great War. The County Rifle Meeting was held at Whitburn Ranges, for the first time since the war. The battalion won the County Shield. Camp was during the last week of July and the first week of August and was held at Ripon. As usual, the battalion had a good turnout. It was also at camp that the sergeants adopted the red sash, brass chain and whistle for walking out to divine service.

One sad event occurred at camp. Private John R. Chisholm, who had only joined the battalion a few months previously, went with some other members of the battalion to Ripon Races. On the way out, the crowds being very heavy at the exits, they decided to climb a fence. Private Chisholm fell and was injured. He returned to camp and was then taken to York Hospital by motor car. His arm was found to be broken and he was admitted to the hospital less than an hour after the accident. He seemed to be doing well but blood poisoning set in, probably owing to dirt getting into the wound. He died of lockjaw and his body was taken back to Sunderland, where he was buried with full military honours.

In the region of about a dozen men missed attendance at camp and were subsequently fined, the amounts ranging from 10s (50p) to 40s (£2). Various reasons in their defence were put forward, including ill health, not being able to get the time off work, having just got married and being out of pocket.

Bugler W.F. Fairweather won the Silver Bugle, which was presented by Colonel Vaux, and Corporal H. Platts was awarded the Territorial Efficiency Medal. The colours of the 2/7th Durham Light Infantry, which had served in North Russia, were now laid up in Durham Cathedral along with a number of other colours of the service battalions of the regiment.

During the year one officer resigned, eleven men left to join the Regular Army, two men joined the Royal Navy, 101 were discharged and four died (Privates W.G. Cook, C.W. Fisher J.W. Thompson and J.R. Chisholm). Second Lieutenant G.L. Robson, who had previously served with the Malvern OTC, joined the battalion, and 101 men enlisted. On 31 December, the strength of the battalion was fourteen officers and 610 other ranks. During the year the change of establishment was implemented.

The year 1923 also saw the start of the 7th Durham Light Infantry Old Comrades Association, following a letter from J. Coates asking for former comrades to contact him. One of the first rules was that no NCOs were allowed and membership was limited to those who had served with the battalion in France. The former rule proving unpopular, it was soon cancelled and membership was granted to anyone who had served with the battalion. The Association was a place where men could have a cup of tea and a biscuit, and a game of cards or dominoes, and generally enjoy the old comradeship that had built up during the war years. It met in various locations until it purchased its own premises in Norfolk Street, Sunderland. The Old Comrades Association ran until the 1970s, when, due to falling numbers, it closed and the building was sold.

In April 1925, Captain C.D. Bowdery, MC took over as adjutant of the battalion from Captain F.J. Thomas, who was appointed quartermaster, and Captain McBeath was appointed to the TA Reserve. Camp was at Pwllheli, North Wales, set in very pleasant surroundings. The weather was inclement, with the march back from the camp to the station having to be carried out in torrential rain. It was here that the battalion officers adopted the custom of the 1st Battalion of sitting during the loyal toast.

On 31 March, Captain McBeath TD (Territorial Decoration) retired after twenty-five years' service. He had joined the 3rd Volunteer Battalion Durham Light Infantry in January 1900, becoming RQMS in 1912 and being commissioned lieutenant and quartermaster of the 3/7th Durham Light Infantry. He served in France and Flanders from 1916 with the 8th Durham Light Infantry. After May 1918, he joined the training cadre at Rouen as an instructor. In 1919, he returned to England for demobilzation, rejoining the battalion on its reformation in 1921 as quartermaster. During the war he was Mentioned in Despatches and received the Territorial Efficiency Medal, Territorial Force War Medal and Territorial Decoration, a combination of awards believed to be unique.

Sadly, Honorary Colonel Ernest Vaux, CMG, DSO, VD died suddenly at a Newcastle nursing home on 21 November 1925. He was sixty years old. Ernest Vaux originally joined the Artillery Volunteers, rising to the rank of major and earning the Volunteer Decoration for twenty years' service. During the Boer War he saw service with the Imperial Yeomanry, commanding two Maxim gun detachments. For his service during this war he became the recipient of the Distinguished Service Order. His time with the 7th Durham Light Infantry commenced when he was appointed to command the battalion in 1912. He continued to

*The band in 1925.*

command the battalion through most of the war until April 1918, when he had to go into hospital, and he relinquished command to Lieutenant Colonel A.H. Birchall, MC. General Sir Percival Wilkinson aptly described the 7th Battalion as 'Colonel Vaux and his happy family'. During the Great War he was twice Mentioned in Despatches and had conferred upon him the CMG (Companion of the Order of St Michael and St George) for his distinguished services. In June 1922, he became Honorary Colonel of the Battalion. Quite a number of the battalion, past and present, attended his funeral. The bearer party was comprised of Regimental Quartermaster Sergeant H. Blenkinsop, Company Sergeant Major H. Langford, Company Sergeant Major J. Stoker DCM, Sergeant T. Prior, Sergeant R. Scott and Sergeant R. Oxberry. The firing party consisted of a detachment of whom all had served for a considerable period under Colonel Vaux.

November 1925 was an unlucky month for the battalion, for on the 26th the death of Major Robert Charles Hudson occurred in tragic circumstances. Major Hudson was accidentally killed at Bishopwearmouth Church, where he had gone to prepare the bells for the muted peals to mark the funeral of Queen Alexandra. It was surmised that as he was putting on the leather cover over the tongue to muffle the bell, the bell slipped and hit his head and, as he fell, caught him again on the back of the neck and shoulders and pinned him between the wheels of the bell and an adjoining bell. Major Hudson, although commissioned into the Royal Army Service Corps, had been the battalion transport officer and had gone with them to France in April 1915. He served in France until the end of the war and was twice Mentioned in Despatches.

A detachment of the battalion was present at a memorial service for the late Queen Alexandra. The Territorial Efficiency Medal was awarded to Private W. Varley.

A guard of honour was formed on 24 February 1926 for HRH the Princess Mary, Viscountess Lascelles, on the occasion of her visit to Sunderland when she came to open the new wing of the Royal Infirmary. The guard comprised 100 other ranks, with the band and bugles, under Captain R. Horan, with Lieutenants G.M. Johnson and G.L. Robson, the latter carrying the King's Colour.

Changes in the command structure took place on 27 April 1926, when Lieutenant Colonel W.F. Laing, MC took over the command of the battalion from Brevet Colonel A.H. Birchall, MC. During the General Strike of May 1926, the battalion raised a section of fifty-six men for the Civil Constabulary Reserve, which stayed in being until the end of the strike. Annual camp was held at Catterick again this year, from 25 July to 7 August.

Colonel Spain TD was gazetted as honorary colonel of the battalion on 22 December. On the outbreak of the war he had been in command of B Company and had been invalided home after the Second Battle of Ypres in 1915.

Corporal M.J. Boyes was awarded the Territorial Efficiency Medal during 1926.

On 14 March 1927, Captain and Adjutant Bowdery, MC, Captains C.W. Wilson, TD, and G.M. Johnson and Lieutenants L. Strother and G.S.F. Ritson and Second Lieutenant W.E. Blackburn attended a levee at St James's Palace and were presented to the king.

The new drill hall at Dykelands Road was officially opened on 23 April 1927 by General Sir Charles H. Harrington GBE, KCB, DSO, the guard of honour being under the command of Captain C.W. Wilson of the battalion. The drill hall at Dykelands Road is still in use today by the Territorial Army. The old drill hall at the garrison field was demolished in the 1970s and the central police station built on the site of the garrison field.

Annual camp took place at Ripon from 24 July to 7 August. The Territorial Efficiency Medal was awarded to Company Sergeant Major D. Stirling.

The first Old Comrades dinner, which was well attended, was held at the North of England Café in Fawcett Street, Sunderland. Company Sergeant Major A.G. Williams arrived from the Coldstream Guards to take up the appointment as regimental sergeant major. It was with pleasure that the outgoing Regimental Sergeant Major Drew, who had joined the regiment in 1901 as a boy and had served continuously, except for a short period, until November 1928, was gazetted lieutenant and quartermaster.

During the year the following were promoted to sergeant: Lance Sergeants Collier, McGuire, Taylor, Turney, Turley Corporal Thompson and Private Rogers.

Annual Camp for 1928 was held at Marske, in Yorkshire. On 10 September 1928, Captain and Quartermaster Frederick James Thomas died unexpectedly. He was fifty-four years old. He had been a regular soldier serving with the 1st Battalion during the Boer War, and was awarded two medals with five clasps. He joined the 7th Battalion in 1908 as a permanent staff instructor, based at South Shields. In 1910 he was appointed regimental sergeant major and was attached to the headquarters element at Sunderland. During the Great War he was appointed quartermaster of the second line of the battalion and went with them to Russia in 1918. On the reformation of the battalion in 1920 he was appointed quartermaster, a position he held until his death.

Captain C.D. Bowdery, MC, who had been the adjutant, left the battalion on completion of his tour of duty on 31 March 1929 and returned to the 1st Battalion of the regiment. He was presented with a silver salver as a token of appreciation. Lieutenant T. O'Brien, from the 1st Battalion, took over the duties of adjutant for a four-year tour of duty.

Annual camp was once again held at Ripon, Yorkshire. The weather deciding to be cruel, it rained most of the time. This did not, however, dampen the spirits of the troops, who made the most of the opportunity for training. The battalion sports day was held at camp on 3 August, many visitors from Sunderland arriving for the occasion.

One of the highlights of the year was the provision of a guard of honour for HRH The Duke of York on the occasion of the opening of the new Wearmouth Bridge. The guard, a hundred strong with the band and bugles, was commanded by Captain T.C. Squance, with Lieutenants H.T. Wilcox and G.S.F. Ritson, the latter carrying the King's Colour.

Another old soldier of the battalion passed away in October 1929. Captain William Ebenezer Liebrecht, aged seventy, died at his home. He had originally served in the Essex Regiment in the Egyptian War of 1882 before coming to Sunderland as a staff sergeant major in 1896. In 1908 he was placed in charge of recruiting. At the outbreak of the war Sergeant Major Liebrecht played a prominent part in organizing the mobilization of the national reserve in Sunderland and surrounding district. He was commissioned captain shortly afterwards. He was buried at Sunderland Cemetery with full military honours.

On 19 October, Major L. Laing, TD, being promoted to lieutenant colonel, took over the command of the battalion from Lieutenant Colonel W.F. Laing, MC, who moved to the TA Officers' Reserve. It is not often that brothers relieve each other as commanding officer of the same battalion.

The Territorial Efficiency Medal was awarded to Sergeant J. Wilson. During the year, Corporal W.T. Thompson, Bugler Corporal H.G. Hood, Private F. Sawyer and Lance Sergeant T. Arkley were all promoted to sergeant.

A change in the way battalion orders were issued occurred in January 1930, when they started to appear every Wednesday, at various post offices throughout Sunderland. These were the days when post offices were plentiful.

Reorganization of the Territorial Army took place again during 1930. Prior to 1 April, the battalion was formed as HQ Wing, A, B, C and D companies, and from that date D Company was converted into a machine gun company, with a strength of ninety-two without officers, compared to a rifle company of 114. Training for this had already taken place during 1929. The change introduced eight Vickers machine guns into a Territorial Army battalion for the first time. It had previously only been four, and at platoon strength. At a battalion parade on 11 June 1930, following an inspection by the brigade commander, Efficiency Medals were presented to Company Sergeant Major R.W. Wigham, Company Quartermaster Sergeant W. Harding, Sergeant T.W. Coxon, Sergeant G. Potts and Privates C.E. Davis and N. Cadas. In October it was announced in *The London Gazette* that 2646570 Warrant Officer Class II A.G. Williams, Coldstream Guards, Acting Regimental Sergeant Major 7th Battalion Durham Light Infantry had been awarded the Long Service and Good Conduct Medal.

The battalion went to annual camp on Sunday, 22 June 1930 for fifteen days to Catterick Camp. This was a remarkable occasion because all the Durham Light Infantry battalions were together at the same time, with the exception of the 2nd Battalion, which was serving abroad.

Sports always played a large part in the life of a battalion and in early 1931 it was announced that Lieutenant W.B. Allan, from the battalion, had been selected to play Rugby football for the Territorial Army against a Regular Army team at Bristol on 25 February 1931.

The battalion went further afield this year for its annual camp. Sunday, 26 July saw the battalion depart for Halton Camp, Lancashire. The weather seemed to have been the worst for a number of years but the training continued as planned and everyone returned to Sunderland at the end of the training having apparently enjoyed the experience. The brigade boxing tournament took place on 6 August at camp; the battalion were runners-up to the 8th Durham Light Infantry, which was a good effort on the part of the battalion. A team of boxers was formed to represent the battalion at the 50th Divisional Tournament at St George's drill hall, Newcastle upon Tyne, in February. The winners were to represent the division in the Territorial Army Boxing Championship in London in March. Private W. Renney of the battalion was declared the winner of the Bantam Weight Class.

In the previous year it had been announced that there would be not annual camps for the Territorial Army during 1932, which was a great disappointment to all concerned. However, weekend training took place at Ponteland Camp and these were well attended. Although they could not replace the fifteen-day camps, full use was made of the time.

In April, 4334783 Sergeant R.M. Vardy, 1st Durham Light Infantry, Permanent Staff Instructor with the 7th Durham Light Infantry, was awarded the Long Service and Good Conduct Medal. In November, Captain and Quartermaster W. McBeath, TD, retired from the Territorial Army, having served with the battalion throughout the Great War.

This year saw the first ever battalion children's Christmas party, held on 28 December, for the children (aged from five to fourteen) of warrant officers, senior non-commissioned officers and serving members of the battalion. About 270 children attended, and each was given tea, a present and some fruit. The party was well supported by the wives of members of the battalion and other volunteers.

Annual camp restarted in 1933, with the battalion going to Marske, Yorkshire, from 30 July to 13 August. Once again it was a brigade camp, with the battalion having the second largest turnout.

Private W. Renney was again selected to take part in the Territorial Army Boxing Championships in London in March 1933. Lieutenant W.B. Allan, who had been previously selected in 1932, was again selected, along with Lieutenant J. Storey, to play for the Territorial Army XV against the Regular Army XV at Aldershot in March. In October, Major R. Horan was promoted to lieutenant colonel and assumed command of the battalion from Lieutenant Colonel L. Laing, TD.

From December 1933, the Machine Gun Company changed its name and was known as the Support (S) Company.

The following year proved to be a quiet one, with annual camp taking place, once again at Ripon, from 29 July to 12 August, with a good attendance, the strength being 550 all ranks. A party of one officer and twenty other ranks attended a service of consecration of the additions to the Memorial Chapel (Regimental) at Durham Cathedral on 30 October.

King George V celebrated his Silver Jubilee during 1935, and the battalion attended the celebrations in Sunderland at the invitation of His Worship the Mayor on Monday, 6 May.

The Silver Jubilee Medal was bestowed upon Lieutenant Colonel R. Horan, Captain and Quartermaster W.R. Drew, Regimental Quartermaster Sergeant H. Blenkinsop, Sergeant R. Oxberry and Private J.W. Beck.

Honorary Colonel, Colonel J. Spain, OBE, TD, died at his home in Wakefield on 12 March 1935. He was sixty-four. At the outbreak of the war he had been a captain in the 7th Battalion Durham Light Infantry and rose to the rank of lieutenant colonel, eventually commanding the 6th Battalion Durham Light Infantry. After the war he established a practice as a valuer in Newcastle. Later he was appointed the county valuer for Durham, the first county valuer to be appointed for the county. He left a widow and two sons. His memorial service was attended by the commanding officer and a number of other officers of the battalion, past and present. Colonel William Basil Greenwood, OBE, DSO, succeeded Colonel Spain as honorary colonel of the battalion.

The annual battalion inspection took place on 5 July at Ashbrooke Cricket Ground, the troops marching through the town from the drill hall at Livingstone Road. The inspection was carried out by Colonel W.B. Greenwell, CBE, DSO. It was during this inspection that Territorial Efficiency Medals, for long service, were presented to the following: Sergeants J.J. Hope, R.W. Boxer and S. Rowe; Lance Sergeant N.T. Callender; Corporal G. Hudson; Lance Corporal M. McArdle; and Privates L. Farrer, J. Taylor, G.W.W. Chipps and J. Johnson.

Camp this year was at Catterick, from 28 July to 11 August, and for once the weather was kind to the battalion.

Sad news was received in February 1936, when it was announced that the 7th Battalion Durham Light Infantry had been selected by the War Office, under the Government's Air Defence Scheme, to be converted to an anti-aircraft battery, forming part of the new 2nd AA Division. This announcement was very much regretted by all ranks but, conscious of the importance of air defence in any coming conflict, it was looked upon as an honour to be chosen. As a result, all officers and a large proportion of the other ranks elected to serve with the new unit, which was titled the 47th (Durham Light Infantry) AA Battalion RE (TA).

Regimental Sergeant Major Fisher and the other permanent staff instructors left the battalion on 10 December to return to the regiment. The new permanent staff instructors from the Royal Engineers arrived on 2 November for the formal handover. The battalion's strength was in the region of 525 when December came around. The new establishment for the battery would be forty-two officers and 1,200 men. Consequently, recruitment of men with the right skills for the Royal Engineers became a big issue to bring the new unit up to strength. It did not take place straight away but new recruits could register their interest. Men would not be attested until the new buildings had been constructed to house all the equipment.

The old colours of the Sunderland Volunteer Infantry, which had been removed from Bishopwearmouth Parish Church during its reconstruction, were replaced on 12 January. The battalion paraded at 9.30 am and escorted the colours and colour party to the church, where Lieutenant Colonel Horan handed them back to the rector for safekeeping. The colours of the 20th Durham Light Infantry, which had similarly been removed, were handed back by Colonel Leather. The colour party consisted of Second Lieutenant Russell, Second Lieutenant Kirkup, Company Quartermaster Sergeant Harding, Sergeants Taylor, Budd and Davison, and Lance Sergeant Stuart. The colours were placed on the tower at the west end of the church. They have since been moved. Those of the Sunderland Volunteer Infantry are now preserved in the

*1937 – 7th Durham Light Infantry as 47 AA (BN) RE.*

Regimental Museum, Durham, and those of the 20th Battalion have joined those of the other battalions in the Regimental Chapel in Durham Cathedral.

The brigade camp took place at Redcar from 12 to 26 July. The battalion furnished a company, at war strength, which assisted by a motor detachment and a machine-gun platoon gave a demonstration of a company attack. On 24 July the officers of the battalion were entertained to dinner by the other officers of the brigade. The next day, a ceremonial parade was held in honour of the battalion. After speeches and prayers the battalion marched past the remainder of the brigade – a very moving ceremony for those who took part.

After camp, training for the new role began. A number of officers and NCOs attended a demonstration of anti-aircraft work, comprising searchlights and guns, at Haltwhistle, Northumberland, from 1 to 3 August. The following weekend, two officers and ten NCOs were attached to the 6th City of London Rifles, who had recently been converted to the anti-aircraft role, at Mytchett Camp. A lot of information was gained from this visit as to the future role of the battalion.

At 23.59 hours, 9 December 1936, the 7th Battalion Durham Light Infantry ceased to exist, and at 00.01 hours, 10 December 1936, the 47th (Durham Light Infantry) AA Battalion RE (TA) came into being. The officers serving with the battalion on this date were as follows:

| | |
|---|---|
| Lieutenant Colonel R. Horan, TD | Commanding Officer |
| Major T.C. Squance | Second in Command |
| Major J.G. Peckston | Commanding HQ Wing |
| Captain W.G. Blackburn | Commanding S Company |
| Captain J. Iliff | Commanding A Company |
| Captain K.W. Black | Commanding B Company |
| Captain W.B. Allan | Commanding C Company |
| Lieutenant J. Storey | S Company |
| Lieutenant A.C. Dixon | S Company |
| Lieutenant J.C. McNaughton | C Company |
| Lieutenant C.J.P. Hope | S Company |
| Lieutenant F.S. Ritson | HQ Wing |
| Lieutenant S.D. Russell | B Company |
| Second Lieutenant R.B. Kirkup | A Company |
| Second Lieutenant R.H. Bell | B Company |
| Second Lieutenant A.P. Muir | A Company |
| Second Lieutenant A.K. Steel | C Company |
| Second Lieutenant B.S.R. Rambaut | Not posted |
| Captain & QM W.R. Drew | |
| Major P. Hickey, Royal Army Medical Corps | Medical |
| Captain H.A. Eccles Royal Army Medical Corps | |
| Captain Rev S. Gibson RA Chaplains Department | |
| Captain D.S. Norman, East Yorks Regiment | Adjutant |

# Epilogue

T he story of the 47th (Durham Light Infantry) AA Battalion RE (TA) does not form part of this book. It deserves to have its own book, written by someone else. Over the years I have interviewed a number of veterans from the battalion, therefore a few words regarding their subsequent lives is in order before this story comes to an end.

Private Stanley Douglass, B Company, recalled what happened to him when he returned to Sunderland:

> I was demobilized shortly after the war through being a miner, they wanted miners quick. I had a few days' leave before I reported. I had to report for the mines. Well that was another thing; I didn't intend to go back to any mines. A mate of mine got me into the shipyard, down Barton's. I was there only about a month or six weeks when I got a letter from the War Office: 'Return to the mines for which you were sent from France, or go back to France.'
>
> My mother nearly had a fit. After nearly four years out there that's the way they treat you. I had to leave and to go to the mines. My mother said that I wasn't going back to France. I was there until I was sixty-five. I worked at Wearmouth Colliery.
>
> During the war I was hit in the hand, just a bit of shrapnel. I got a week or two down with that, 'course it was only a flesh wound. I was hit in both knees, just shrapnel, flesh wounds, but it got me out of the line for a week or two.
>
> I still have nightmares. The wife often wakes me up, I've been shouting, screaming and she's frightened I get hold of her and strangle her. This has lasted ever since the war [the interviews took place in the 1970s]. I can look upon a field now if I was in the country and imagine thousands of dead lying there, especially the cornfield. I can see it as it is now and as it was when we saw it when we went through them cornfields. The only time you could find your dead was by the smell. Mind they do smell; they say, 'The sweet smell of death.' It has a funny sweet smell. And even that, it comes on often. I can still see everything as it happened; it seems as if it gets on your mind and you cannot shift it, there's nothing that happens now you can forget another day but you cannot with that.
>
> I'm glad I saw it but to go through it again? No! No! Not for anything!

Private Stanley Douglass died in the 1980s.

Lance Corporal Joseph Robson, C Company, after having been gassed for a second time during the battles of 1918, found himself after convalescence working on the lighting system at a POW camp at Ripon. He remembered:

> I was there [at Ripon] until 1919 and I was discharged from there. They sent me from there to the 4th Durham Light Infantry, at Seaham Harbour. When I got up there to

Certificate presented to Private Douglass by Sunderland Town Council. One was presented to each person who served in the armed forces.

their headquarters at the drill hall they wanted to know who I was, they had no papers, nothing belonging me. I was there two days before my papers came through. They did not know who I was, where I had come from, nothing.

When I was at Ripon, the secretary of my works at Osborne & Graham, Mr Rowntree, sent letters to the headquarters of all the lads, to come back to their jobs who were serving their time. So we were discharged out of the Army. Until I got my discharge I was C3 category, that's disabled; because I was going home to work they marked my papers A1.

For being in the Army five years I received a gratuity of £39, I received a shilling a day when I was in. Our sergeant, they called him Billy Dickerson, sergeant of the signals section, would have received more gratuity than me being a sergeant. He came out and there was a fried fish shop over the road to Rutland Street, in Hylton Road, he took over that place. He was there for quite a long while. I was in the British Legion, the branch used to be in Vine Place. Major King used to be the head and Charlie Lamb was the Secretary. They got on to me about the gas, they said that they had prepared a letter for me to go through to St Mary's Place, Newcastle, and see the medical people through there, to see if I could get a pension. My mother said she would come with me. I told her it would be a trial for her and that I did not know how long I would be there. We had to be there at ten o'clock in the morning and we had to get through the best way we could. Well we got there about ten o'clock and we were sitting there about a quarter of an hour before they asked me into a room, my mother remained outside. I was going from one room to another and there were about four doctors in each room and they were talking Latin to each other. They said to go to the next room. I would go out to the next room. I went into the room and they got a chair and told me to do step-ups. I did not get three steps before I was on the floor. They had to bring me round; they knew what it was like. Anyway that went on until four o'clock in the afternoon and they never came to my mother and said, 'Here is a cup of tea for you.' I never had a cup of tea.

We were glad to get outside to go and get a cup of tea in the first place we could come to. They said that I would be notified in a day or two. I received a letter, they could not grant me a pension for the gas because it had not been poison gas, with it being mustard gas it would clear up.

When you get mustard gas the doctors tell me you get blebs [blisters] inside your stomach and when one of them bursts you have a bad attack for a minute or two. I used to have a bad do every month or so. Nobody could do anything for me, they just left me 'til I came round, then I had to run to the bathroom and was sick. It was just like mustard coming up, yellow. When that came up I was alright. This went on for a year or two and I still never received a penny off them. The only thing I could do was to go down to Seaburn for the sea air. I got myself pulled together but I've had a bad chest ever since.

And Lance Corporal Robson's last words on the war: 'You had some funny times, some dangerous times, some happy times. We used to make the best of it.'

Private Frank Surtees was, as mentioned, a member of the battalion band both before and during the war. When he was demobilized he continued with his musical talents, joining various orchestras, working in theatres and eventually becoming lead cornet at the Theatre Royal, Newcastle upon Tyne. Frank's brother, Thomas Whyburn Surtees, also served during the war and was killed in action on 2 June 1918, while serving with the 9th Durham Light Infantry.

Finally, Private Edwin Patterson, B Company, was home on leave when the Armistice was announced and remembered that he did not see any excitement in the town on that day. However, as he was still a serving soldier with the battalion he had to return to France after his leave was over and await demobilization. His last comments were:

*Lance Corporal Joe Robson in the 1920s.*

I got £20 gratuity. I got a letter from Durham HQ: 'Dear sir, as we have overpaid you and your mother 7/6d would you please return the same to keep our books straight.'

Your top coat, if you took it down to the railway station to the sorting office you got £1. Mine went in.

If it hadn't been for the Territorials when war broke out it would have been a sad lookout. We hadn't any men, the old army had gone. We filled the gaps. If it hadn't been for that I reckon we would have lost the war. The Territorials saved the war.

I was glad when the war was finished. I went back [to the shipyards] the foreman was standing at the door. He said, 'I suppose you want some work then?' I only stayed about a fortnight and then went up the river to another yard. I was a joiner; I could work in the shipyard, on the houses or as a cabinet maker. I had the pick of all three. You had to be a good joiner in the shipyard.

Private Patterson married the sister of Private Surtees and the men remained close well into their nineties.

Arthur Speight, who had been captured during the Aisne battles and spent the rest of the war in a prisoner of war camp, left a written account of his time there, which is deposited at the Imperial War Museum, London. This is how he described his return home from the prisoner of war camp:

*Private Thomas Surtees (brother of Frank Surtees), killed in action 2 June 1918 with 9 Durham Light Infantry.*

*50th Divisional band.*

about fifty of us packed up our traps, marched through the gates and down to Wesel, where, in spite of the station master, and his sword, we boarded a train which took us to Zevenaar. Just over the Dutch frontier. Here we left the train and after a good a meal we were put onto the train for Rotterdam where we arrived in the dark, at the Waterside Station. From here we marched through the city and took up our abode in a large warehouse on the dockside. We were here for two days and then a vessel arrived to take us to Blighty. She was one of the LMS boats, called *Londonderry*.

We were all given a small flag and a bar of chocolate when we went aboard. It lay off the Hook of Holland all night. The next day was very foggy so we were unable to proceed but on the next we crossed over to Cromer, where we lay all night. Early next morning we entered the

*Brass plaque to the SNCOs of the battalion, which also hangs in Dykelands Road Drill Hall.*

*7th Durham Light Infantry Roll of Honour, which hangs in the Drill Hall, Dykelands Road, Sunderland.*

*The King's Colour, hanging at Bishop Auckland Drill Hall.*

*The Regimental Colour, hanging at Bishop Auckland Drill Hall.*

IN MEMORY OF
THE OFFICERS AND MEN
7th (PIONEER) BATTALION
DURHAM LIGHT INFANTRY
YPRES SALIENT
1915 – 1918

*Plaque to the battalion installed in St George's Church, Ypres.*

Humber, passing through lines of torpedo boats and drifters, all of whom gave us a grand howl on their whistles. It made one's back hair curl to hear this rousing welcome. The food on the ship was a dream. Bread and butter, tinned rabbit and bottles of stout at each meal. We landed at the Riverside Station at Hull and boarded a train for Ripon, from whence I was demobbed and arrived in Sunderland on 10 December looking quite plump and absolutely giving the lie to all my tales of misery.

Most returning servicemen returned to their pre-war employment or found work in the shipyards or mines in the area. However, for some ex-servicemen times were hard and they took to selling items on street corners to make a few coppers. Here is a poem printed at the time to explain their circumstances:

### Unemployed Ex-Service Man

*Help him by buying*
*It is just a simple story,*
*That I want to tell you,*
*Yet, in spite of its simplicity,*
*It is, alas, too true.*

*I'm but a disabled soldier,*
*One who answered duty's call,*
*Now forgotten by my country –*
*Left to wither and to fall.*

*When I saw that I was needed,*
*I enlisted full of pride –*
*They said I was a hero then,*
*But now I am cast aside.*

*Like the song they call* Playthings,
*I am one of England's toys,*
*Life is but a drama*
*With its sorrows and its joys.*

*I have tramped along the highways*
*I have searched each city through,*
*But good luck never comes my way,*
*I can find no work to do.*

*And this is England's gratitude*
*To the men who fought and bled,*
*They rewarded us with a medal,*
*Then we're left to want for bread.*

*So now you know my story,*
*I ask you if you can,*
*To try and spare a trifle*
*For a poor ex-Service man.*

# Awards

**Order of St Michael & St George**
Vaux, Ernest, Lieutenant Colonel (DO), 13 June 1916

**Order of the British Empire**
Bradley, William Alan, T/Captain, OBE, 3 June 1919, France
Broad, Arthur Nowell, Lt A/Captain, MBE, 3 June 1920, Russia 2/7
Priestley, William, Major, OBE, 3 June 1919
Swan, Robert Arhur, Major (Essex), OBE, 3 June 1920, Russia 2/7

**Distinguished Service Order**
Wilson, Percy Phillipe, Major, 26 July 1918, 7th att 9th
'For conspicuous gallantry and devotion to duty during recent operations. He showed great coolness and skill while in command of the battalion, particularly on one occasion when the brigade on his right was forced back. Also he stayed in the trenches for four days after being wounded in the foot. He is a fine example to his men.'

**Military Cross**
Bell, James Alan, Captain, 1 January 1919

Bewley, Isaac, Lt A/Captain, 15 October 1918, 7th att 13th
'For conspicuous gallantry and devotion to duty during an enemy attack. He showed great skill in handling of his men, and kept his battalion commander well in touch with the situation by sending back accurate reports. When the attack broke down he organized a party and brought in several prisoners. Next morning when the positions of the enemy were still obscure, he made a personal reconnaissance and brought back valuable information besides accounting for two of the enemy. He has previously done fine work.'

Birchall, Arthur Harold. Lt A/Captain, 17 September 1917
'For conspicuous gallantry and devotion to duty during an attack. Regardless of personal danger, he moved along the top of his trench under fire of every description, encouraging his men. Afterwards he went out with a sergeant and located a number of enemy snipers, bringing four of these back unwounded to our line. He set a very fine example of keenness and fearlessness.'

Bradley, William Alan, Lt T/Captain, 3 June 1918, 7th att Hy. Arty

Broadley, John, QM & Hon Captain, 3 June 1918

Davies, William Herbert, 2Lt T/Lt, 4 February 1918, 7th att 14th
'For conspicuous gallantry and devotion to duty. After a very heavy bombardment his company was attacked and forced back from its trenches. Though he had been buried three times by enemy shells, he led a counter-attack with the greatest skill and determination and recaptured the position.'

Dickson, Cecil, T/Lt (Cheshire Regt), 3 October 1919, att 2/7th Russia
'When in command of the British sector of the Allied mission which left Archangel on 8 March 1919 and arrived at Omsk 21 May 1919 to establish communications with the Serbian Army under Admiral Kolchak, he showed great courage and initiative behind the enemy lines and in dealing with superior enemy forces by which to a large extent the success of the mission was secured.'

Dobson, George Dodds Rowell, Lt A/Major, 26 July 1918
'For conspicuous gallantry and devotion to duty during a retirement. He showed exceptional zeal and by his cheerful and resourceful manner and disregard for personal safety, did much to keep up the spirits of the men.'

Dunn, Thomas, A/Captain, 1 January 1919, 2/7th att MGC Salonika

Goodrick, Walter Robert, Lt T/Captain, 25 November 1916
'For conspicuous gallantry and devotion to duty in action. When in command of two companies of Pioneers under intense fire, he carried out his work with great courage and determination. He set a splendid example to his men.'

Howey, Thomas Windlow, Lt A/Captain, 1 January 1919, 8th att 7th

MacIntyre, Reginald George, Captain, 1 January 1918

Mackinnon, Mervyn Alexander, T/Captain, 14 November 1916
'For conspicuous gallantry and devotion to duty during operations. He reconnoitred ground and sited trenches under difficult and dangerous conditions. On one occasion he led his company through a barrage, and linked up with two positions under very heavy shellfire. He has set a fine example.'

Noble, Arthur Rogerson Brinkler, 2Lt, 11 January 1919, 7th att 2/5th LF
'He led his patrol with great gallantry and vigour to capture an important trench junction, which he did with success, and then with only four survivors, he repelled an enemy bombing attack and defeated a second counter-attack by well-aimed rifle fire. His coolness and judgement gave great confidence to his men.'

Readhead, Stanley, Captain, 25 November 1916
'For conspicuous gallantry in action. He sited a trench, placing his men in position, and kept them working under intense fire, displaying great courage and determination throughout.'

Rushworth, Tom, Lieutenant, 24 September 1918, 7th att 6th
'For conspicuous gallantry and devotion to duty. He held a bridgehead with a small party of men under heavy machine-gun fire until completely outflanked. He then withdrew his party successfully and took up another position in the rear, where he kept in touch under circumstances of great difficulty with the division on the right.'

Short, Leonard Highton, Lieutenant, 26 July 1918 7th att 10 Sqn RAF
'For conspicuous gallantry and devotion to duty in bringing in many excellent and accurate patrol reports and owing to adverse weather conditions, having to fly very low. On one occasion his observer was wounded from fire from the ground, and he was attacked by three enemy aeroplanes but he brought him safely back. On another occasion his observer was wounded when bombing enemy troops from 1,000 feet.'

Sutton, Thomas Ridley, A/Captain, 3 June 1919, 7th att 2nd Carrier Company, Tank Corps

Welch, Thomas Ridley, 2 Lieutenant, 1 January 1918 7th att 14

Windle, Maurice Bentley, 2 Lieutenant, 2 December 1918, 7th att 8th Liverpools
'For conspicuous gallantry and devotion to duty. He commanded his platoon with great initiative during an enemy attack, and was responsible for driving off the attack and inflicting heavy losses on the enemy. Later he led his men in a most determined manner in an attack and captured and consolidated his objective. His good leadership was an inspiration to all ranks.'

## DISTINGUISHED FLYING CROSS
James, Reginald Vyse, T/Lieutenant, 8 February 1919, 7th att RAF
'This officer has taken part in seventeen bomb raids, thirteen of which he personally led. The success of these has been largely due to the determination and courage Captain James displayed, combined with leadership of high merit.'

## DISTINGUISHED CONDUCT MEDAL
Benneworth, W, 1162, CSM, 3 September 1918
'For conspicuous gallantry and devotion to duty. He made a personal reconnaissance under heavy machine-gun fire over 800 yards of ground, thus saving a very dangerous position. Later, when in command of a post, he showed great courage and skill in covering the retirement of other troops, killing six of the enemy himself. He set a fine example to all.'

Borthwick, D.N., 2276, Sergeant, 21 June 1916
'For consistent good work as Transport Sergeant. He has shown great courage in trying circumstances.'

Coleman, T. (MM), 275428, CSM, 3 September 1918
'For conspicuous gallantry and devotion to duty during a retirement. One day he killed twelve of the enemy who had crossed a canal, thereby allowing a platoon to complete its retirement. Throughout the operations he showed a fine example to his men.'

Dunlop, W., 3 CSM, 11 March 1916
'For conspicuous gallantry. He went out several times under heavy fire, and carried in wounded men to shelter where it was possible to have their wounds dressed. He also exhibited great bravery and determination in rallying men of various regiments and leading them forward.'

Handyside, E., 22/327, Private, 3 September 1919
'He has repeatedly displayed great coolness and gallantry in action, particularly on the morning of 25 March 1918, near Morchain. When the enemy was attacking he rallied men in his vicinity, and in spite of numerically superior forces he held on to his post, and inflicted heavy casualties on the enemy. On previous occasions he has displayed great gallantry and coolness, and throughout these operations his conduct had a very inspiring effect on his comrades.'

Kilpatrick, J., 275028, Sergeant, 25 August 1917
'Conspicuous gallantry and devotion to duty in assisting his officer to capture a hostile sniping post. He set a splendid example to the men during the operation, displaying the greatest courage and coolness on this, as on all other occasions.'

Parker, W.B., 275002, CSM, 17 April 1918
'For conspicuous gallantry and devotion to duty. By his energy and zeal he has brought his company to a high state of efficiency, and has inspired his men by his splendid example and encouragement.'

Stoker, J., 65, CSM, 11 March 1916
'For conspicuous gallantry when in charge of a machine gun. For a period of three weeks he had no officer over him, and his courage, energy and resource has been at all times of the highest standard.'

Wardropper, R.W., 275004, CSM, 21 October 1918
'For conspicuous gallantry and devotion to duty. This warrant officer, during an extended period of service, has on many occasions rendered services of a conspicuously valuable description, displaying under heavy fire a most fearless disregard for his own duties, which he has carried out in a manner worthy of the highest praise.'

## MILITARY MEDAL
### 1/7th Battalion

| | | | |
|---|---|---|---|
| Allen, F. | 42736 | Corporal | 7 October 1918 |
| Bittlestone, L.A. | 2543 | L/Sergeant | 9 December 1916 |
| Boutflower, R. | 1510 | Sergeant | 6 January 1917 |
| Brown, J.T. | 2756 | Corporal | 27 October 1916 |
| Campbell, J.W. | 1798 | Sergeant | 27 October 1916 |
| Coleman, T. | 2416 | Sergeant | 21 December 1916 |
| Collins, J.B. | 275486 | Private | 21 October 1918 |
| Craig, W. | 203564 | Sergeant | 6 August 1918 |

| Davey, A. | 2566 | Sergeant | 21 December 1916 |
| Davidson, A. | 15744 | Sergeant | 27 October 1916 late 14th |
| Dodds, J. | 257446 | Corporal | 7 October 1918 |
| Edmonds, A. | 275410 | L/Corporal | 7 October 1918 |
| French, T.C. | 4225 | Private | 9 December 1916 |
| Gasston, F. | 323040 | Sergeant | 21 October 1918 |
| Green, F. | 3911 | Private | 22 January 1917 |
| Hampton, C. | 3185 | L/Corporal | 27 October 1916 |
| Hart, G.M. | 275511 | Private | 10 June 1920 |
| Hodgson, J. | 1119 | L/Sergeant | 27 October 1916 |
| Hutton, R. | 277288 | Private | 6 August 1918 |
| Langford, H. | 1375 | CSM | 27 October 1916 |
| Laverick, H. | 275397 | CSM | 13 March 1919 |
| Maguire, R. | 2284 | Private | 9 December 1916 |
| Marsh, A.H. | 1720 | Sergeant | 3 June 1916 |
| Mottram, S. | 2365 | Sergeant | 27 October 1916 |
| Nixon, G. | 2119 | Sergeant | 27 October 1916 |
| Richardson, J. | 45299 | Private | 21 October 1918 |
| Robinson, A. | 1467 | Sergeant | 27 October 1916 |
| Rodley, D. | 275177 | Corporal | 6 August 1918 |
| Russell, A.S. | 1813 | Private | 27 October 1916 |
| Scully, J. | 903 | Private | 17 June 1919 |
| Smeaton, A. | 275810 | Private | 6 August 1918 |
| Thompson, G. | 275049 | Corporal | 21 October 1918 |
| Thompson, G.E. | 275988 | Private | 7 October 1918 |
| Tweddle, J. | 2612 | Corporal | 27 October 1916 |

**2/7th Battalion for North Russia**

| Brown, J. | 80125 | Private | 17 June 1919 |
| Colman, J. | 276342 | Sergeant | 22 January 1920 |
| Neesam, F. (DCM) | 277699 | CSM | 22 January 1920 |

# MERITORIOUS SERVICE MEDAL
## 1/7th Battalion for France

| Blenkinsopp, H. | 275022 | CQMS | 17 June 1918 |
| Kelly, T. | 30157 | Cpl A/Sgt | 3 June 1919 |
| McArdle, B. | 275216 | Private | 3 June 1919 |
| Rackstraw, R. | 275898 | Private | 22 March 1919 |
| Reeves, F.G. | 22/412 | Sgt A/CQMS | 3 June 1919 |
| Saxon, N. | 275527 | Sergeant | 3 June 1919 |
| Steele, A.S. | 275396 | CQMS | 3 June 1919 |
| Trenholme, W. | 275400 | Sergeant | 17 June 1918 |
| Wilson, J.A. | 22/13 | QMS | 18 January 1919 |
| Wilson, R.E. | 275512 | L/Corporal | 17 June 1918 |

*Company Sergeant Major McArdle MSM.*

## 2/7th Battalion for North Russia

| | | | |
|---|---|---|---|
| Barber, A.H. | 351396 | Pte A/Sgt | 3 January 1920 |
| Edgar, M. | 275970 | CSM | 22 January 1920 |
| Irwin, J. | 277512 | CSM | 22 January 1920 |
| Occomore, T.R. | 109707 | Sergeant | 22 January 1920 |
| Ward, A.E. | 109836 | Cpl (CQMS) | 13 August 1919 |

## MENTIONED IN DESPATCHES
### 1/7th Battalion for France

| | | | |
|---|---|---|---|
| Aitcheson, J.J. | 275367 | Private | 25 May 1917 |
| Armstrong, E.A. | 22/340 | Pte A/Cpl | 9 July 1919 |
| Blenkinsopp, T. | 275022 | CSM | 21 December 1917 |
| Bradley, W.A. | | Lt T/Capt | 9 Sept 1921 |
| Brown, J.W. | | Lieutenant | 9 July 1919 |
| Charlton, R.H. | 77135 | CQMS | 28 December 1918 |
| Coates, J. | 275448 | Cpl A/Sgt | 9 July 1919 |
| Carswell-Hunt, W.D. | | 2Lt T/Major | 1 January 1916 |
| Dobson G.D.R. | | 2Lt A/Capt | 21 December 1917 and 24 May 1918 |
| Down, J. | 2141 | L/Sergeant | 4 January 1917 |
| Eccles, J.E. | 1961 | Sergeant | 25 May 1917 |
| Graham, F. | 275535 | Pte A/L/Cpl | 9 July 1919 |
| Green, G. | 22/435 | L/Corporal | 9 July 1919 |
| Hart, G.M. | 275511 | Private | 30 January 1920 |
| Henshaw, J.T. | 276528 | Sergeant | 9 July 1919 |
| Howey, S. | 275364 | CQMS | 25 July 1917 |
| Lee, J. | 2628 | Corporal | 4 January 1917 |
| McBeath, W. | | QM & Hon Lt | 21 December 1917 and 28 December 1918 |
| MacIntyre, R.G. | | Lt T/Capt | 4 January 1917 |
| Mottram, S. | 2365 | Sergeant | 4 January 1917 |
| Murtha, J. | 275024 | L/Corporal | 21 December 1917 |
| Nixon, G. | | 2nd Lieutenant | 21 December 1917 and 28 December 1918 |
| Smith, T. | 275377 | Sergeant | 25 May 1917 |
| Taylor, E.W.A. | 351393 | Private | 9 July 1919 |
| Thompson, G. | 275049 | Corporal and Sergeant | 24 May 1918 28 December 1918 |
| Tweedle, J. | 2612 | Corporal | 1 January 1916 |

### 2/7th Battalion for North Russia

| | | | |
|---|---|---|---|
| Bezer, H. | 78142 | Pte. A/Sgt | 3 February 1920 |
| Colman, J. | 276342 | Sgt A/CSM | 3 February 1920 |
| Fielding, A.E. | | Lt A/Capt | 3 February 1920 |

| Fillingham, G.S. | | Lt A/Capt | 3 February 1920 |
| Lavie, H.E. | | Lt Colonel | 24 May 1918 |
| | | | and 6 April 1920 |
| | | and Maj T/Lt Col | 21 May 1920 |

In addition to those listed above, the following members of the battalion were also mentioned in despatches while attached to other units:

| Dunn, T. | | 2Lt T/Lt | 28 November 1917 |
| | | att MGC | Salonika |
| Wilson, P.P. | | Maj A/Lt Col | 28 December 1918 |
| | | att 4th West Riding | and 9 July 1919 |
| | | Regt | |

**BELGIUM**
**(CROIX DE GUERRE)**

| Lee, J. | 275514 | Cpl, L/Sgt | 12 July 1918 |

**FRANCE**
**(CROIX DE GUERRE)**

| Wilson, P.P. | | Major | 7 October 1919 |

**(MEDAILLE MILITAIRE)**

| Stoker, J. | 65 | CSM | 24 February 1916 |

**ITALY**
**(BRONZE MEDAL FOR VALOUR)**

| McCormick, J. | 1117 | CSM, A/RSM | 26 May 1917 |

# Appendix One

Members of the 3rd Volunteer Battalion Durham Light Infantry known to have served in the Volunteer Companies during the Boer War:

| Name | Rank | Number | Company |
|------|------|--------|---------|
| Bowman, J.B. | Lieutenant | | 1 |
| Strangeways, E.S. | Captain | | 3 |
| Wilson, P.P. | Lieutenant | | 3 |
| | | | |
| Annandale, W. | Private | 8244 | 1 |
| Armour, J.A. | Private | 8280 | 1 |
| Batty, N. | Private | 8108 | 1 and with 3 Coy |
| Berry, R.W. | Private | 8109 | 1 |
| Bradford, F. | Private | 9297 | 2 |
| Bramley, J. | Private | 8111 | 1 |
| Brine, J.H. | Private | 8233 | 2 |
| Brown, C.M. | Corporal | 8221 | 2 |
| Brown, S.E. | Private | 8112 | 1 |
| Brown, T.A. | Private | 8113 | 1 |
| Bryan, J.E. | Private | 8114 | 1 |
| Colquhoun, J. | Private | 9298 | 2 |
| Colquhoun, M. | Private | 9299 | 2 |
| Colquhoun, R.J. | Private | 9300 | 2 |
| Colquhoun, W. | Private | 9301 | 2 |
| Craven, F. | Private | 8115 | 1 |
| Douglass, M. | Private | 8228 | 2 |
| Ellison, S. | Private | 8117 | 1 |
| Gay, J. W. | Private | 8202 | 2 |
| Grey, L. | Corporal | 8222 | 1 |
| Hepple, M.R. | Pte, L/Cpl | 8226 | 2 |
| Herbert, J.W. | Private | 8118 | 1 |
| Horan, T.H. | Private | 8119 | 1 |
| Horn, F.W. | Private | 8120 | 1 |
| Hunter, C. | Sergeant | 8105 | 1 |
| Jefferson, J.T. | Private | 8121 | 1 |
| Judson, A. | Private | 8245 | 2 |
| Kirkup, G. | Sergeant | 9296 | 2 |
| Lawton, J.R. | Private | 8234 | 2 |
| Lindsay, D. | Private | 8281 | 2 |
| Metcalf, R.E. | Corporal | 8106 | 1 |
| Murray, W. H. | Private | 9303 | 2 |

| | | | |
|---|---|---|---|
| Orr, W. | L/Corporal | 8122 | 1 |
| Pedersen, A. | Private | 8123 | 1 |
| Phillips, T.H. | Private | 8124 | 1 |
| Reas, A.E. | Private | 8125 | 1 |
| Reay, J.M. | Pte, L/Cpl | 8130 | 2 |
| Redpath, J. | Private | 8227 | 2 |
| Rogers, P. | Private | 8107 | 1 |
| Sawyer, J.D. | Private | 8232 | 2 |
| Scott, R. | Private | 8231 | 2 |
| Stainton, R.A.N. | Private | 8126 | 1 |
| Swan, T. | Private | 8229 | 2 |
| Tate, J.G. | Private | 8225 | 1 |
| Tindall, W. | Private | 8224 | 2 |
| Usher, T.W. | Private | 8223 | 2 |
| Willis, J. | Private | 8127 | 1 |

Orr, Alexander, Bugler, 9058
Died of wounds at Preesant Pan Farm, Boshof, Orange River Colony, on 22 July 1901. No medals were issued. He was killed while out foraging for wood with another member of the corps, who escaped.

# Appendix Two

All members of the battalion who landed in France before 31 December 1915 would be entitled to the 1914/15 Star, together with the British War Medal and Victory Medal. However, one of the rarest First World War medals is the Territorial Force War Medal, which was awarded to members of the Territorial Force who were members of a unit on 4 August 1914 or who rejoined before 30 September 1914. To be eligible to receive the award the soldier, or nurse, must have volunteered for overseas service, on or before 30 September 1914, served abroad between 4 August 1914 and midnight 11/12 November 1918 and been ineligible for either the 1914 or 1914/15 Star. Only 33,944 were awarded compared to approximately 2,366,000 1914/15 Stars.

The following is a list of members of the battalion who received the medal taken from the Durham Light Infantry medal rolls. There may be others who served with other formations such as the Machine Gun Corps.

Major Wilson, P.P.
Captain Page, T.A.
Quartermaster & Lieutenant McBeath, W.
Lieutenant Corbett, G.

| | | |
|---|---|---|
| Allan, W. | Private | 1997 |
| Barker, J. | Private | 1884 |
| Croisdale, T.C. | A/RQMS | 275027 |
| Dickinson, E. | Sergeant | 275040 |
| Holborn, H. | Sergeant | 275140 |
| Irwin, J. | CSM | 277512 |
| Johnson, E. | Private | 1174 |
| Logan, J.F. | Private | 2476 |
| McVay, S.P. | CSM | 275015 |
| Norton, E. | Sergeant | 277640 |
| Phillips, J. | Sergeant | 275342 |
| Southern, A. | Private | 2295 |
| Stephenson, W. | Private | 2003 |
| Storey, R. | Sergeant | 275250 |
| Timothy, R. | Private | 204230 |
| Warrener, T. | Private | 375280 |

# Appendix Three

## Battle Honours

| | | | |
|---|---|---|---|
| Gravenstafel | St Julien | Frezenberg | Bellewaarde |
| Ypres 1915 | Flers-Courcelette | Le Transloy | Ancre Heights |
| Somme 1916 | Scarpe 1917 | Passendaele | Ypres 1917 |
| St Quentin | | Rosieres | Somme 1918 |
| Estaires | | | |
| Lys | Aisne 1918 | Arras 1918 | Ypres 1918 |

# Appendix Four

## List of officers of the 7th Durham Light Infantry

| Name | Rank | Casualty | Dates |
|------|------|----------|-------|
| Adamson, R.W. | Second Lieut. | KIA 26/05/1915 | 1914 - 1915 |
| Allan, W.B. | Captain | | 1927 - 1936 |
| Athy, E.B.F. | Second Lieut. | Wounded & POW 27/5/1918 | 1917 - 1921 |
| Ayton, R.G. | Lieut. | Seconded to Royal Engineers | 1916 - 1921 |
| Bailes, J.R. | Second Lieut. | Commissioned from 18 DLI | 1917 - 1921 |
| Bannehr, H.J.T | Lieut. | KIA 5/11/1916 | 1915 - 1916 |
| Barker, A.S. | Second Lieut. | Died 15/09/1917 | 1915 - 1916 |
| Barron, G. | Second Lieut. | | 1918 - 1921 |
| Barry, R.A. | Second Lieut. | | 1918 - 1921 |
| Belfitt, J. | Lieut. | Att. 9 DLI – wounded April 17 | 1915 - 1921 |
| Bell, J.A. | Captain | | 1913 - 1921 |
| Bell, E.W. | Second Lieut. | | 1918 - 1919 |
| Bell, R.H. | Second Lieut. | | 1935 - 1936 |
| Bennett, L. | Captain | POW 27/05/1918 | 1915 - 1920 |
| Beveridge, R.E. | Major | RAMC | 1894 - 1909 |
| Bewley, I. | Captain | KIA 8/10/18 with 13 DLI | 1915 - 1918 |
| Birchall, A.H. | Lieutenant Col. | | 1915 - 1926 |
| Black, K.W. | Captain | | 1927 - 1936 |
| Black, W. | Lieut. | | 1914 - 1919 |
| Blackburn, W.E. | Captain | | 1926 - 1936 |
| Bosuston, G.W. | Lieut. | | 1915 - 1921 |
| Bowker, W.J. | Lieutenant Col. | 2/7 DLI North Russia | 1918 - 1919 |
| Bowman, J.B. | Major | | 1908 - 1921 |
| Bowman, J.H. | Captain | | 1914 - 1921 |
| Bradley, W.A. | Captain | Died 23/12/1919 | 1915 - 1919 |
| Broadley, J. | Captain | | 1914 - 1921 |
| Broadley, J.F. | Lieut. | | 1917 - 1921 |
| Brogden A.T. | Lieut. | Att. MGC | 1915 - 1921 |
| Boutflower, R.S. | Lieut. | | 1917 - 1919 |
| Bowes, A.S. | Captain | | 1914 - 1919 |
| Bowhill, C.F. | Lieut. | | 1915 - 1918 |
| Brotherton, N.J. | Lieut. | | 1915 - 1921 |
| Brown, A.W. | Lieut. | Att. MGC | 1917 - 1919 |
| Brown, J. | Lieut. | | 1916 - 1921 |
| Brown, J.W. | Second Lieut. | | 1919 - 1921 |
| Byers, H.S. | Lieut. | | 1915 - 1919 |
| Byers, T.D. | Captain | | 1915 - 1917 |

| | | | |
|---|---|---|---|
| Campbell, W.L. | Second Lieut. | | 1915 - 1921 |
| Carswell-Hunt, W.D. | Major | Died 5/04/1917 | 1913 - 1917 |
| Carter, S.N. | Lieut. | | 1915 - 1921 |
| Coates, W. | Second Lieut. | | 1909 - 1911 |
| Colling, F. | Second Lieut. | | 1918 - 1921 |
| Cook, A.C. | Second Lieut. | Transferred to RAF | 1915 - 1918 |
| Coppard, A.J. | Lieut. | | 1915 - 1920 |
| Corbett, G. | Second Lieut. | | 1915 - 1921 |
| Cox, R.B. | Second Lieut. | Joined RAF | 1933 - 1935 |
| Cree, A.T.C. | Lieut. | KIA 12/05/1915 | 1914 - 1915 |
| Crosby, W.H. | Second Lieut. | | 1914 - 1918 |
| Dalziel, C.S. | Second Lieut. | KIA 8/01/1917 | 1915 -1917 |
| Darling, H.A. | Lieut. | Att. MGC | 1915 - 1921 |
| Davies, W.H. | Lieut. | Att. 14 DLI | 1915 - 1921 |
| Dawson, W | Lieut. | | 1906 - 1910 |
| Dickinson, A.V. | Lieut. | | 1915 - 1918 |
| Dickson, R. | Major | KIA 27/05/1918 | 1917 - 1918 |
| Ditcham, H.J. | Second Lieut. | Att. 2 DLI | 1917 - 1921 |
| Dixon, A.C. | Second Lieut. | | 1927 - 1936 |
| Dobson, G.D.R. | Major | | 1915 - 1921 |
| Dobson, P. | Second Lieut. | | 1918 - 1921 |
| Dodds, T.E. | Lieut. | | 1917 - 1922 |
| Dove, J.G. | Lieut. | | 1915 - 1921 |
| Drew, W.R. | Lieut. | | 1920 - 1936 |
| Dunlop, W. | Lieut. | | 1915 - 1921 |
| Dunn, T. | Captain | Att. MGC | 1915 - 1921 |
| Eccles, H.A. | Lieut. | RAMC | 1927 - 1936 |
| Ellis, F.R. | Lieut. | | 1915 - 1921 |
| Ellis, R.G. | Captain | Att. MGC | 1915 - 1921 |
| Errington, J. | Captain | KIA 30/08/1915 | 1908 - 1915 |
| Evans, W.J. | Lieutenant Col | | 1896 - 1911 |
| Farrow, A.H. | Major | | 1904 - 1921 |
| Fielding, A.E. | Captain | | 1915 - 1921 |
| Foreman, J.G. | Second Lieut. | | 1922 - 1924 |
| Forrest, W.R. | Second Lieut. | KIA 12/09/1918 | 1918 - 1918 |
| Forster, T.F. | Captain | KIA 31/10/1917 | 1915 - 1918 |
| Foster, L.J. | Lieut. | | 1915 - 1921 |
| Gargett, H.S. | Lieut. | | 1915 - 1921 |
| Gillies, J.N. | Lieut. | | 1916 - 1921 |
| Goodrick, W.R. | Captain | KIA 01/01/1917 | 1915 - 1917 |
| Graham, F. | Lieut. | POW 27/05/1918 | 1915 - 1921 |
| Graham, R.N. | Second Lieut. | | 1911 - 1914 |
| Grayston, A.V. | Lieut. | POW | 1915 - 1921 |
| Green, J.F. | Lieut. | KIA 5/11/1916 Att. 9DLI | 1915 - 1916 |

| | | | |
|---|---|---|---|
| Greenwood, P.M. | Captain | | 1910 - 1921 |
| Grey, J.P.R. | Lieut. | Att. 15 DLI | 1915 - 1920 |
| Grieves, R. | Lieut. | | 1915 - 1919 |
| Grindell, J.F.L. | Captain | KIA 20/06/1917 Att. 22 DLI | 1915 - 1917 |
| Haley, U. | Lieut. | | 1915 - 1919 |
| Hardy, R.T. | Captain | | 1914 - 1921 |
| Harrison, R.B. | Captain | | 1897 - 1907 |
| Heslop, H.L. | Captain | RAMC Died 30/10/1917 | 1910 - 1917 |
| Hines, S.W. | Major | KIA 26/05/1915 | 1897 - 1915 |
| Hodkinson, P. | Second Lieut. | KIA23/10/1918 Att. 15 DLI | 1917 - 1918 |
| Holland, T.C.B. | Lieut. Col | 2/7 DLI | 1919 - 1919 |
| Hope, C.J.P. | Lieut. | | 1931 - 1936 |
| Hopper, B.H. | Lieut. | | 1916 - 1921 |
| Hopper, F.A. | Captain | | 1900 - 1908 |
| Hopper, J. | Lieut. | | 1915 - 1921 |
| Hopson, A.E. | Lieut. | KIA 11/04/1918 Att. 10 DLI | 1916 - 1918 |
| Horan, R. | Lieut. Col | | 1921 - 1936 |
| Hudson, A.T.R. | Captain | KIA 12/04/1918 | 1915 - 1918 |
| Hugall, J.G. | Lieut. | | 1918 - 1921 |
| Hughes, P.B. | Captain | | 1915 - 1921 |
| Hunter, J.A. | Second Lieut. | | 1918 - 1921 |
| Iles, F.J. | Captain | | 1915 - 1921 |
| Iles, R.V. | Captain | | 1915 - 1921 |
| Iliff, J. | Captain | | 1926 - 1936 |
| Jacks, H. | Captain | Died 27/01/1919 | 1910 - 1919 |
| James, R.V. | Lieut. | Seconded to RFC | 1915 - 1917 |
| Johnson, G.M. | Captain | | 1922 - 1933 |
| Johnson, R.S. | Captain | | 1915 - 1921 |
| Johnson, R.H. | Lieut. | | 1021 - 1924 |
| Johnson, C.F. | Lieut. | | 1917 - 1918 |
| Jones, R.A. | Major | KIA 21/05/1916 Att. R War R | 1910 - 1916 |
| Jopling, T.R.S. | Lieut. | | 1930 - 1936 |
| Joseph, H.H. | Captain | | 1911 - 1922 |
| Keates, A.S. | Captain | 2/7 DLI | 1920 - 1921 |
| Keirl, J.H. | Lieut. | | 1915 - 1919 |
| Kirkup, P.A. | Captain | Died 11/04/1917 Att. RFC | 1911 - 1917 |
| Kirkup, R.B. | Second Lieut. | | 1934 - 1936 |
| Knight, J.P. | Lieut. | KIA 26/03/1918 | 1915 - 1918 |
| Liang, L. | Lieut. Col | | 1910 - 1933 |
| Liang, W.F. | Lieut. Col | POW 27/05/1918 | 1915 - 1932 |
| Larkham, S.H.M. | Captain | | 1915 - 1919 |
| Lawson, R. | Lieut. | KIA 27/05/1918 | 1915 - 1918 |
| Lawson, W.T. | Lieut | | 1915 - 1921 |
| Laye, P.A.W. | Major | | 1916 - 1916 |

| | | | |
|---|---|---|---|
| Liebrecht, W.H. | Captain | | 1915 - 1926 |
| Liebrecht, W.E. | Captain | | 1914 - 1919 |
| Little, H.J. | Lieut. | KIA 26/03/1918 | 1915 - 1918 |
| Lloyd, H.P. | Lieut. | | 1911 - 1913 |
| Lockey, J.O. | Lieut. | Att. MGC | 1915 - 1921 |
| Lorraine, J.D. | Lieut. | Att. Ox & Bucks LI & RFC | 1915 - 1918 |
| Low, H.B. | Captain | transferred to RAMC | 1907 - 1915 |
| Lynch, G.E. | Lieut. | KIA 21/03/1918 Att. 7 RIR | 1917 - 1918 |
| Mail, M.E. | Major | | 1908 - 1921 |
| Mair, A.P. | Second Lieut. | | 1935 - 1936 |
| Manley, E.R. | Lieut. | | 1915 - 1921 |
| Marsham, R.B. | Lieut. | | 1918 - 1921 |
| Martyr, E.G.W. | Lieut. | | 1915 - 1921 |
| Massey, J.H.R. | Lieut. | | 1915 - 1921 |
| Meek, J. | Second Lieut. | KIA 24/05/1915 | 1914 - 1915 |
| Moon-Ord, C.D. | Lieut. | DOW 2/12/1916 | 1915 - 1916 |
| Moore, M. | Captain | | 1898 - 1911 |
| Morant, W.M. | Captain | KIA 11/04/1918 | 1914 - 1918 |
| Morris, F.D. | Captain | | 1915 - 1921 |
| Morton-Smith, F. | Captain | | 1921 - 1927 |
| Mullus, A.E. | Lieut. | | 1915 - 1919 |
| McBeath, W. | Captain | | 1915 - 1925 |
| McCann, W.R. | Second Lieut. | DOW 11/10/1916 | 1915 - 1916 |
| McCaughey, C.H. | Lieut. | | 1918 - 1921 |
| McDonald, P. | Second Lieut. | KIA 21/04/1917 | 1917 - 1917 |
| MacIntyre, R.G. | Captain | | 1914 - 1920 |
| MacKinnon, E.A. | Major | | 1914 - 1921 |
| McLeaman, J. | Lieut. | | 1915 - 1921 |
| MacNair, J. | Lieut. | | 1920 - 1921 |
| McNaughton, J.C. | Lieut. | | 1930 - 1936 |
| Nelson, R.D. | Lieut. | | 1927 - 1932 |
| Nesbitt, F.W.R. | Lieut. | Died 19/04/1918 | 1915 - 1918 |
| Nesbitt, T.T. | Second Lieut. | | 1911 - 1911 |
| Nichol, J.M. | Major | Trans to RAMC | 1908 - 1915 |
| Nicholson, E.T. | Major | | 1914 - 1919 |
| Nixon, G. | Lieut. | | 1916 - 1921 |
| Noall, A. | Lieut. | Att. MGC | 1914 - 1921 |
| Noble, A.R.B. | Lieut. | Att. 2/5 Lancashire Fusiliers | 1917 - 1921 |
| Norman, C.C. | Lieut. Col | | 1918 - 1918 |
| Page, T.A. | Major | | 1910 - 1921 |
| Pallister, J.L. | Second Lieut. | | 1915 - 1916 |
| Parker, R.W.W. | Captain | | 1920 - 1922 |
| Parkin, A. | Lieut. | | 1915 - 1919 |
| Peckston, J.G. | Major | | 1918 - 1936 |

| | | | |
|---|---|---|---|
| Pickersgill, C. | Captain | | 1914 - 1921 |
| Polge, A.H. | Lieut. | | 1915 - 1921 |
| Potts, A.L.L. | Second Lieut. | KIA 5/11/1916 Att. 9DLI | 1915 - 1916 |
| Preistly, W. | Major | | 1904 - 1921 |
| Prest, A.M.G. | Second Lieut. | | 1914 - 1915 |
| Price, A.T. | Lieut. | Trans to 12 & 15 DLI | 1915 - 1915 |
| Probert, S. | Lieut. | KIA 27/05/1918 | 1914 - 1918 |
| Rabett, H.W. | Lieut. | | 1918 - 1921 |
| Rambaut, B.S.R. | Second Lieut. | | 1936 - 1936 |
| Raynes, L. | Captain | | 1915 - 1924 |
| Redhead, S. | Major | | 1914 - 1921 |
| Rhodes, A. | Second Lieut. | KIA 24/05/1915 | 1914 - 1915 |
| Richardson, C.S. | Lieut. | | 1915 - 1918 |
| Riddles, E.P. | Lieut. | Att. MGC | 1915 - 1921 |
| Ridoutt, W.A. | Lieut. | KIA 31/10/1917 | 1915 - 1917 |
| Ritson, F.S. | Lieut. | | 1933 - 1936 |
| Ritson, G.S.F. | Captain | | 1925 - 1934 |
| Robson, G.L. | Lieut. | | 1924 - 1931 |
| Rowstron, N.S. | Lieut. | | 1921 - 1930 |
| Rushworth, T. | Captain | Att. 6 DLI | 1915 - 1921 |
| Russell, S.D. | Lieut. | | 1933 - 1936 |
| Rutledge, J.H. | Lieut. | Att. MGC | 1915 - 1919 |
| Rudge, G.P. | Lieut. | | 1915 - 1919 |
| Salmon, H.E. | Second Lieut. | | 1914 - 1915 |
| Sanderson, W.S. | Captain | | 1914 - 1921 |
| Sayer, C.O. | Lieut. | DOW 7/06/1915 | 1913 - 1915 |
| Schaffer, P.P. | Captain | | 1914 - 1921 |
| Scott, J.E. | Captain | KIA 27/05/1918 | 1915 - 1918 |
| Scott, T.C. | Captain | | 1916 - 1921 |
| Shepherd, L.G. | Captain | | 1916 - 1936 |
| Shepherd, N.R. | Captain | KIA 4/11/1916 | 1915 - 1916 |
| Shield, J.W. | Lieut. | | 1915 - 1921 |
| Short, L.H. | Lieut. | Trans to RFC | 1915 - 1917 |
| Smith, C.F. | Major | | 1915 - 1917 |
| Smith, C.W. | Lieut. | | 1915 - 1921 |
| Smith, J.D. | Lieut. | | 1915 - 1918 |
| Smith, L.F. | Lieut. | | 1915 - 1921 |
| Spain, J. | Lieut. Col | | 1898 - 1921 |
| Squance, A.H.P. | Lieut. | | 1904 - 1911 |
| Squance, T.C. | Major | | 1917 - 1936 |
| Steel, A.K. | Second Lieut. | | 1936 - 1936 |
| Stewart, H. | Captain | | 1915 - 1921 |
| Stockdale, A.W.S. | Second Lieut. | KIA 24/05/1915 | 1914 - 1915 |
| Storey, J. | Lieut. | | 1927 - 1936 |

| | | | |
|---|---|---|---|
| Storey, M. | Major | | 1907 - 1921 |
| Strangeways, E.S. | Major | | 1895 - 1911 |
| Strother, L. | Captain | | 1922 - 1934 |
| Sutcliffe, T.F. | Captain | | 1909 - 1916 |
| Sutton, W. | Captain | Att. Tank Corps | 1915 - 1921 |
| Swan, R.A. | Lieut. Col | 2/7 DLI | 1918 - 1919 |
| Tait, J. | Captain | KIA 16/06/1917 | 1915 - 1917 |
| Taylor, K.W. | Lieut. | | 1915 - 1921 |
| Taylor, W.K. | Captain | Att. 2 DLI | 1914 - 1921 |
| Tetley, J.C. | Lieut. | | 1915 - 1918 |
| Thomas, F.J. | Captain | | 1914 - 1925 |
| Thompson, A.R. | Lieut. | | 1908 - 1911 |
| Thompson, G.F. | Second Lieut. | | 1916 - 1917 |
| Thompson, H. | Captain | KIA 28/03/1918 | 1915 - 1918 |
| Thompson, J.L. | Lieut. | | 1908 - 1909 |
| Thompson, L.A. | Captain | | 1914 - 1921 |
| Thompson, S.W. | Second Lieut. | | 1914 - 1914 |
| Thornton, W.T. | Lieut. | | 1917 - 1921 |
| Tilbrook, F.C. | Lieut. | DOW 10/04/1918 | 1915 - 1918 |
| Tindle, K. | Second Lieut. | KIA 26/03/1918 | 1917 - 1918 |
| Troughton, E.R. | Captain | | 1915 - 1921 |
| Troup, E. | Lieut. | Transferred to 6 DLI | 1920 -1924 |
| Tully, J.S. | Lieut. | | 1917 - 1922 |
| Turnbull, R.J. | Second Lieut. | | 1918 - 1920 |
| Turner, W.H. | Lieut. | | 1921 - 1923 |
| Turner, W.H.T. | Lieut. | | 1918 - 1921 |
| Vaux, E. | Lieut. Col | | 1910 - 1922 |
| Walker, P. | Lieut. | | 1916 - 1921 |
| Walker, S. | Second Lieut. | KIA 15/08/1917 | 1915 - 1917 |
| Waller, G.S. | Second Lieut. | | 1905 - 1911 |
| Walton, H. | Lieut. | | 1915 - 1921 |
| Wardlaw, J. | Lieut. | | 1915 - 1921 |
| Wardle, J.P. | Major | | 1908 - 1921 |
| Wawn, F.M. | Captain | KIA 25/05/1915 | 1899 - 1915 |
| Webb, H. | Lieut. | | 1915 - 1919 |
| Welch, T.R. | Lieut. | | 1916 - 1921 |
| Welsh, E.A. | Lieut. | | 1914 - 1921 |
| Wild, J. | Lieut. | | 1920 - 1921 |
| Willcox, T.H. | Captain | | 1921 - 1932 |
| Williamson, A.R. | Captain | | 1910 - 1921 |
| Wilson, C.W. | Major | | 1917 - 1931 |
| Wilson, D. | Lieut. | | 1915 - 1921 |
| Wilson, E. | Second Lieut. | KIA 26/03/1918 | 1916 - 1918 |
| Wilson, P.P. | Major | | 1900 - 1921 |

| | | | |
|---|---|---|---|
| Windle, M.B. | Lieut. | Att. 8 Liverpool Regiment | 1918 - 1921 |
| Winterschladen, J.C. | Second Lieut. | | 1936 - 1936 |
| Wishart, A.E. | Captain | | 1914 - 1919 |
| Wood, H.H. | Captain | | 1910 - 1921 |
| Wood, J.R.W. | Captain | | 1914 - 1921 |
| Yeaman, C.H. | Second Lieut. | Died 15/09/1916 | 1916 - 1916 |
| Zacharias-Jessel, V.A.V | Lieut. | KIA 6/04/1917 Att. 15 DLI | 1915 - 1917 |

## Abbreviations

| | |
|---|---|
| Att | Attached |
| DLI | Durham Light Infantry |
| DOW | Died of Wounds |
| KIA | Killed in Action |
| MGC | Machine Gun Corps |
| Ox & Bucks L.I. | Oxfordshire & Buckinghamshire Light Infantry |
| POW | Prisoner of War |
| RAF | Royal Air Force |
| RAMC | Royal Army Medical Corps |
| RFC | Royal Flying Corps |
| RIR | Royal Irish Regiment |
| R. War. R. | Royal Warwickshire Regiment |

# Appendix Five

## Other ranks who landed with the battalion in April 1915

This list is as near complete as is possible to make. I apologise for any omissions which may have been caused by the individual soldier changing regiments or corps.

| Name | Rank | Number | TF Number | Died | Buried | Remarks |
|------|------|--------|-----------|------|--------|---------|
| Abbott M. | Cpl. | 1976 | 275240 | | | Disembodied |
| Adams D. | Pte. | 2714 | 320062 | 31/05/18 | | KIA with 6DLI |
| Adamson R. W. | | 601 | | 26/05/15 | Menin Gate | Discharged to Commission |
| Adcock R. | Pte. | 2456 | | | | Disembodied |
| Adey W. | Pte. | 2574 | 275500 | | | Disembodied |
| Airey C. | Sgt. | 1507 | 277368 | 04/05/18 | Leuze Communal Cem. Belgium | |
| Aiston M. | Pte. | 2532 | | 16/10/15 | Cite Bonjean Military Cem. France | |
| Aitchison J.J. | Pte. | 2281 | 275367 | | | Disembodied |
| Alcock J. | Pte. | 1910 | | 04/03/19 | Sunderland (Ryhope Road) Cem. | |
| Alderson E. | Pte. | 1642 | 350787 | 11/04/18 | Ploegsteert Memorial | KIA with W.Yorks |
| Aldridge J. | Pte. | 1823 | 275182 | 24/03/18 | Pozieres Memorial | |
| Allan J. | Bandsman | 440 | | | | Trans to Royal Engineers |
| Allan W. | Pte. | 2438 | 300147 | | | |
| Allen A. | Pte. | 1987 | 350373 | 24/05/15 | Menin Gate | |
| Anderson D. | Pte. | 2865 | | | | |
| Anderson J. | Sgt. | 243 | | | | |
| Anderson J. | Pte. | 2507 | | | | Discharged |
| Angus R. | Pte. | 2195 | 275338 | | | Discharged |
| Archbold J. | Pte. | 2366 | | | | Disembodied |
| Archer R. | Pte. | 2138 | 275305 | 26/05/15 | Menin Gate | Trans to Royal Engineers |
| Armstrong G. | Pte. | 2345 | 275391 | | | Discharged |
| Armstrong J. | L/Cpl. | 1518 | | | | Disembodied |
| Armstrong W. | Pte. | 1355 | | | | Discharged |
|  |  |  |  |  |  | Discharged |

| Name | Rank | No. | No. | Date | Memorial / Cemetery | Fate |
|---|---|---|---|---|---|---|
| Atkinson G.H. | Pte. | 675 | | | | Discharged |
| Atkinson J. | Pte. | 1887 | 275204 | | | Trans to RAF |
| Atkinson J.A. | Pte. | 2408 | 275423 | | | Discharged |
| Atlay T.A. | CQMS | 844 | 275029 | | | Discharged to Commission |
| Austin R. | Pte. | 667 | | | | Discharged |
| Austin S. | Pte. | 2369 | 275403 | | | |
| Baharie J.G. | Pte. | 2482 | | 26/05/15 | Menin Gate | |
| Bailey J. | Pte. | 2280 | | 15/05/15 | Menin Gate | |
| Bailey T.W. | Pte. | 1573 | | | | Discharged |
| Bainbridge D. | Pte. | 2024 | 275261 | | | Disembodied |
| Ball R. | Pte. | 3245 | | 16/05/15 | Menin Gate | |
| Bamlett J.H. | Cpl. | 2761 | 350320 | | | Discharged |
| Bannister J.H. | Pte. | 2560 | 275494 | | | Discharged |
| Barclay L.T. | Pte. | 2501 | | | | Class Z Reserve |
| Barker A.S. | Pte. | 3528 | | | | Discharged |
| Barker W. | Pte. | 3824 | 276061 | 13/04/18 | Ploegsteert Memorial | |
| Barkes T. | Pte. | 1783 | 275164 | | | |
| Barnes R. | Sgt. | 311 | | | | Discharged |
| Barrass J. | Pte. | 2920 | | 31/08/15 | Chapelle-D'-Armentieres Old Military Cem. | |
| Barrow T. | Pte. | 2034 | 275264 | | | Class Z Reserve |
| Barry R.H. | Cpl. | 1524 | 275073 | | | Disembodied |
| Batchelor G. | Pte. | 2732 | | | | Discharged |
| Baxter F.W. | Cpl. | 2804 | 275601 | | | Disembodied |
| Bayliss W.T. | Pte. | 2746 | 275567 | | | |
| Beattie J. | Pte. | 1901 | 202543 | | | Disembodied |
| Beck T. | Pte. | 1787 | 275167 | | | Disembodied |
| Begg W. | Cpl. | 1249 | 275048 | | | Disembodied |
| Bell A. | Pte. | 2122 | 275299 | | | Disembodied |
| Bell A. | Pte. | 2452 | | | | Discharged |
| Bell E. | Sgt. | 1056 | | 26/05/15 | Menin Gate | |
| Bell F. | Pte. | 2550 | | 26/05/15 | Menin Gate | |
| Bell J.T. | Pte. | 2858 | | 26/05/15 | Menin Gate | |
| Bell L. | Pte. | 2653 | 275523 | | | Disembodied |
| Bell T. | Pte. | 1224 | 350313 | | | Discharged |
| Bellairs J.H. | Pte. | 2690 | 275542 | 26/10/18 | Niederzwehren Cem. | |

| Name | Rank | Regt. No. | Service No. | Date | Cemetery/Memorial | Fate |
|---|---|---|---|---|---|---|
| Bellas G. | Cpl. | 2705 | 295039 | | | Disembodied |
| Belton E. | Sgt. | 7122 | 277308 | 27/05/18 | Germany Soissons Memorial | |
| Benison F. | Pte. | 2996 | 275697 | | | Disembodied |
| Benison J.W. | Pte. | 2995 | | 21/09/16 | Bazentin-Le-Petit Communal Cem. Ext. | |
| Berston R. | Pte. | 2091 | | | | Discharged |
| Bisset J. | Pte. | 2906 | 275651 | | | Disembodied |
| Bittlestone L.A. | Sgt. | 2543 | 275483 | 05/10/18 | Sunderland (Bishopwearmouth) Cem. | |
| Black D. | Pte. | 2371 | | | | Disembodied |
| Blair-Allen F. | Pte. | 2678 | 275404 | 24/05/15 | Menin Gate | |
| Blanchflower J.M. | Pte. | 2637 | | | | Discharged |
| Blenkinsop H. | RQMS | 445 | 275022 | | | Discharged to Commission |
| Bolam J.G. | Pte. | 7107 | 277293 | 23/06/17 | St. Martin Calvaire British Cem. France | |
| Bond T. | Pte. | 3127 | | | | Discharged |
| Bond T.H. | Pte. | 1759 | 275774 | 02/05/15 | Menin Gate | |
| Booth F.W. | Pte. | 2780 | 275584 | 05/11/17 | Poelcapelle | Killed with 9DLI |
| Borthwick D.N. | Sgt. | 2276 | 275366 | | | Disembodied |
| Bourne J. | Pte. | 1313 | | | | Discharged |
| Boutflower R. | Sgt. | 1510 | 275069 | | | Discharged to Commission |
| Bowles T.F. | Pte. | 2316 | 275382 | | | Disembodied |
| Bowman J.M. | Pte. | 2652 | 275522 | | | Disembodied |
| Bowman W.H. | Pte. | 2760 | 275575 | | | Disembodied |
| Boyling C.H. | Pte. | 2378 | | | | Discharged |
| Bradley J.E. | Pte. | 1611 | | | | Discharged |
| Brady R.H. | Pte. | 2942 | | | | Discharged |
| Brashier W. | Pte. | 2436 | | 18/05/15 | Boulogne Eastern Cem. France | |
| Brennan G. | Pte. | 2597 | | | | Discharged |
| Brennan R.H. | Pte. | 2410 | 275425 | | | Disembodied |
| Bridgewood G. | Sgt. | 2917 | 275655 | | | Disembodied |
| Broadhurst W.H. | Pte. | 3061 | | | | Disembodied |
| Brockbanks H.S. | Pte. | 2358 | | | | Disembodied |
| Brodie G.W. | Pte. | 2044 | 275266 | 26/05/15 | Menin Gate | |

| Name | Rank | No. | No. | Date | Cemetery / Memorial | Fate |
|---|---|---|---|---|---|---|
| Brotherston R.T. | Pte. | 2605 | | 06/05/15 | Boulogne Eastern Cem. France | |
| Brow G. | Cpl. | 2238 | | 05/05/15 | Bailleul Communal Cem. Ext. France | |
| Brown A.W. | Pte. | 2469 | 275450 | | | Discharged |
| Brown B. | Pte. | 2656 | | 26/05/15 | Menin Gate | |
| Brown F | Pte. | 2297 | | | | Discharged |
| Brown F. | Pte. | 2757 | 275419 | | | Transferred to RAF |
| Brown G. | Pte. | 2403 | | | | Disembodied |
| Brown J.A. | Pte. | | 275176 | | | Disembodied |
| Brown J.T. | Cpl. | 2756 | | | | Trans to Glos. Regt |
| Brown J.W. | Pte. | 1536 | | 24/05/15 | Perth Cem. Belgium | |
| Brown R. | Pte. | 690 | | | | Discharged |
| Brown R.H. | Pte. | 2460 | 205360 | | | Discharged |
| Brown W. | Pte. | 2564 | 275671 | | | Discharged |
| Brown W. | Pte. | 2616 | | 26/05/15 | Menin Gate. | |
| Brown W. | Pte. | 2952 | | 19/06/15 | Bailleul Communal Cem. Ext. France | |
| Brown W.H. | CQMS | 288 | | | | Disembodied |
| Bruce A. | Sgt. | 2350 | | 07/07/16 | La Laiterie Military Cem. Belgium | |
| Bryan T. | Pte. | 2912 | | | | Discharged |
| Bryant A. | Pte. | 1992 | 275248 | | | Disembodied |
| Brydon T. | Pte. | 2528 | | | | Class Z Reserve |
| Burke P. | Pte. | 2500 | 103086 | | | Transferred to Labour Corps |
| Burn A. | Pte. | 2430 | | | | Discharged |
| Burn W. | Pte. | 2422 | | 10/06/15 | Menin Gate. | |
| Burns A. | Pte. | 2700 | 275549 | | | Discharged |
| Burnside J. | Pte. | 1369 | | | | Discharged |
| Burnside J. | Pte. | 1775 | | | | Discharged |
| Byers M.J. | Cpl. | 836 | | | | |
| Cadas N. | Pte. | 2908 | 275652 | | | Disembodied |
| Caine J.W. | Pte. | 1529 | 275076 | | | Disembodied |
| Calvert R. | Pte. | 2380 | | | | |
| Campbell E. | Pte. | 1635 | 275114 | | | Disembodied |
| Campbell G.A. | Sgt. | 1755 | | 05/11/16 | Warlencourt British Cem. | |

| Name | Rank | No. | No. | Date | Location | Status |
|---|---|---|---|---|---|---|
| Campbell J.W. | Sgt. | 1798 | 275169 | | | Disembodied |
| Campbell W.H. | Pte. | 2120 | 275298 | | | Discharged |
| Carden D. | Pte. | 2809 | | | | Disembodied |
| Carmichael A. | Pte. | 2395 | 327114 | | | |
| Carpenter J.E. | Pte. | 1890 | | | | |
| Carr J.E. | Pte. | 3032 | 275718 | | | Disembodied |
| Carr J.F. | Pte | 1701 | | 12/07/17 | Vis-en-Artois British Cemetery | KIA with 11 Sqd. RFC |
| Carr R. | Sgt. | 1097 | 275036 | 21/04/17 | Hibers Trench Cem. France | |
| Carroll J.T. | Pte. | 1622 | 275111 | | | Disembodied |
| Carter E.P. | Pte. | 2459 | 277315 | | | Class Z Reserve |
| Carter F. | Sgt. | 2611 | 275506 | | | Discharged to Commission |
| Carter W.K. | Pte. | 2663 | 275529 | | | Disembodied |
| Cassels G. | Pte. | 1830 | 275185 | | | Discharged |
| Cassidy E. | Pte. | 2535 | | 22/06/15 | Bailleul Communal Cem. Ext. France | |
| Chambers C.V. | L/Cpl. | 2662 | 275528 | 03/02/19 | Les Baraques Mil. Cem. Sangatte | |
| Chapman G. | Pte. | 1816 | 275180 | | | Disembodied |
| Charlton E. | Pte. | 1221 | 275042 | | | Disembodied |
| Charlton W. | L/Cpl. | 2254 | | | | |
| Cheal J. | Pte. | 2115 | 275297 | 24/05/15 | Menin Gate. | Disembodied |
| Cheal J.W. | Pte. | 2093 | | | | Discharged |
| Christian C. | Pte. | 1993 | 275249 | 17/08/18 | Sunderland (Bishopwearmouth) Cem. | |
| Clark J.W. | Pte. | 2132 | 275303 | | | Discharged |
| Clark R. | Pte. | 3145 | | 26/05/15 | Menin Gate. | Disembodied |
| Clark W.B. | CSM | 296 | 204048 | | | Discharged |
| Clarke W.E. | Pte. | 1663 | | | | Discharged |
| Claxton J.H. | Pte. | 2837 | 275622 | | | Disembodied |
| Clough J. | L/Cpl. | 2793 | 203456 | 30/10/17 | Boulogne Eastern Cem. | DOW with 5DLI |
| Coates A. | Pte. | 2775 | | | | Discharged |
| Coates J. | Cpl. | 2461 | | | | Disembodied |
| Cockburn F. | Bugler | 1225 | 275448 | | | Discharged |

| Name | Rank | Number | Renumber | Date | Location | Notes |
|---|---|---|---|---|---|---|
| Cogden G. | L/Cpl. | 2740 | 251903 | | | Discharged to Commission |
| Cohen T.M. | Pte. | 2598 | 275504 | | | Disembodied |
| Coleman T. | CSM | 2416 | 275428 | 11/04/18 | Ploegsteert Memorial Belgium | |
| Colling W. | Sgt. | 2418 | 275430 | | | Disembodied |
| Collingwood N.M. | Sgt. | 1428 | 275060 | | | Discharged |
| Collins G.W. | Pte. | 1583 | | 26/05/15 | Menin Gate | |
| Collins J.B.A. | Pte. | 2546 | 275486 | | | Disembodied |
| Collins N. | Pte. | 1492 | 275065 | | | Discharged |
| Colman J.G. | Pte. | 3031 | | | | Transferred to Labour Corps |
| Colquhoun J.W. | Pte. | 1802 | | 26/05/15 | Menin Gate | |
| Cook J.E. | Pte. | 2642 | | 26/05/15 | Menin Gate | |
| Cook M. | L/Cpl. | 2688 | 275540 | | | Discharged |
| Cooney H. | Pte. | 2228 | 275350 | 13/04/18 | Ploegsteert Memorial Belgium | |
| Cooney N. | Pte. | 2427 | | 27/03/16 | Lijssenthoek Military Cem. Belgium | |
| Cooper G. | Pte. | 3357 | 275884 | | | Disembodied |
| Cooper T.G. | Pte. | 3374 | | | | Class Z Reserve |
| Coppin J. | Cpl. | 2015 | 43449 | | | Class Z Reserve |
| Corder A. | Pte. | 2584 | | 26/05/15 | Boulogne Eastern Cem. France | |
| Cornish W.H. | Pte. | 1387 | | | | Transferred to Labour Corps |
| Cororan J. | Pte. | 2823 | | | | |
| Costigan P. | Pte. | 363 | | 27/05/15 | Longuenesse (St Omer) Souvenir Cem. | |
| Coulson T. | Pte. | 1314 | | | | Discharged |
| Coulthard W. | L/Cpl. | 2676 | | | | Transferred to RFC |
| Coupland G. | L/Cpl. | 2308 | | | | Disembodied |
| Coupland J.B. | Pte. | 2310 | 275379 | | | Discharged |
| Coupland T.N. | Pte. | 1634 | | | | Transferred to HLI |
| Coupland W. | Sgt. | 2275 | 275365 | | | Disembodied |
| Cowey J. | Pte. | 2627 | 350725 | | | Discharged |
| Cowie J.M. | L/Cpl. | 791 | | | | Discharged |
| Cowley R. | Pte. | 317 | | | | Discharged |
| Cox S.R. | Cpl. | 1354 | | 26/05/15 | Menin Gate | |

| Name | Rank | No. | No. | Date | Cemetery/Memorial | Fate |
|---|---|---|---|---|---|---|
| Coxon J. | Cpl. | 1595 | | 15/09/16 | Contalmaison Chateau Cem. France | Re-enlisted in RNR |
| Crabbe D. | Pte. | 2522 | | | | Discharged |
| Craig J.D. | Drummer | 1346 | | | | |
| Cranmer J.W. | Pte. | 1774 | 275159 | 07/11/18 | Terlincthun British Cem. France | |
| Crathorne R. | Pte. | 2232 | 275352 | 13/04/18 | Ploegsteert Memorial Belgium | |
| Crinson G. | Sgt. | 2214 | 275343 | | | Disembodied |
| Crosby S. | Sgt. | 2926 | 275658 | | | Disembodied |
| Cruickshanks J.W. | Pte. | 2412 | 275426 | | | Discharged |
| Crute A. | Pte. | 2357 | 275398 | | | Discharged to Commission |
| Cunningham C.S. | Sgt. | 2651 | 275521 | 28/10/16 | Thiepval Memorial | |
| Cunningham J. | Sgt. | 2718 | 275558 | 13/04/18 | Le Grand Hasard Military Cem. France | |
| Currell R.H. | Pte. | 3174 | | | | Discharged |
| Currie J.E. | Pte. | 2258 | | | | Disembodied |
| Curry J. | Cpl. | 2699 | | | | Class Z Reserve |
| Curry J.D. | Sgt. | 2293 | 275360 | | | Discharged |
| Curry T.W. | Pte. | 2759 | 275372 | | | Discharged |
| Curtis M.C. | Pte. | 2824 | 275614 | | | Disembodied |
| Dale E. | Pte. | 1614 | 275108 | | | Discharged |
| Dammery J. | Pte. | 2324 | 277354 | | | Discharged |
| Davey A. | Sgt. | 2566 | | 14/11/16 | Thiepval Memorial | |
| Davie G. | Pte. | 2798 | 275596 | | | Disembodied |
| Davis C. | Pte. | 783 | | | | Discharged |
| Davis T. | Pte. | 2164 | | 08/01/16 | Longuenesse (St Omer) Souvenir Cem. | |
| Davison A. | Pte. | 3152 | 275787 | | | Disembodied |
| Davison G.W. | Pte. | 1761 | | | | Transferred to RAF |
| Davison R.L. | Pte. | 2222 | 275348 | | | Discharged to Commission |
| Dawson J. | Pte. | 2303 | | 29/06/15 | Lindenhoek Chalet Military Cem. | |
| Dawson N. | Cpl. | 1754 | 275154 | | | Disembodied |
| Day J. | Cpl. | 1840 | 275189 | | | Disembodied |
| Deacon T. | Pte. | 2684 | | | | Disembodied |

| Name | Rank | | | Date | Cemetery / Memorial | Fate |
|---|---|---|---|---|---|---|
| Deacon W. | Pte. | 2745 | | | | Discharged |
| Deans J. | Pte. | 2904 | | | | Disembodied |
| Dearden W. | Pte. | 1652 | 275650 | | | Disembobied |
| Dennis C. | Pte. | 1129 | | 25/07/15 | La Chapelle D'Armentieres Communal Cem. | |
| Dent J. | Sgt. | 355 | 204824 | | | Discharged |
| Dent T. | Pte. | 2184 | 275328 | | | Disembodied |
| Devine F. | Pte. | 3249 | 275830 | | | Discharged |
| Dewhurst L. | Cpl. | 2638 | 204825 | | | Discharged |
| Dickens A. | Pte. | 2251 | | | | Trans to KOSB |
| Dickinson J.G. | Pte. | 2801 | 275599 | | | Disembodied |
| Divers T. | Pte. | 2979 | | | | Disembodied |
| Divers W.H. | Pte. | 2893 | | | | Disembodied |
| Dixon R. | Pte. | 1487 | 275064 | | | Disembodied |
| Dixon T. | Sgt. | 250 | 275012 | | | Disembodied |
| Dobson G.D.R. | Sgt. | 2671 | | | | Discharged to Commission |
| Dobson W.G. | Pte. | 2742 | | | | Discharged |
| Docherty J. | Pte. | 2937 | | | | Disembodied |
| Docherty W. | Pte. | 1861 | 275197 | 24/05/15 | Menin Gate | |
| Dodds G. | Pte. | 3086 | | 10/06/15 | Harlebeke New British Cem. Belgium | |
| Dodds J. | Cpl. | 2457 | 275446 | | | Disembodied |
| Dodds V. | L/Sgt. | 1482 | | 17/06/15 | Southend-On-Sea (Sutton Road) Cem. | |
| Dodds W.G. | Pte. | 2477 | 275455 | | | Disembodied |
| Donald J | Pte. | 2938 | | | | Discharged |
| Donaldson H. | Cpl. | 2279 | 350455 | | | Class Z Reserve |
| Donkin C. | Pte. | 2189 | 275333 | 26/03/18 | Pozieres Memorial | |
| Donnelly G. | Pte. | 3078 | 275747 | | | Disembodied |
| Donohue L. | Pte. | 3278 | 351693 | | | Disembodied |
| Dorrian D.N. | Pte. | 2542 | 275482 | | | Discharged |
| Douglas G. | Pte. | 2677 | | | | Trans to NF |
| Douglas S. | Pte. | 1957 | 275231 | | | Disembodied |
| Douglass W. | Pte. | 2806 | 275603 | | | Discharged |
| Dowd P. | Pte. | 1899 | | 15/05/15 | Menin Gate | |
| Down J. | Sgt. | 2141 | 275306 | 13/02/18 | Nine Elms British Cem | |

| Name | Rank | Number | Number | Date | Commemoration / Cemetery | Remarks |
|---|---|---|---|---|---|---|
| Drakesmith H. | Pte. | 3010 | | 26/05/15 | Belgium Menin Gate | |
| Drew J. | Pte. | 1793 | | | | Discharged |
| Drummond A. | Pte. | 1344 | | | | |
| Dryden J.H. | L/Cpl. | 2390 | 275432 | 07/06/15 | Boldon Cem. | Discharged |
| Duke G.H. | L/Cpl. | 2423 | 275093 | | | |
| Duncan W. | Cpl. | 1567 | | | | Class Z Reserve |
| Duncan W.B. | Pte. | 1501 | 275161 | 21/07/15 | South Shields (Harton) Cem. | |
| Dundas T. | Pte. | 1780 | | | | Disembodied |
| Dunlop W. | WO11 | 3 | | | | Discharged to Commission |
| Dunn G.J. | Pte. | 2259 | 275361 | | | Discharged |
| Dunn R.P.B. | Pte. | 2984 | 275691 | | | Transferred to Labour Corps |
| Dunn W. | Pte. | 2730 | | 29/06/15 | Bailleul Communal Cem. Ext. France | |
| Dunnigham J.M. | Pte. | 1791 | | | | Discharged |
| Dunning C. | Pte. | 2023 | | 26/05/15 | Menin Gate | |
| Dunville C. | Pte. | 3228 | 350726 | | | Discharged |
| Dwerryhouse J.E. | Pte. | 2710 | | 28/03/16 | Spoilbank Cem. Belgium | |
| Dykes J. | Pte. | 2658 | 275525 | | | Discharged |
| Eccles J.E. | Sgt. | 1961 | | | | Discharged to Commission |
| Edgar A. | Pte. | 2766 | | | | Discharged |
| Edmunds A. | Pte. | 2382 | 275410 | | | Disembodied |
| Edmundson M. | Pte. | 2409 | 275424 | | | Disembodied |
| Edmundson T.T. | Pte. | 2648 | | 26/04/15 | Menin Gate | |
| Edwards D. | Pte. | 2498 | 275462 | 25/05/15 | Bailleul Communal Cem. Ext. France | Discharged |
| Edwards J.W. | Pte. | 2035 | | 25/05/15 | Menin Gate | |
| Eggleston W. | Pte. | 3151 | | | | Disembodied |
| Elliott C. | Pte. | 3140 | 275780 | | | Discharged |
| Elliott D.L. | Pte. | 2752 | | | | |
| Elliott J.W. | Pte. | 2973 | | 27/08/15 | Chapelle-D'-Armentieres Old Military Cem. | |
| Elliott W. | L/Sgt. | 1540 | 275081 | | | Disembodied |
| Elliott W. | Pte. | 3134 | 350316 | | | Class Z Reserve |
| Elvin S.W. | Pte. | 2629 | | | | Tranfereed to RAF |
| Emerson J.C. | Pte. | 2552 | | | | Discharged |

| Name | Rank | Number | Number | Date | Place | Status |
|---|---|---|---|---|---|---|
| Emmerson E. | Pte. | 1655 | 275123 | | | Discharged |
| Emmerson J.G. | Pte. | 3115 | 275766 | | | Discharged |
| Emmerson W. | Pte. | 2769 | | 05/11/16 | Warlencourt British Cem. France | |
| Emms G. | Bugler | 2094 | | | | |
| Evans J. | Sgt. | 2338 | | 26/04/15 | Menin Gate | |
| Fairley J.L. | Pte. | 2233 | | | | Discharged |
| Fairweather R.R. | Pte. | 2489 | 275353 | | | Discharged |
| Falkous J. | Pte. | 2102 | | 16/05/15 | | Discharged |
| Faller H.E. | Cpl. | 1145 | 275784 | | Menin Gate | |
| Fathers G. | Pte. | 3146 | | 24/05/15 | Menin Gate | Disembodied |
| Fawcett B. | Pte. | 2744 | | 24/05/15 | Sanctuary Wood Cemetery Belgium | |
| Fenton E.S.L. | Pte. | 2127 | | 16/06/15 | | |
| Finnigan J. | Pte. | 2776 | 245046 | | | Discharged |
| Fletcher J.G. | Sgt. | 910 | | | | Transferred to RAF |
| Flynn C. | Pte. | 2153 | 275311 | | | Discharged |
| Flynn F. | Pte. | 2515 | 350319 | | | Discharged |
| Forbes J. | Pte. | 1386 | | | | Discharged |
| Ford J.W. | Pte | 2727 | 203454 | | | Disembodied |
| Ford R.W. | Pte | 3128 | 205235 | | | Transferred to Labour Corps |
| Foreman J.E. | Pte. | 1671 | 203443 | | | Discharged |
| Fothergill J.E. | Pte. | 1530 | 275077 | | | Disembodied |
| Fox T.W. | Pte. | 2066 | | 26/05/15 | Menin Gate | |
| Fraser A. | L/Cpl. | 2372 | | 26/05/15 | Menin Gate | |
| Fryer J. | Pte. | 1900 | | | | Discharged |
| Galbraith R. | L/Cpl. | 2755 | 275572 | 06/11/17 | Cement House, Belgium. | Discharged |
| Gallagher J. | CSM | 1736 | | | | Discharged |
| Gardner W. | Pte. | 2803 | | | | Tran to Manchester Regt |
| Gartland J. | Pte. | 432 | 5/8416 | | | Discharged |
| Garvey F. | Pte. | 1927 | 275220 | 21/09/16 | Bazentin-Le-Petit Communal Cem. Ext. | Disembodied |
| Gaughan J. | L/Cpl. | 1590 | | | | |
| Gedling T.A. | Pte. | 2639 | 275517 | | | Disembodied |
| Gettings M.W. | Pte. | 2565 | 275497 | 25/03/18 | Pozieres Memorial | Disembodied |
| Gibbon T. | Pte. | 2830 | 275617 | | | |

| Name | Rank | Number | Date | Cemetery/Memorial | Fate |
|---|---|---|---|---|---|
| Gibbon W. | Pte. | 1972 | | | Disembodied |
| Gibbons R. | Cpl. | 1556 | | | Disembodied |
| Gibney A. | Pte. | 1607 | | | Discharged |
| Gibson J. | Pte. | 3009 | 275238 / 275096 / 275704 | 27/06/17 | Dundee Western Necropolis Cem. |
| Gibson J.L. | Pte. | 1406 | 275055 | 24/05/15 | Menin Gate | Class "W" - T.F. Reserve |
| Gibson M. | L/Cpl. | 2762 | | 24/05/15 | Menin Gate |
| Gillan L.A. | Pte. | 1905 | | 17/10/15 | Bailleul Communal Cem. Ext. France |
| Gillies J.N. | Cpl. | 2591 | | | | Discharged to Commission |
| Gooch W. | Pte. | 3257 | | 09/06/15 | Harlebeke New British Cem. Belgium |
| Goodfellow T. | Pte. | 2911 | | 24/05/15 | Menin Gate |
| Gordon J.T. | Sgt. | 586 | 275025 | | | Disembodied |
| Gosling A. | Pte. | 2520 | | 28/09/16 | Thiepval Memorial | KIA with W. Yorks |
| Graham A. | Cpl. | 1374 | | | | Discharged |
| Graham F. | Pte. | 2680 | 275535 | | | Disembodied |
| Graham J. | Pte. | 1820 | 275181 | | | Discharged |
| Graham J.A. | Pte. | 2270 | | 09/10/16 | Contalmaison Chateau Cem. France |
| Graham T. | Pte. | 2205 | | | | Discharged |
| Gray G. | Pte. | 906 | | | | Discharged |
| Gray J.D. | Pte. | 461 | | 27/04/15 | Hazebrouck Communal Cem. France |
| Grayston A.V. | Sgt. | 1618 | | | | Commissioned |
| Green A.J. | Pte. | 2623 | | 26/05/15 | Menin Gate |
| Green J.G. | Pte. | 967 | | | | Discharged |
| Green J.H.D. | Pte. | 2128 | 275301 | 05/11/18 | Etaples Military Cem. France |
| Green W. | Pte. | 2715 | 275557 | | | Discharged |
| Greenhalgh J. | Pte. | 2980 | | | | Trans to Royal Engineers |
| Greenwood J.H. | L/Cpl. | 2618 | | 24/05/15 | Menin Gate |
| Greenwood T.C. | Pte. | 3200 | 275808 | | | Disembodied |
| Gregory R. | Pte. | 2157 | 275314 | | | Disembodied |
| Grey F. | Pte. | 2827 | | 14/07/15 | Lindenhoek Chalet Military Cem. |

| Name | Rank | No. | No. | Date | Cemetery / Memorial | Status |
|---|---|---|---|---|---|---|
| Habgood J. | Sgt. | 2264 | 204049 | | | Class Z Reserve |
| Hadden W. | Sgt. | 1242 | | | | Discharged |
| Haddock G.F. | Pte. | 2647 | | 26/05/15 | Menin Gate | |
| Hagel F. | Pte. | 2139 | | | | Discharged |
| Hagel G.F. | Cpl. | 1408 | 275056 | | | Discharged |
| Hails W. | Pte. | 2256 | | 30/05/16 | La Laiterie Military Cem. Belgium | |
| Hair R. | Pte. | 3370 | | | | Disembodied |
| Halcrow F. | Pte. | 1964 | 275888 | | | Discharged |
| Hall D.S. | Pte. | 3148 | | 14/09/15 | Strand Military Cem. Belgium | |
| Hall E.L. | Pte. | 1494 | | | | Discharged |
| Hall H. | Pte. | 2320 | 275383 | | | Disembodied |
| Hall H.E. | Pte. | 2617 | 275510 | | | Disembodied |
| Hall S. | L/Cpl. | 1613 | | | | Discharged |
| Hamilton W. | Pte. | 1516 | | 29/04/15 | Menin Gate | |
| Hancock W.C. | Pte. | 1500 | | 29/05/15 | Wimereux Communal Cem. France | |
| Hanking J. | Pte. | 1845 | | 16/06/16 | La Laiterie Military Cem. Belgium | |
| Harbord T.G. | Pte. | 2333 | | | | Discharged |
| Hardy F. | Cpl. | 1349 | | | | Discharged |
| Hardy J.R. | Pte. | 5982 | | | | Discharged |
| Harkess G. | Cpl. | 1895 | | | | Disembodied |
| Harle J. | Cpl. | 2721 | 275209 | 15/10/16 | Dernancourt Communal Cem. Ext. | |
| Harper G.H.A.L. | Cpl. | 2508 | 275465 | | | Discharged |
| Harper J.W. | Pte. | 2799 | 275597 | | | Discharged |
| Harrison G. | Pte. | 2315 | 275381 | | | Discharged |
| Harrison J. | Pte. | 2150 | | 22/05/15 | Menin Gate | |
| Harrison J.W.S. | Pte. | 2555 | | | | Discharged |
| Harrison R. | Pte. | 2826 | 275615 | | | Disembodied |
| Hart G.M. | Pte. | 2624 | 275511 | | | Discharged to Commission |
| Hart R. | Pte. | 1653 | 350771 | | | Class Z Reserve |
| Hart W. | Pte. | 2388 | | | | Discharged |
| Haswell G. | Pte. | 1756 | 203446 | | | Discharged |

| Name | Rank | Number | Date | Location | Status |
|---|---|---|---|---|---|
| Haswell W. | Pte. | 3102 | | | Discharged |
| Haugh H.J. | Pte. | 2538 | | | Disembodied |
| Hauxwell G.W. | Sgt. | 1675 | | | |
| Hawkins W. | Pte. | 1713 | | | Disembodied |
| Hawkins W. | Cpl. | 2161 | | | Disembodied |
| Hayburn J. | Pte. | 2381 | 26/05/15 | Menin Gate | |
| | | | 03/09/18 | Sunderland (Bishopwearmouth) | |
| Hayes W. | Pte. | 2822 | | | Discharged |
| Hays J. | Pte. | 2383 | | | Discharged |
| Heath A. | Pte. | 1913 | | | Disembodied |
| Hedley G. | Pte. | 983 | | | Discharged |
| Hedley T.R. | Cpl. | 2704 | | | Discharged |
| Hellam J.T. | Pte. | 2558 | | | Disembodied |
| Henderson J. | L/Cpl. | 2346 | | | Disembodied |
| Hendy C.W. | Pte. | 2061 | | | Discharged |
| Henshaw J.T. | Sgt. | 728 | | | Discharged |
| Henson F. | Pte. | 2170 | | | Discharged |
| Hepple J.R. | Pte. | 2334 | | | Disembodied |
| Hepple T. | Pte. | 2131 | | | Discharged |
| Herring T. | Pte. | 2342 | | | Discharged |
| Herron E. | Pte. | 1851 | | | Discharged |
| Herron J. | Pte. | 1852 | 26/05/15 | Menin Gate | Discharged |
| Hetherington W. | Pte. | 2723 | 27/05/15 | Hazebrouck Communal Cem. France | |
| Hewison A. | Pte. | 1707 | | | Disembodied |
| Hewison R. | Pte. | 1853 | | | Disembodied |
| Hewitson D. | Pte. | 7039 | | | Discharged |
| High A. | Pte. | 3237 | 28/05/15 | Boulogne Eastern Cem. France | |
| Hillerby W. | Pte. | 2782 | | | Transferred to RFC |
| Hobbs W. | Pte. | 1422 | | | Trans to Royal Engineers |
| Hobson H. | Pte. | 1956 | | | Disembodied |
| Hodgkiss T. | Pte. | 2301 | | | Discharged |
| Hodgson A.F. | Pte. | 2496 | | | Discharged |
| Hodgson H.F. | Pte. | 2082 | | | Disembodied |
| Hodgson J. | Sgt. | 1119 | | | Disembodied |

| Name | Rank | Number | Date | Cemetery | Fate |
|---|---|---|---|---|---|
| Hodgson J. | Pte. | 1678 | | | Discharged to Commission |
| Hodgson J. | Pte. | 3075 | | | Disembodied |
| Hodson G.P. | Pte. | 2668 | | | Transferred to RDC |
| Hoggart G.M. | Pte. | 2981 | | | |
| Holland T.H. | Pte. | 2167 | | | Disembodied |
| Holliday P. | Pte. | 3303 | 13/06/15 | Courtrai (St Jean) Comm. Cem. | |
| Holmes E. | Sgt. | 358 | | | Discharged |
| Holt H.J. | Pte. | 2853 | | | Disembodied |
| Hood W.S. | Cpl. | 1854 | | | Discharged |
| Hope F.W. | Pte. | 3064 | | | Discharged |
| Hope J.A. | Pte. | 1704 | 10/11/15 | Bailleul Communal Cem. Ext. France | |
| Hopper D. | Pte. | 3511 | 09/06/15 | Harlebeke New British Cem. Belgium | Died as prisoner |
| Hopper J. | Pte. | 2592 | | | Discharged to Commission |
| Horn E.H. | Pte. | 2405 | | | Disembodied |
| Horn H. | Cpl. | 2944 | | | Disembodied |
| Horn J.W. | Pte. | 2329 | 16/05/16 | Menin Gate | |
| Horn W.A. | Pte. | 2632 | | | Discharged |
| Horsburgh J. | Pte. | 2247 | | | Disembodied |
| Howard W. | Pte. | 2473 | | | Discharged |
| Howey S. | Sgt. | 2267 | | | Discharged |
| Hubbard A. | Pte. | 1359 | | | Discharged |
| Hudson J. | Sgt. | 1233 | | | Disembodied |
| Hull F. | Pte. | 2454 | 26/05/15 | Bailleul Communal Cem. Ext. France | |
| Hulley F. | Pte. | 2305 | | | Discharged |
| Humble H. | Pte. | 1020 | | | Disembodied |
| Hunter B.O. | Sgt. | 1679 | | | Disembodied |
| Hunter J. | Cpl. | 2349 | | | Discharged |
| Hunter J.W. | Pte. | 2011 | | | Discharged |
| Hunter R.W. | Pte. | 1327 | | | Discharged |
| Hunter T. | Pte. | 1562 | | | Discharged |
| Hutchins J.R.H. | Pte | 2726 | | | Disembodied |
| Hutchinson R.C. | Pte. | 3172 | | | Discharged |

| Name | Rank | No. | No. | Date | Place | Fate |
|---|---|---|---|---|---|---|
| Innes W.T. | Pte. | 1811 | | | | Disembodied |
| Isherwood J.T. | Pte. | 2763 | 275576 | | | Discharged |
| Isherwood W. | Pte. | 2810 | 275606 | | | Disembodied |
| Jackson D. | Pte. | 2009 | 275256 | | | Discharged |
| Jackson H.E. | Pte. | 1348 | | 26/05/15 | Menin Gate | |
| Jackson I. | Pte. | 2578 | | 16/05/15 | Bedford House Enclosure No2, Ypres | |
| Jackson J.J. | Pte. | 3264 | 350374 | | | Discharged |
| Jackson T. | Pte. | 2643 | 275518 | | | Discharged |
| Jackway T. | Pte. | 2664 | | 24/05/15 | Menin Gate | |
| Jacoby H. | Pte. | 2579 | 275502 | | | Disembodied |
| Jameson R.D. | Pte. | 2330 | 201476 | | | Discharged |
| Jeffels J. | Pte. | 2712 | | | | Discharged |
| Jefferson H.B. | Pte. | 1564 | 275092 | | | Disembodied |
| Johnson A. | Pte. | 3164 | | | | Transferred to Tank Corps |
| Johnson B. | Pte. | 2327 | 275384 | | | Disembodied |
| Johnson C.R. | Pte. | 332 | 275017 | | | Trans to Royal Engineers |
| Johnson D.E. | Pte. | 1657 | 275125 | | | Discharged |
| Johnson J. | Pte. | 2706 | 275554 | | | Discharged |
| Johnson W. | Pte. | 1511 | | | | Trans to Gordon Highlanders |
| Johnson W. | Pte. | 2474 | 275453 | | | Disembodied |
| Jones J. | Pte. | 2615 | | | | Discharged |
| Jones R. | Pte. | 2510 | 275467 | | | Disembodied |
| Jones W. | Cpl. | 1542 | 275083 | 30/03/18 | St. Sever Cem. Ext. France | |
| Jones W. | Pte. | 1806 | 203447 | | | Class Z Reserve |
| Kay J. | Sgt. | 138 | | | | Discharged |
| Keelan P.J. | Pte. | 1658 | 275126 | | | Disembodied |
| Keelin T. | Pte. | 2772 | 103063 | | | Continued Serving |
| Keenan W. | Pte. | 1385 | | | | Discharged |
| Kelly J | Pte. | 3386 | | | | Discharged |
| Kelly J. | Pte. | 2353 | | 23/01/17 | Flatiron Copse Cem. France | |
| Kelly J. | Pte. | 2354 | 350723 | | | Discharged |
| Kemp T. | Pte. | 2470 | 275451 | | | Discharged |
| Kent E. | Pte. | 2670 | 275531 | | | Disembodied |

| Name | Rank | No. | No. | Date | Cemetery | Status |
|---|---|---|---|---|---|---|
| Kerr G. | Pte. | 2972 | 275685 | | | Disembodied |
| Kerr J.W. | Pte. | 3025 | 275713 | | | Disembodied |
| Kilpatrick J. | Sgt. | 810 | 275028 | | | Transferred to RDC |
| King J. | Pte. | 3277 | | | | Disembodied |
| Kirkhouse J.T. | Pte. | 1782 | 275163 | 25/03/18 | Brie British Cem. France | |
| Knox J. | Pte. | 2429 | | 26/05/15 | Bailleul Communal Cem. Ext. France | |
| Laidler R. | Pte. | 2765 | 275577 | | | Discharged |
| Lake H. | Pte. | 2754 | 275571 | | | Discharged |
| Lamb C. | Pte. | 2490 | 275458 | | | Discharged |
| Lamb H. | Pte. | 3240 | 275825 | | | Discharged |
| Lamb W. | Pte. | 2534 | | | | Transferred to Labour Corps |
| Lambert H.J. | Pte. | 1576 | 275097 | | | Discharged |
| Lambert J.W. | Sgt. | 1758 | 275156 | | | Disembodied |
| Lambie J. | Pte. | 1824 | 275183 | | | Disembodied |
| Langford H. | T/RSM | 1375 | 275052 | | | Disembodied |
| Langham E. | Pte. | 2905 | 350784 | | | Discharged |
| Larkman R. | Pte. | 1978 | | 14/05/15 | Brandhoek Military Cem. Belgium. | |
| Lavender W. | Sgt. | 74 | | | | Disembodied |
| Laverick H. | Pte. | 2352 | 275397 | | | Disembodied |
| Lawrence C. | L/Cpl. | 2479 | 275457 | 21/04/17 | Faubourg D'Amiens Cem. Arras | |
| Lawson G. | Pte. | 2802 | 275600 | 26/11/18 | Sunderland (Mere Knolls) Cem. | |
| Lawson T. | Cpl. | 1785 | 275165 | | | Discharged |
| Lax C. | Cpl. | 1563 | 350786 | | | Discharged |
| Laybourne A. | Cpl. | 2486 | 323041 | 03/11/17 | Wimereux Communal Cem. France | |
| Laycock F. | Pte. | 2805 | 275602 | | | Discharged |
| Leach R.H. | Cpl. | 2582 | | | | Disembodied |
| Leadbitter G. | Pte. | 1417 | | | | Discharged |
| Leask R. | Pte. | 2735 | 202481 | 24/05/15 | Menin Gate | |
| Leavesley J.H. | Pte. | 1480 | | 24/05/15 | Menin Gate | |
| Leavesley W. | Pte. | 1878 | 275202 | | | Disembodied |
| Lee J. | Cpl. | 2628 | 275514 | | | Disembodied |

| Name | Rank | Number | Service No. | Date | Cemetery/Memorial | Fate |
|---|---|---|---|---|---|---|
| Lee S. | Pte. | 963 | | 28/06/15 | Boulogne Eastern Cem. France | |
| Leighton J. | Pte. | 1985 | 275246 | | | Disembodied |
| Leonard A. | Sgt. | 2788 | 275589 | | | Disembodied |
| Leonard B. | Pte. | 3350 | | | | |
| Lewis E. | Pte. | 2862 | | 26/05/15 | Menin Gate | |
| Lewis G. | Pte. | 3129 | 202586 | 26/05/15 | Menin Gate | |
| Lewis J. | Sgt. | 1977 | 275241 | | | Disembodied |
| Liddle R.E. | Pte. | 3093 | 275757 | | | Transferred to Labour Corps |
| Liddle W.A. | Sgt. | 2226 | 203549 | | | Discharged |
| Liebrecht W.H. | CSM | 6 | | | | Discharged to Commission |
| Loades C.S. | Pte. | 49 | 275228 | 27/03/18 | Humbercamps Communal Ext | |
| Locke A. | Pte. | 2634 | | 24/05/15 | Menin Gate | |
| Lodge J. | Pte. | 382 | | | | Discharged |
| Logan A. | Pte. | 1373 | | | | Discharged |
| Long J. | Cpl. | 933 | 103282 | | | Discharged |
| Longstaff R. | Pte. | 2880 | 275643 | | | Disembodied |
| Lovell R. | Pte. | 2943 | | | | Discharged |
| Lowes H.P. | Pte. | 1602 | | 12/07/18 | Sunderland (Bishopwearmouth) Cem. | |
| Lunn G.O. | Pte. | 2633 | | | | Discharged to Commission |
| Lynn S. | L/Cpl. | 2572 | | | | Discharged |
| Mackel J. | Pte. | 2502 | 350778 | | | Transferred to Labour Corps |
| Maddison A. | Pte. | 2506 | | | | Disembodied |
| Maddison J. | Sgt. | 1638 | 275116 | | | Disembodied |
| Maddison J.C. | Pte. | 2175 | 273324 | | | |
| Mallam M.S. | Pte. | 2719 | | 08/05/15 | Le Treport Military Cem. France | |
| Mallan J. | Pte. | 2526 | 275474 | 26/05/15 | Menin Gate | |
| Mallin J. | Pte. | 2495 | | | | Discharged |
| Marsh A.H. | Pte. | 1720 | 275146 | | | Disembodied |
| Marshall J.L. | Pte. | 2593 | 204740 | | | Disembodied |
| Martin P. | Cpl. | 1908 | 275215 | | | Disembodied |
| Martin W.L.F. | Pte. | 259 | | | | Discharged |
| Mason J.A. | Pte. | 1999 | | | | Discharged |

| Name | Rank | Number | Service No. | Date | Cemetery / Memorial | Remarks |
|---|---|---|---|---|---|---|
| Matthews R.C. | Pte. | 2739 | 202538 | | | Disembodied |
| Mattison S. | Cpl. | 897 | | | | |
| Maw A. | Pte. | 2512 | 275468 | | | Disembodied |
| McAlroy H.W. | Pte. | 2758 | 275574 | | | Disembodied |
| McAndrews J. | L/Cpl. | 1912 | 275218 | 26/04/15 | Menin Gate | |
| McArdle B. | Pte. | 1909 | 275216 | 20/01/18 | Ypres Reservoir Cem. Belgium | |
| McBreasty J.W. | Pte. | 1121 | | | | Disembodied |
| McCarty P. | Cpl. | 1134 | 350453 | | | Discharged |
| McCormick J. | Sgt. | 1117 | 275038 | 28/07/18 | Terlincthon Cem. | |
| McDermott J.G. | Pte. | 1894 | 275208 | | | Discharged |
| McGorian J. | Pte. | 1420 | | | | Discharged to Commission |
| McGough T. | Pte. | 1838 | 275188 | | | Disembodied |
| McGuire J.C. | Pte. | 2949 | 275669 | | | Transferred to Labour Corps |
| McHugh R. | Pte. | 2283 | 236938 | | | Disembodied |
| McIntosh D. | Pte. | 2367 | | | | Discharged |
| McIntosh E. | Pte. | 2348 | 275394 | | | Trans to Royal Engineers |
| McKenna A. | Pte. | 2196 | | | | Trans to Royal Engineers |
| McKenna M. | Sgt. | 691 | 203501 | | | Discharged to Commission |
| McKennie J. | L/Cpl. | 2294 | | | | Trans to York & Lancs Regt |
| McKenzie W. | Pte. | 1911 | 275217 | | | Discharged |
| McLaren R. | Pte. | 1575 | | | | Disembodied |
| McLoughlin J. | Pte. | 1770 | 350314 | | | Discharged |
| McLoughlin J.L. | Pte. | 2105 | 275292 | | | Discharged |
| Mercer J. | Pte. | 3063 | | 26/05/15 | Menin Gate | |
| Metcalfe D. | Pte. | 1413 | | 26/05/15 | Menin Gate | |
| Milburn H. | Cpl. | 2621 | | | | Discharged |
| Miller R. | Pte. | 1571 | 275094 | | | Discharged |
| Miller R. | Cpl. | 3349 | 275881 | | | Disembodied |
| Miller T.H. | Pte. | 2838 | | 04/06/15 | Sunderland (Ryhope Road) Cem. | |
| Miller W.M. | Bandsman | 1548 | 295011 | | | Discharged |
| Milligan C. | Pte. | 1656 | 275124 | | | Discharged |
| Milligan R. | A\CSM | 297 | | | | Discharged |
| Mills M.E. | Pte. | 1116 | 350312 | | | Discharged |

| Name | Rank | No. | No. | Date | Cemetery / Memorial | Status |
|---|---|---|---|---|---|---|
| Mitchell W. | Pte. | 1778 | 275160 | 06/11/18 | Sunderland (Ryhope Road) Cem. | Discharged |
| Monro D. | Pte. | 1930 | | | | Discharged |
| Monte T. | Pte. | 2518 | 204875 | 26/05/15 | Menin Gate | |
| Mooney W. | Pte. | 2274 | | | | Discharged |
| Moore E. | Pte. | 2683 | 275537 | | | Discharged |
| Moran F. | CSM | 2691 | 275543 | 12/09/17 | Sunderland (Bishopwearmouth) Cem. | |
| Morris N. | Pte. | 2487 | | | | Discharged |
| Morrison T.E. | Bugler | 2930 | | 11/07/15 | Lindenhoek Chalet Military Cem. | Discharged |
| Morrison W.A. | Pte. | 2441 | 275439 | | | Discharged |
| Morse M. | Pte. | 3002 | 350781 | | | Trans to Royal Engineers |
| Morton W. | Pte. | 2581 | | 30/05/15 | Roulers Communal Cem. Belgium | |
| Moses W.H. | Pte. | 2311 | | | | Transferred to Labour Corps |
| Mottram S. | Sgt. | 2365 | 275402 | | | Discharged |
| Mountain J.W. | Pte. | 2173 | 275322 | 26/05/15 | Menin Gate | |
| Mulley G. | Pte. | 2021 | | | | Discharged |
| Mulley J.F. | Cpl. | 2285 | 277388 | | | Disembodied |
| Murtha J. | Pte. | 521 | 275024 | | | Disembodied |
| Mushens R. | Pte. | 2774 | 350457 | | | Discharged |
| Mustard J. | Pte. | 1550 | 275086 | 11/04/18 | Aire Communal Cem. France | |
| Mutch J. | Pte. | 1875 | 275201 | | | Disembodied |
| Myers F. | Pte. | 679 | | | | Discharged |
| Nairn J. | Cpl. | 323 | 275016 | | | Disembodied |
| Nairn O.T. | L/Cpl. | 2446 | | 26/04/15 | Menin Gate | |
| Nairn W. | Bugler | 1366 | | 22/06/15 | Bailleul Communal Cem. Ext. France | |
| Nash A. | Pte. | 2080 | 203460 | | | Transferred to RAF |
| Nash W. | Pte. | 3308 | 275391 | | | Class Z Reserve |
| Naylor A.R. | Pte. | 2791 | 275596 | | | Transfered to AOC |
| Naylor A.R. | Pte. | | | | | Signaller |
| Nelson A.J. | Pte. | 2521 | 275471 | | | Disembodied |

| Name | Rank | Number | Number | Date | Place | Fate |
|---|---|---|---|---|---|---|
| Nelson R.G. | Pte. | 2067 | 275278 | 11/04/18 | Merville Communal Cem. Ext. France | Discharge |
| Nelson T. | Pte. | 2176 | 275325 | | | Discharged |
| Nelson W. | Cpl. | 703 | | | | Discharged |
| Newby W.A. | Pte. | 2741 | | | | Discharged |
| Nichol J. | Pte. | 333 | 7398 | | | Discharged |
| Nicholson J. | Cpl. | 3466 | 275934 | | | Disembodied |
| Nicholson T. | Pte. | 2689 | 275541 | 04/05/20 | South Shields (Harton) Cem. | |
| Nicholson W. | Pte. | 2544 | 275484 | | | Discharged |
| Nixon G. | Sgt. | 2119 | | | | Discharged |
| O'Hara J. | Sgt. | 2265 | 275363 | 21/04/17 | Hibers Trench Cem. France | Discharged to Commission |
| Ohlsson A. | Pte. | 2856 | | 26/05/15 | Menin Gate | |
| Old T. | Pte. | 1869 | | 09/06/15 | Harlebeke New British Cem. Belgium | |
| Oliphant J.B. | Cpl. | 348 | 275019 | | | Disembodied |
| Oliver A. | Cpl. | 2948 | 275668 | | | Disembodied |
| Oswald C. | Pte. | 2417 | | | | Transferred to Labour Corps |
| Ousby W.J. | Cpl. | 245 | 275011 | | | Disembodied |
| Oxberry R. | Pte. | 1549 | 275085 | | | Disembodied |
| Page A.E. | Pte. | 2931 | | | | Disembodied |
| Palfreyman J. | Pte. | 1508 | 275068 | | | Disembodied |
| Pallas H. | L/Cpl. | 1592 | | | | Transferred to RDC |
| Pallins J.Y. | L/Cpl. | 2650 | | 24/05/15 | Menin Gate | |
| Parker W.B. | CSM | 23 | 275002 | | | Discharged |
| Parkin E. | Pte. | 1646 | 275119 | | | Disembodied |
| Parkin S. | Cpl. | 2750 | 275570 | | | Disembodied |
| Parkin W. | Pte. | 3013 | 275707 | | | Disembodied |
| Parkinson C. | Cpl. | 2396 | 277372 | | | Discharged |
| Parton E. | Pte. | 2339 | 275387 | | | Disembodied |
| Patterson E. | Bandsman | 1544 | 275084 | | | Disembodied |
| Patterson J. | | 802 | | | | Discharged |
| Pattison C.L. | Pte. | 2661 | | 24/05/15 | Menin Gate | |
| Pattison G.W. | Pte. | 2364 | | 24/05/15 | New Irish Farm Cem. Belgium | |

| Name | Rank | No. | Service No. | Date | Cemetery/Memorial | Status |
|---|---|---|---|---|---|---|
| Pattison J. | Pte. | 2985 | | | | Discharged |
| Pattison L. | Pte. | 1582 | | 26/05/15 | Menin Gate | Discharged |
| Pattison R. | Pte. | 1946 | 295015 | 12/04/18 | Pernes British Cem. France | Disembodied |
| Pattison S. | Pte. | 749 | | | | Disembodied |
| Paul W. | Pte. | 1103 | | | | Discharged |
| Payne W.H. | Pte. | 1458 | 275061 | 19/07/21 | Gateshead East Cem. | Discharged |
| Peacock A. | Pte. | 1960 | 275233 | | | Discharged |
| Pearce E. | Cpl. | 1311 | 350780 | | | Discharged |
| Pearce J.W. | Pte. | 2644 | 275519 | | | |
| Peat T.W. | Pte. | 139 | 275008 | | | |
| Pentland J. | Pte. | 2255 | | | | |
| Pescodd J.S. | Pte. | 2870 | | 29/04/15 | Menin Gate | Disembodied |
| Peters G.H. | Cpl. | 2002 | 275251 | | | Discharged |
| Peterson J. | L/Sgt. | 2697 | | | | Discharged |
| Petty W. | Pte. | 1641 | | | | |
| Pickering E. | Pte. | 1547 | | 15/07/15 | Bailleul Communal Cem. Ext. France | |
| Place T. | Pte. | 1398 | | | | Discharged |
| Plews W. | Pte. | 1715 | | 15/05/15 | Menin Gate | |
| Pollard J.W. | Cpl. | 2682 | 275142 | | | Disembodied |
| Polson W. | Pte. | 1710 | 275544 | | | Disembodied |
| Pooley C. | L/Cpl. | 2695 | | 27/10/17 | Bard Cottage, Belgium. | |
| Porter A. | Pte. | 2468 | | | | Discharged |
| Potter J. | Pte. | 217 | | | | Discharged |
| Potts C. | Pte. | 2437 | | 24/05/15 | Menin Gate | |
| Potts F. | Pte. | 1332 | | | | Discharged |
| Potts J. | Pte. | 2088 | 275288 | | | Disembodied |
| Potts J. | Pte | 2551 | 275490 | | | Discharged |
| Potts R. | Pte. | 1898 | | | | Disembodied |
| Potts R.W. | Pte. | 1737 | 275149 | | | Disembodied |
| Potts T. | Pte. | 2517 | 203554 | | | Disembodied |
| Potts W. | Pte. | 1357 | | | | Discharged |
| Preece C.W. | Pte. | 2527 | 275475 | | | Discharged |
| Price F. | Sgt. | 1752 | 275153 | | | Disembodied |
| Queenan A. | Pte. | 1318 | 275050 | | | Disembodied |

| Name | Rank | No. | No. | Date | Cemetery / Memorial | Status |
|---|---|---|---|---|---|---|
| Rae R. | Pte. | 1855 | 275194 | | | Disembodied |
| Raine W. | Pte. | 2613 | 275508 | | | Discharged to Commission |
| Raine W.A. | Pte. | 2163 | 350372 | | | Class Z Reserve |
| Ramshaw C.F. | L/Cpl. | 1495 | 275066 | | | Disembodied |
| Ramshaw W.G. | Sgt. | 3221 | | 28/05/15 | Ypres Reservoir Cem. Belgium | |
| Rarity E. | Sgt. | 1093 | | | | Discharged |
| Raw V.W. | Pte. | 2620 | 251904 | | | Disembodied |
| Rawson T. | Pte. | 2269 | | | | Transferred to ASC |
| Read A.E. | L/Sgt. | 2337 | | 30/07/15 | La Chapelle D'Armentieres Communal Cem. | |
| Reardon R. | Cpl. | 2795 | 275595 | 13/04/18 | Ploegsteert Memorial Belgium | |
| Reay S. | Sgt. | 1904 | | | | Discharged |
| Redpath J. | Pte. | 2889 | 275496 | 26/05/15 | Menin Gate | |
| Reed A. | Pte. | 2563 | | | | Disembodied |
| Reed G. | Pte. | 1466 | | | | Discharged |
| Reed G.T. | Pte. | 2016 | 277390 | | | Disembodied |
| Reed J. | Pte. | 2530 | 350375 | | | Discharged |
| Reed R. | Pte. | 3578 | 106043 | | | Discharged |
| Reid J.W. | Pte. | 3356 | | 30/06/15 | Lindenhoek Chalet Military Cem. | |
| Renwick E.F. | Pte. | 2398 | 203452 | | Lille Southern Cem. France | |
| Riceborough W. | L/Cpl. | 1863 | 275198 | | | Discharged |
| Richardson J.W. | Pte. | 1767 | 275157 | | | Disembodied |
| Richardson T. | Pte. | 2448 | | 11/07/15 | Lindenhoek Chalet Military Cem. | |
| Richardson T.H. | Cpl. | 1353 | | 16/05/15 | Menin Gate | |
| Richardson W. | Pte. | 1748 | | 30/10/15 | Houplines Communal Cem. France | |
| Richardson W. | Pte. | 2548 | 275488 | | | Disembodied |
| Riddell C.R. | Pte. | 1154 | | | | Discharged |
| Ridyard R. | Pte. | 3191 | | 12/07/15 | Lindenhoek Chalet Military Cem. | |
| Rigg W. | Pte. | 2792 | 275592 | | | Disembodied |

| Name | Rank | No. | Service No. | Date | Cemetery | Fate |
|---|---|---|---|---|---|---|
| Robe J. | Pte. | 1539 | | | | Disembodied |
| Roberts W. | Pte. | 2692 | 275080 | 16/05/15 | Menin Gate | |
| Robertson J.B. | Sgt. | 2377 | 275407 | | | Disembodied |
| Robertson J.C. | Pte. | 2877 | 201313 | | | Disembodied |
| Robertson W. | Pte. | 2941 | | 24/05/15 | Sunderland (Bishopwearmouth) Cem. | |
| Robins T. | Pte. | 2847 | 204785 | | | Class Z Reserve |
| Robinson A. | Sgt. | 1467 | 275063 | | | Discharged |
| Robinson G. | Pte. | 2764 | | 02/05/15 | Menin Gate | |
| Robinson J. | Pte. | 2687 | 275009 | | | Discharged |
| Robson A.F. | Pte. | 198 | 275368 | | | Discharged |
| Robson H.C. | Pte. | 2282 | | 30/05/19 | South Shields (Harton) Cem. | |
| Robson H.J. | Pte. | 3399 | | | | Discharged |
| Robson J. | Pte. | 2126 | | 02/03/16 | Larchwood (Railway Cuttings) Cem. | |
| Robson J. | Pte. | 2210 | | | | Discharged |
| Robson J.C. | Pte. | 2619 | | | | Transferred to MGC |
| Robson M. | Pte. | 3101 | | 30/10/15 | Houplines Communal Cem. France | |
| Robson W.W. | Pte. | 2070 | 275280 | | | Discharged |
| Rodgers I. | Cpl. | 1239 | 275177 | | | Discharged |
| Rodley D. | Sgt. | 1810 | | | | Disembodied |
| Rodley V. | Pte. | 2124 | | 26/04/15 | Menin Gate | |
| Rogers T.W. | CQMS | 781 | 275026 | | | Disembodied |
| Roll J. | Pte. | 2743 | 275566 | | | Disembodied |
| Rooks W. | Pte. | | 275804 | 24/05/15 | Menin Gate | |
| Roscamp E.J. | Pte. | 1862 | | | | Transferred to RAOC |
| Ross F | Pte. | 1619 | | | | Discharged |
| Ross H. | Pte. | 3197 | | | | Discharged |
| Ross R.A.V. | Pte. | 2097 | 350143 | | | Disembodied |
| Ross T.H. | Pte. | 1858 | | | | Discharged |
| Ross W.O. | Pte. | 2493 | 275459 | | | Disembodied |
| Roumph A. | Pte. | 2063 | | | | Discharged |
| Routledge W. | Pte. | 2242 | 275355 | | | Discharged to Commission |
| Rowntree H.S. | Pte. | 3348 | 275880 | | | Disembodied |

| Name | Rank | No. | No. | Date | Cemetery / Memorial | Remarks |
|---|---|---|---|---|---|---|
| Ruddick C. | Pte. | 3405 | | | | Trans to Royal Engineers |
| Rundle W. | Pte. | 2385 | | | | Discharged |
| Russell T. | Sgt. | 2111 | | 26/05/15 | Menin Gate | |
| Rylance T. | Pte. | 1361 | | | | Discharged |
| Ryles J. | Pte. | 1503 | | | | Discharged |
| Ryles J. | Pte. | 2030 | 275263 | | | Discharged |
| Ryles T. | Pte. | 2901 | | | | |
| Sache W. | Pte. | 3090 | | 25/05/15 | Menin Gate | Disembodied |
| Sanderson T. | Bugler | 1872 | 275755 | 25/05/15 | Klein-Vierstraat British Cem. | |
| Sands G. | L/Cpl. | 2577 | 275501 | | | Discharged to Commission |
| Savage G.A. | Pte. | 1769 | 275158 | | | Disembodied |
| Sawyer J.A. | Pte. | 2549 | 275489 | 12/03/17 | Heath Cem. Harbonnieres France | |
| Saxon N. | Sgt. | 2660 | 275527 | | | Disembodied |
| Sayers C. | Pte. | 2734 | 275562 | | | Discharged |
| Scarlett J. | Pte. | 1371 | | | | Discharged |
| Scorer J. | Pte. | 3425 | | | | Discharged |
| Scorer W. | Pte. | 2464 | | 02/02/19 | Sunderland (Mere Knolls) Cem. | |
| Scott R. | Sgt. | 234 | | 24/05/15 | Menin Gate | Discharged |
| Scott R. | L/Cpl. | 2231 | | 07/11/16 | Becourt Military Cem. France | Discharged |
| Scott R.W. | Cpl. | 1797 | 275010 | | | |
| Scott T.C. | CQMS | 19 | | | | Discharged to Commission |
| Scott T.C. | Pte. | 1935 | 275224 | | | Disembodied |
| Scouler J. | Pte. | 2401 | 275418 | | | Discharged |
| Scrowther J.C. | L/Cpl. | 1416 | | 07/11/16 | Dernancourt Communal Cem. Ext. | |
| Seaman A. | Pte. | 2927 | | | | Discharged |
| Settle R.E. | Bugler | 7476 | 201219 | 31/12/18 | Sunderland (Bishopwearmouth) Cem. | |
| Sharkey J. | Pte. | 2879 | | | | Discharged |
| Sharp A. | Pte. | 1568 | | 14/05/15 | Bedford House Enclosure No2, | |
| Sheraton G. | Pte. | 2993 | | | | Discharged |

| Name | Rank | Number | Number | Date | Cemetery | Fate |
|---|---|---|---|---|---|---|
| Shore T. | Pte. | 2218 | 275345 | | | Disembodied |
| Shuttleworth C.H. | Pte. | 1363 | | 21/01/17 | St. Sever Cem. Ext, Rouen | |
| Siddle W. | Pte. | 2666 | 275318 | | | Transferred to Tank Corps |
| Sidney P.C. | L/Cpl. | 2165 | 350315 | | | Disembodied |
| Sills T. | Pte. | 2332 | 275291 | | | Discharged |
| Simpson J. | L/Cpl. | 2101 | 277373 | | | Disembodied |
| Sinclair W.K. | Cpl. | 2531 | 275113 | | | Discharged |
| Slater S. | Cpl. | 1633 | | | | Disembodied |
| Slater T. | Pte. | 1649 | | | | Discharged |
| Slavin J. | Pte. | 2248 | 277376 | | | Discharged |
| Sloanes J. | Pte. | 1788 | 275168 | | | Disembodied |
| Smales W.H. | Pte. | 2421 | 275431 | | | Disembodied |
| Smallman R. | Pte. | 1740 | 275150 | | | Disembodied |
| Smiles T. | Pte. | 1424 | 277392 | | | Disembodied |
| Smiles W. | Pte. | 1781 | 275162 | | | Disembodied |
| Smith E. | Pte. | 2794 | | | | Trans to NF |
| Smith J. | Pte. | 1617 | 275109 | | | Disembodied |
| Smith J.D. | Pte. | 2649 | | | | Discharged to Commission |
| Smith J.G. | Bugler | 1860 | 275196 | | | Discharged |
| Smith J.W. | Pte. | 2013 | | | | Discharged |
| Smith R.M. | Pte. | 1792 | | 07/05/16 | Weston-Super-Mare Cem. | |
| Smith R.W. | Pte. | 3051 | 275732 | | | Discharged |
| Smith T. | Sgt. | 2304 | 275377 | | | Released to Munitions |
| Smith W. | Sgt. | 2659 | | | | Disembodied |
| Smoat H. | Pte. | 2724 | | | | Discharged to Commission |
| Softley W.G. | Pte. | 919 | | 27/08/15 | Chapelle-D'-Armentieres Old Military Cem | |
| Sollas P.W. | Pte. | 2376 | | 26/04/15 | Menin Gate | |
| Souter L. | Pte. | 2335 | 350776 | 30/07/15 | La Chapelle D'Armentieres Communal Cem | |
| Southern J.G. | Pte. | 3097 | | | | Discharged |
| Sparling J.W. | Cpl. | 271 | | | | Discharged |
| Speight A. | Cpl. | 2007 | 275255 | | | Discharged Class Z Reserve |

| Name | Rank | No. | No. | Date | Cemetery / Memorial | Fate |
|---|---|---|---|---|---|---|
| Speight H.W. | Sgt. | 1700 | | 14/07/15 | Lindenhoek Chalet Military Cem. | |
| Spence R. | Pte. | 2180 | 203499 | | | Class Z Reserve |
| Spencer G. | Pte. | 2604 | 203558 | | | Discharged |
| Spencer J. | Pte. | 2404 | | | | Discharged |
| Spooner T. | CSM | 1238 | 275047 | 27/05/18 | Soissons Memorial | |
| Sproat W. | Pte. | 2696 | 275545 | | | Discharged |
| Sproxton J.W. | Pte. | 1460 | 270535 | | | Trans to Royal Engineers |
| Squance E. | Pte. | 3569 | | 24/05/15 | Menin Gate | |
| Stabler W. | Pte. | 1601 | 275103 | 16/10/18 | Glageon Communal Cem. Ext. | |
| Stafford T.E. | Pte. | 2773 | 275120 | | | Discharged |
| Stainsbey H. | Pte. | 1647 | 275101 | | | Disembodied |
| Stamp J. | Pte. | 1596 | 275293 | | | Disembodied |
| Stead W.M. | Pte. | 2108 | 275396 | | | Disembodied |
| Steele A.S. | CQMS | 2351 | 275035 | | | Disembodied |
| Steinberg A. | Pte. | 1070 | | | | Transferred to RAF |
| Stephenson D. | Pte. | 1532 | | | | Discharged |
| Stephenson J. | Pte. | 2158 | 275315 | | | Discharged |
| Stevens J. | Pte. | 2902 | | 26/05/15 | Menin Gate | |
| Stevenson H. | Cpl. | 1561 | 275090 | | | Disembodied |
| Stevenson J.R. | Pte. | 3080 | 275749 | | | Disembodied |
| Stevenson R. | Pte. | 2065 | 275277 | | | Class Z Reserve |
| Stewart J. | Pte. | 2400 | | | | Discharged |
| Stewart J. | Cpl. | 2626 | 203453 | | | Discharged |
| Stidolph W. | Sgt. | 1841 | 270147 | | | Class Z Reserve |
| Stobbs H. | Sgt. | 2636 | 10618 | 26/10/17 | Poelcapelle British Cemetery | |
| Stoker J. | CSM | 65 | | | | Discharged to Commission |
| Stoker R. | Pte. | 2933 | 275005 | 26/05/15 | Menin Gate | |
| Stonley R.E. | Pte. | 1766 | | | | Disembodied |
| Stothard J. | Pte. | 1906 | 275214 | 21/04/18 | Ploegsteert Memorial Belgium | Transferred to RAF |
| Stracham F.W.A. | Pte. | 1825 | 201392 | | | Discharged |
| Straker T. | Pte. | 2449 | | 24/05/15 | Aeroplane Cemetery, Belgium | |

| Name | Rank | No. 1 | No. 2 | Date | Cemetery/Memorial | Status |
|---|---|---|---|---|---|---|
| Strratton E. | Pte. | 2324 | | | | Discharged |
| Struthers W. | Pte. | 3276 | 275844 | | | Disembodied |
| Stubbs S. | Pte. | 3033 | 275719 | | | Disembodied |
| Studd J.W. | Pte. | 3137 | 275779 | | | Disembodied |
| Sullivan J. | L/Cpl. | 1903 | 275213 | 15/10/18 | Niederzwehren Cem. Germany | |
| Sumby K.W. | Pte. | 2407 | 275422 | 30/04/15 | Menin Gate | |
| Sumby R. | Pte. | 2313 | | | | Disembodied |
| Surtees E.R. | Pte. | 2813 | 275607 | | | Disembodied |
| Surtees F. | Pte. | 1068 | 275034 | | | Disembodied |
| Surtees F. | Pte. | 1168 | | | | Discharged |
| Swales J.E. | Pte. | 2375 | 275406 | | | Discharged |
| Swanson G.E. | Pte. | 1751 | 350722 | | | Discharged |
| Swinhoe J. | Pte. | 2114 | 275296 | | | |
| Swinney A. | Pte. | 2211 | | 01/10/16 | Theipval Memorial | |
| Tardito J. | Pte. | 2428 | | 27/06/15 | Lindenhoek Chalet Military Cem. | |
| Tasker J. | Pte. | 3123 | 275772 | | | Dsiembodied |
| Tate A. | Pte. | 2453 | 275443 | 17/04/17 | Tilloy British Cem. France | |
| Tate G. | Pte. | 912 | | | | Discharged |
| Taylor A.L. | Pte. | 2665 | | 30/05/15 | Harlebeke New British Cem. Belgium | |
| Taylor C. | Pte. | 1848 | | | | Transferred to Worc. Regt |
| Taylor D. | Pte. | 2062 | 275275 | 13/04/18 | Le Grand Hasard Military Cem. | |
| Taylor M. | Pte. | 1362 | | | | Discharged |
| Taylor T.W. | Pte. | 2426 | 276169 | 26/06/17 | Bailleul Road East Cem. France | |
| Taylor W. | Pte. | 1586 | 275098 | | | Discharged |
| Teasdale J. | Pte. | 1334 | | | | Discharged |
| Teasdale R. | WOII | 2235 | 275354 | | | Disembodied |
| Teasdale T. | Pte. | 2686 | | | | Disembodied |
| Telford W. | Pte. | 1199 | 275041 | | | Disembodied |
| Tetley T. | Pte. | 1871 | 275200 | 24/07/18 | Glageon Communal Cem. Ext. France | |

| Name | Rank | No. | No. | Date | Cemetery / Memorial | Fate |
|---|---|---|---|---|---|---|
| Thompson A. | Pte. | 2800 | | | | Class Z Reserve |
| Thompson D.H. | Pte. | 2753 | | | | Disembodied |
| Thompson F. | Pte. | 334 | 275049 | | | Discharged to Commission |
| Thompson G. | Cpl. | 1310 | | 26/04/15 | Menin Gate | |
| Thompson H. | Cpl. | 2669 | | 28/03/18 | Cerisy-Gailly French National Cemetery | |
| Thompson J. | Pte. | 1409 | | 24/05/15 | Menin Gate | |
| Thompson J. | Pte. | 2547 | 275487 | | | Disembodied |
| Thornton L. | Pte. | 2432 | | | | Discharged |
| Thornton R. | Cpl. | 3219 | | 01/10/16 | Flatiron Copse Cem. France | |
| Thornton T. | Pte. | 1805 | 275173 | | | Disembodied |
| Thornton W. | Pte. | 2078 | | 26/04/15 | Menin Gate | |
| Tierney W. | Pte. | 2373 | 275405 | | | Disembodied |
| Tindell R. | Pte. | 2645 | | 07/10/15 | Houplines Communal Cem. France | |
| Tindle H. | Pte. | 3263 | | | | Discharged |
| Todd B. | Pte. | 1226 | 275043 | | | Transferred to ASC |
| Todd B. | Pte. | 2575 | | 24/05/15 | Menin Gate | |
| Todd C.A. | Pte. | 2787 | 275588 | | | Transferred to ASC |
| Todd O. | Pte. | 336 | 275018 | | | Discharged |
| Tomkinson F. | Cpl. | 2883 | | | | Disembodied |
| Tones R. | Pte. | | | 09/07/15 | Lindenhoek Chalet Military Cem. | |
| Trenholm W. | Cpl. | 2361 | 275400 | | | Disembodied |
| Trewick J.J. | Pte. | 1779 | | 06/06/15 | Sunderland (Mere Knolls) Cem. | |
| Troughton W. | L/Cpl. | 1938 | 275226 | 02/11/17 | Mendinghem Military Cem. Belgium | |
| Tunstall E. | Pte. | 1591 | 275100 | | | Discharged |
| Turnbull T. | Pte. | 1579 | 350721 | | | Class Z Reserve |
| Tweddle J. | Cpl. | 2612 | | | | Trans to Royal Fusiliers |
| Tweedale F. | Sgt. | 1705 | 275139 | | | Disembodied |
| Tye C. | Pte. | 2344 | 275390 | | | Disembodied |
| Tyson R. | Pte. | 2536 | 275479 | | | Disembodied |
| Tyson R.H. | Sgt. | 1247 | 203785 | | | Discharged |

| Name | Rank | No. | No. | Date | Cemetery / Memorial | Status |
|---|---|---|---|---|---|---|
| Udale H. | Cpl. | 2444 | | | | Disembodied |
| Upfold R.A. | Cpl. | 2291 | 275441 | | | Discharged |
| Urwin G. | Sgt. | 1345 | | 26/05/15 | Menin Gate | Discharged |
| Usher R. | Pte. | 2466 | 275449 | | | Discharged |
| Usher W. | Pte. | 2431 | 275436 | | | |
| Vipond R.H. | Pte. | 2386 | | 29/04/15 | Menin Gate | |
| Wailes T. | Pte. | 2573 | | 25/07/15 | La Chapelle D'Armentieres Communal Cem. | |
| Waiter G. | A/CSM | 1849 | | 26/06/16 | Kemmel Chateau Military Cem. | |
| Wake T.W. | Pte. | 3042 | 275724 | | | Discharged |
| Wales W.W. | Pte. | 2391 | 275413 | | | Discharged |
| Walker C. | Pte. | 2392 | 275414 | | | Disembodied |
| Walker J. | Pte. | 2485 | | | | Transferred to RAF |
| Walker J. | Pte. | 2833 | 275619 | | | Disembodied |
| Walker J.W. | Pte. | 1870 | | 21/11/16 | Dernancourt Communal Cem. Ext. | |
| Walker P. | CSM | 2631 | 275473 | | | Discharged to Commission |
| Wallis G. | Pte. | 2524 | | 02/11/17 | Solferino Farm Cem. Belgium | |
| Walshaw T. | Pte. | 2994 | 275696 | | | Disembodied |
| Walton H. | Sgt. | 1695 | | | | Discharged to Commission |
| Walton J. | Pte. | 2533 | | 11/07/15 | Lindenhoek Chalet Military Cem. | |
| Wanlass J.J. | Pte. | 2151 | 275415 | | | Disembodied |
| Ward F. | Pte. | 2394 | 275074 | | | |
| Wardle W.S. | Pte. | 1525 | 275004 | | | Disembodied |
| Wardropper R. W. | CSM | 41 | 275393 | | | Disembodied |
| Waters R. | Pte. | 2347 | 275393 | 28/03/18 | Pozieres Memorial | |
| Watson A. | Cpl. | 1376 | 204325 | 14/04/18 | Etaples Military Cem. France | |
| Watson M. | Pte. | 2601 | 275505 | | | Disembodied |
| Watson T.B.T. | Pte. | 2737 | 275564 | | | Disembodied |
| Watson T.J. | Pte. | 2362 | | | | Discharged |
| Watson W.H. | Pte. | 1982 | | | | Trans to Royal Engineers |
| Watt J.W.T. | Pte. | 2236 | | | | Discharged |

| Name | Rank | Number | | Date | Cemetery / Memorial | Fate |
|---|---|---|---|---|---|---|
| Weatherston A. | Pte. | 2698 | 275547 | | | Disembodied |
| Welsh R. | Pte. | 3138 | | 05/07/15 | Lindenhoek Chalet Military Cem. | |
| Weston G. | Cpl. | 2110 | 275295 | | | Disembodied |
| Whale J. | L/Sgt. | 1721 | | | | Trans to School of Musketry |
| Whillians J. | Pte. | 3301 | | | | Discharged |
| White J.G. | L/Cpl. | 2694 | | 13/07/15 | Lindenhoek Chalet Military Cem. | |
| White J.H. | Pte. | 2467 | | | | Discharged |
| White J.T. | Pte. | 1915 | | 31/10/17 | South Shields (Harton) Cem. | |
| Whyles C. | Pte. | 1364 | 275045 | | | Discharged |
| Whyte W. | Pte. | 1236 | 275376 | | | Discharged |
| Wigham R.W. | Sgt. | 2302 | | | | Disembodied |
| Wigham T. | Pte. | 2478 | | | | Discharged |
| Wilkie J.G. | Pte. | 1865 | | 05/11/16 | Theipval Memorial | |
| Wilkinson E. | Cpl. | 2415 | 275427 | | | Transferred to Tank Corps |
| Wilkinson E.M. | Cpl. | 1717 | 275145 | | | Disembodied |
| Wilkinson G. | Pte. | 3411 | | | | Discharged |
| Willbey J.G. | Cpl. | 1335 | | | | Discharged |
| Williams I. | Pte. | 1394 | | 24/05/15 | Menin Gate | |
| Williams P.K. | Pte. | 2654 | 275524 | | | Disembodied |
| Williamson F. | Pte. | 1808 | 275175 | | | Discharged |
| Williamson W.R. | Sgt. | 2071 | 114578 | | | Continued serving |
| Willis D.T. | Pte. | 2420 | | 26/05/15 | Menin Gate | |
| Willmer C.S. | Pte. | 1698 | | | | Discharged to Commission |
| Wilson A. | Pte. | 2433 | 275437 | | | Disembodied |
| Wilson F.J. | A/L/Cpl. | 1360 | | 29/05/15 | Tuileries British Cem. Belgium | |
| Wilson G. | Pte. | 2545 | 275555 | | | Discharged |
| Wilson H. | Pte. | 2707 | 275613 | | | Disembodied |
| Wilson J. | Cpl. | 2821 | | | | Disembodied |
| Wilson J.E. | L/Cpl. | 1382 | | | | Discharged |
| Wilson R. | Pte. | 1551 | | | | Disembodied |
| Wilson R. | Pte. | 2843 | | | | Disembodied |
| Wilson R.E. | Pte. | 2625 | 275512 | | | Class Z Reserve |

| Name | Rank | No. 1 | No. 2 | Date | Cemetery | Status |
|---|---|---|---|---|---|---|
| Wilson S. | L/Cpl. | 2118 | | 01/10/16 | Flatiron Copse Cem. France | |
| Wilson T.H. | Pte. | 3212 | 275813 | | | Discharged |
| Wilson W.B. | Pte. | 3039 | | | | Discharged |
| Wiltshire T.H. | Pte. | 2171 | 275320 | | | Discharged |
| Winlow R. | Sgt. | 2749 | 275569 | | | Discharged |
| Winter J.C. | Pte. | 2640 | | 26/05/15 | Menin Gate | |
| Wood W. | Pte. | 1745 | 275152 | | | Disembodied |
| Wray H. | Pte. | 1968 | 275236 | | | Disembodied |
| Wright J. | Pte. | 2999 | 201331 | 18/09/18 | Glageon Communal Cem. Ext. France | |
| Wright T. | Pte. | 2731 | | | | Discharged |
| Yates H.S. | Pte. | 2614 | 275509 | 26/05/15 | Menin Gate | Disembodied |
| Young J. | Pte. | 2540 | | | | Discharged |
| Young L. | Pte. | 2481 | | | | Disembodied |
| Young R. | Pte. | 1612 | 275107 | | | Disembodied |
| Young S. | Pte. | 2057 | 275273 | | | Disembodied |
| Young W. | Pte. | 2728 | 275561 | | | Disembodied |
| Younger G. | CQMS | 1599 | 275102 | | | Discharged |
| Youngson J.W. | Cpl. | 2439 | 275438 | | | Discharged |

# Bibliography

Bradford VC, MC, Brigadier General, and his brothers, private publication
Brophy & Partridge, *The Long Trail*
Clutterbuck, Colonel L.A., *The Bond of Sacrifice*, Vol. 2
Dennis, Peter, *The Territorial Army 1907-1940*
*History of the Great War, Military Operations: France and Belgium 1914-18* (usually referred to as the *British Official History*)
Raimes, Major A.L., *The Fifth Battalion The Durham Light Infantry*
Record of Service of Solicitors and Articled Clerks 1914-1918 with His Majesty's Forces
Shepherd N.R., Essays
Thompson & Watts Moses, The War Record of Old Dunelmians
Ward, S.G.P., *Faithful: The story of the Durham Light Infantry*
Wyrall, Everard, *The History of the 50th Division 1914-1919*, P. Lund, Humphries & Co, London, 1939

**Newspapers**
*Durham Advertiser, The*
*Shields Gazette, The*
*Sunderland Echo*

**Unpublished sources held by the Imperial War Museum**
Miller, W.G.
Speight, A.

# Index